'The contrast in social development between Uttar Pradesh and Tamil Nadu is as sharp as it is intriguing. Through this prism, Dipa Sinha's insightful study sheds light on many critical aspects of India's development.'

Jean Drèze, Development Economist and Visiting Professor, Ranchi University, Jharkhand, India

'This book is a must for policy makers, public administrators and community workers. Sinha brilliantly unpackages state performance and highlights . . . the vital importance of women's freedom, state capacity, public accountability, and intra-family as well as community relationships in promoting human development.'

A. K. Shiva Kumar, Economist and Policy Advisor, New Delhi, India

Women, Health and Public Services in India

Why are interstate differences in human development in India so high? What explains regional patterns in which overall the southern region has some of the best human development outcomes in the country while the states in the northern 'heartland' have the worst? In addressing these important questions, this volume provides a detailed analysis of health outcomes in India, especially their effects on women and children. It offers insights into how multiple factors affecting human development, in particular, health, play out differently in various sociocultural and economic contexts.

This book will interest scholars and researchers of sociology, development studies, gender studies, economics and public policy.

Dipa Sinha is Assistant Professor (Economics) at Ambedkar University, New Delhi, India. She studied at Jawaharlal Nehru University, New Delhi, and at the School of Oriental and African Studies (SOAS), University of London, UK. She is involved with issues related to public health, nutrition and right to food as a researcher and activist. She has worked in Andhra Pradesh on a project mobilising communities for better maternal and child health and nutrition, supported by a fellowship from the MacArthur Foundation (administered by Population Council). She was later affiliated with the Office of Commissioners to the Supreme Court (on the Right to Food) and has been part of a number of research and implementation projects with the Centre for Equity Studies (CES) and Public Health Resource Network (PHRN), New Delhi, India.

Critical Political Economy of South Asia

Series editors: C. P. Chandrasekhar and Jayati Ghosh, both at the *Centre for Economic Studies and Planning, Jawaharlal Nehru University, New Delhi, India*

At a time when countries of the South Asian region are in a state of flux, reflected in far-reaching economic, political and social changes, this series aims to showcase critical analyses of some of the central questions relating to the direction and implications of those changes. Volumes in the series focus on economic issues and integrate these with incisive insights into historical, political and social contexts. Drawing on work by established scholars as well as younger researchers, they examine different aspects of political economy that are essential for understanding the present and have an important bearing on the future. The series will provide fresh analytical perspectives and empirical assessments that will be useful for students, researchers, policy makers and concerned citizens.

The first books in the series cover themes such as the economic impact of new regimes of intellectual property rights; the trajectory of financial development in India; changing patterns of consumption expenditure and trends in poverty, health and human development in India, and land relations. Future volumes will deal with varying facets of economic processes and their consequences for the countries of South Asia.

Women, Health and Public Services in India

Why are states different?

Dipa Sinha

Routledge
Taylor & Francis Group

LONDON AND NEW YORK

First published 2016 by Routledge

2 Park Square, Milton Park, Abingdon, Oxfordshire OX14 4RN

52 Vanderbilt Avenue, New York, NY 10017

Routledge is an imprint of the Taylor & Francis Group, an informa business

First issued in paperback 2019

British Library Cataloguing in Publication Data
A catalogue record for this book is available from the British Library

Library of Congress Cataloging-in-Publication Data
A catalog record has been requested for this book

ISBN: 978-1-138-64804-3 (hbk)
ISBN: 978-0-367-17715-7 (pbk)

Typeset in Goudy
by Apex CoVantage, LLC

Contents

Figures

Tables

Acknowledgements

Like most people, I started off not ever wanting to go look at my thesis, once it was done. I am grateful to Jayati Ghosh for making me go back to it and for thinking it was worth sharing with a larger audience. Without her encouragement this book wouldn't have seen the light of day. The book is based on the work I did for my PhD dissertation in JNU. I have been fortunate to have had two supervisors, Jayati Ghosh and Jean Drèze, who guided my research with regular advice. Jean got me excited about Tamil Nadu and the idea of doing a comparative study in the first place.

There are a number of people in Villupuram and Moradabad who made the field work possible. First, all the women I interviewed who welcomed me into their homes, allowed me to ask all kinds of questions and taught me so much in return – I would like to thank each one of them. Sarita in Villupuram and Shilpi in Moradabad helped me with field work. Shanti along with her family and neighbours in Villupuram and Vidyanath and family in Chennai provided me with space to stay, great coffee, enriching discussions and so much affection. Prof Nagraj and the Iruvelpattu team at MIDS, Chennai, for giving me a background of the area and helping me establish initial contacts in the village. Gopinath in Chennai for always being available for any help.

In Moradabad, I had the pleasure of staying with the Palanpur research team at the house they had rented in Pipli village. I shared good food, intense conversations, Palanpur gossip, mosquito bites, monkey menace and long hours waiting for electricity with Dinesh, Gajender, Hemender, Ashish, Archana and Sangeetha – a warm thanks to all of them. Gurminder and Suraj Singh in Bilari for helping me locate villages and bailing me out when I was stranded. Nick Stern, Abhiroop, Ruth and Peter for discussions on Palanpur in Delhi and at the LSE. The Palanpur study has been supported by the DFID.

Many friends and comrades have contributed in different ways and I am deeply indebted to each one of them. Colleagues from the Right to Food campaign have been a source of inspiration and also much fun! Harsh and Biraj, co-travellers, friends and much more for providing such a wonderful workspace. Giuseppe and Prashant who have been a part of this project right from its inception for the long chats, reading my drafts, hearing my stories and always believing in me. I can't thank them enough.

Throughout this process my family has been a source of encouragement and support. My mother, Shantha Sinha, sister, Sudha, cousins and nephews have all taken time out to help me with childcare while I did field work. The children, Tanay and Laya, for coping so beautifully with my frequent travels and for keeping me on the ground. Himanshu has been an integral part of this process, and if there is one thing I want to thank him for, it is for not letting me give up ever.

For my grandparents – Amma, Appa, Nainamma and Tatagaru – for everything they gave us.

Chapter 1

North–south contrast in human development

Does economic growth automatically take care of human development? Should the state focus on enhancing economic growth rather than providing welfare services? Can public services contribute to improved human development outcomes? If state intervention can deliver for the poor, what are the factors that make this happen?

Debates around the relationship between economic growth and human development and the role of the state in direct provision of public services are of course not new, and a lot has been written about this in the Indian context as well. However, these questions continue to be relevant to public policy even today. The current political environment in India is in favour of relying on private-sector-led economic growth to solve the problems of poverty, poor education, malnutrition and ill health of a vast section of the Indian population. Recent developments that include social sector budget cuts and serious threats of dilution of welfare provisions through schemes under the employment guarantee act and food security act all seem to be in the same direction. The present mood is also against public investment in social sector programmes as they are being undermined as having failed, being inefficient and having made no impact on any outcomes.

While India has managed to significantly improve its human development indicators (in relation to literacy, infant mortality, life expectancy, etc.) in the last four decades, the rate of improvement is slow, especially given the experience of high economic growth during this time. India's performance also fails in comparison with other countries in South, Southeast and East Asia, including several with lower per capita incomes. Infant mortality rates (IMRs) in India declined from about 130 to 140 infant deaths per 1,000 live births in the early 1970s to 50 in 2009, representing an annual rate of decline of about 2.5 per cent. On the other hand, countries such as South Korea, Thailand and

Indonesia experienced declines in IMR at rates of 3–4 per cent per year and neighbouring countries such as Sri Lanka and Bangladesh showed even faster declines of 4.3 and 5.6 per cent per year, respectively (Deolalikar 2005). Bangladesh, whose per capita income is only about one half of India's, has a level of IMR that is even lower than India's (Sen 2011). This contradiction of simultaneous high economic growth and slow human development in India has also been examined in the recent book by Amartya Sen and Jean Drèze, *An Uncertain Glory: India and Its Contradictions* (Drèze and Sen 2013). The present book is located within this context, where it examines regional differences in India's human development achievements as it provides some interesting insights and also policy lessons.

Despite improvements in average levels of human development outcomes in India, wide interstate disparities continue to persist and need to be understood further. Broadly, the southern region consisting of Kerala, Tamil Nadu, Andhra Pradesh and Karnataka has some of the best human development outcomes in the country while the states in the northern 'heartland' consisting of Bihar, Jharkhand, Madhya Pradesh, Chhattisgarh, Uttar Pradesh and Rajasthan have the worst.[1] The term 'BIMARU', meaning 'ill' in Hindi, was coined to refer to the undivided northern states of Bihar, Madhya Pradesh, Rajasthan and Uttar Pradesh.[2] It is the popular perception, unfortunately also often supported by evidence that these states are mostly 'backward' with low literacy levels, poor health, poor governance and high levels of poverty.

For instance, an average person in Kerala is expected to live for 12 years longer than her counterpart in Madhya Pradesh (life expectancy at birth (2007–11) in Kerala was 75 years, in Madhya Pradesh the life expectancy for the corresponding period was 63 years) (Government of India 2015). Similarly Kerala has the lowest IMR in the country, with 12 infant deaths per 1,000 births; while IMR is 21 in Tamil Nadu, it is a much higher 54 in Madhya Pradesh and 50 in Uttar Pradesh (Government of India 2014a). The female literacy rate is around 92 per cent in Kerala and 53 per cent in Bihar (Government of India 2011a). If they were different countries, Kerala would be close in its ranking to high human development countries such as Brazil and China in terms of its IMR, while Madhya Pradesh would be among the low human development countries such as Zimbabwe and Liberia (HDR 2014). This difference, especially in the context of varying fertility rates, has often been mentioned in the literature as the 'north–south divide' (Dyson and Moore 1983; Guilmoto and Rajan 1998; Bose 2000, 2007; Dommaraju and Agadjanian 2009).

The results of Census 2011 have once again brought out the stark difference between the northern and southern states in India, especially in relation to demographic indicators. While the average decadal population growth in the last two decades (1991–2011) in Uttar Pradesh and Bihar was around 25 per cent, in the states of Andhra Pradesh, Tamil Nadu and Kerala, the figure was around half of that. More specifically, between 2001 and 2011, Kerala's population grew by just under 5 per cent, while Bihar's population grew by over 25 per cent. While the Census 2011 data show that for the first time there has been a reduction in the population growth rates in the northern states, these are still higher than the average for India as a whole and much higher than the southern states (Khilnani 2011).

This trend of higher fertility rates in northern states compared to the four southern states has been observed over a long period, as shown by Dyson and Moore (1983) for Census data from 1921 onwards. A similar regional pattern in infant and child mortality rates is also seen by Dyson and Moore (1983). Guilmoto and Rajan (1998) find that based on health outcome data in India, we can distinguish five regional groups: southern states, north-western states (Punjab, Haryana, Himachal Pradesh, Maharashtra and Gujarat), large northern Indian states (BIMARU states) and the cluster of eastern states (West Bengal, Orissa and Assam) (Guilmoto and Rajan 1998). A study of interstate differences in sex ratios between 1901 and 1961 by Visaria (1969) showed that throughout the period sex ratios were persistently lower in the northern states than in the southern states (i.e. less females per 1,000 males in the North). This regional pattern continues till today and has even been reinforced by the Census 2011.

While interstate inequality continues to be high, some argue that there has been a tendency towards convergence in IMR over the last few decades (Agrawal 2010). Along with a reduction in the levels of IMR, Chaurasia (2005) finds that there is a decrease in interstate inequality in IMR in India. However, this convergence appears to have slowed down after 1993–5. Deolalikar (2005) finds that in general, there was some (although limited) convergence in infant mortality, so that interstate disparity in infant mortality decreased between 1981 and 2000. Dholakia (2003) looks at regional disparity among major Indian states in relation to different human development indicators for the period 1981–2000 and finds that while there are differences in individual indicators, the overall trend is that regional disparity in human development clearly decreased in the decade of the 1980s, whereas the results for the 1990s are mixed. Disparities increased with respect to poverty but decreased with respect to deaths, literacy and dropout rates.

The India Human Development Report (IHDR) argues that there is a convergence in human development among Indian states, by looking at the improvement in the human development index (HDI) of states between 1990–2000 and 2007–8 (Institute of Applied Manpower Research 2011). This is based on the relatively higher percentage changes in the HDI values in low human development states. However, it cannot necessarily be concluded that there is convergence taking place in human development across states because the backward states have made better progress in terms of percentage change in HDI. Improving human development indicators becomes more and more difficult at higher levels of human development, and therefore percentage change is not a good measure. Other indices such as the 'Sen Improvement Index' have therefore been proposed to take account of the initial level of the outcome indicator and measure the change in relation to that (Sen 1981; Chakraborty 2011). Based on such an index, Chakraborty (2011) argues that the claim of convergence made in the IHDR is incorrect.

Even if there is some convergence, it is still not enough considering the enormous gap that separates the northern states from the rest of the country (Drèze and Khera 2012). For instance, by just looking at simple ratios, we find that while the state with the highest IMR in 1982 (Uttar Pradesh) had an IMR (159) that was four and a half times higher than that of the state with the lowest IMR (Kerala – 35), in 2014 this ratio in IMR between the highest IMR state (Madhya Pradesh – 54) and lowest IMR state (Kerala – 12) is still the same at 4.5. So, even though there might be an overall convergence in IMRs, the issue of regional disparity is a matter of great concern.

To understand the extent of regional inequality, some basic indicators of health and education for different states on the basis of the latest data available are presented in Table 1.1. With regard to literacy rates, Kerala, Himachal Pradesh, Maharashtra, Tamil Nadu and Gujarat are amongst the top five states. Uttar Pradesh, Rajasthan, Jharkhand, Bihar and (surprisingly) Andhra Pradesh are amongst the bottom five. Kerala, Himachal Pradesh and Tamil Nadu are the states that have the highest school life expectancy.[3]

Tamil Nadu is the second best in terms of IMR, following Kerala. The other states amongst the top five are Maharashtra, West Bengal and Punjab. The states with the highest IMR and the maternal mortality ratio (MMR) are Uttar Pradesh, Rajasthan, Assam, Madhya Pradesh

Table 1.1 Education and health indicators across Indian states

	Literacy rate (2011)*	School life expectancy**	Infant mortality rate (2013)***	Maternal mortality ratio (2011–13)†	Life expectancy‡ (2007–11)
Andhra Pradesh	67.7	9.7	39	92	67
Assam	73.2	9.5	54	300	62.7
Bihar	63.8	9.6	42	208	67.2
Chhattisgarh	71	9.3	46	–	–
Gujarat	79.3	8.8	36	112	67.7
Haryana	76.6	9.7	41	127	67.6
Himachal Pradesh	83.8	11.1	35	–	70.5
Jammu & Kashmir	68.7	NA	37	–	–
Jharkhand	67.6	9.7	37	–	–
Karnataka	75.6	9.8	31	133	68
Kerala	93.9	11.3	12	61	74.7
Madhya Pradesh	70.6	9	54	221	63.3
Maharashtra	82.9	9.9	24	68	70.8
Orissa	73.5	8.7	51	222	64.3
Punjab	76.7	9.8	26	141	70.3
Rajasthan	67.1	9.2	47	244	67.2
Tamil Nadu	80.3	10.6	21	79	69.8
Uttar Pradesh	69.7	9.2	50	285	63.5
West Bengal	77.1	8.9	31	113	69.7
India	74	9.6	40	167	67

*GOI (2011a)
**GOI (2015)
*** GOI (2014a)
†GOI (2014b)
‡Suryanarayana et al. (2011)

and Orissa. Further, it is also seen that the gap between states like Tamil Nadu and Maharashtra that are on the top and states that are at the lower end such as Uttar Pradesh and Madhya Pradesh is significantly large. For instance, the IMR in Uttar Pradesh is more than twice that in Tamil Nadu, and the MMR in Uttar Pradesh is more than three times that in Tamil Nadu.

Table 1.2 presents some further indicators of health in the major states in the country. These are indicators related to child survival (percentage

Table 1.2 Index of child health

S. no	State	% of children who survive to age five	% of children who are fully immunised	% of children who are not underweight	% of deliveries assisted by health personnel	Index of child health (normalised)
1	Kerala	98.4	75.3	77.1	99.4	0.98
2	Tamil Nadu	96.4	80.9	70.2	90.6	0.86
3	Punjab	94.8	60.1	75.1	68.2	0.68
4	Jammu & Kashmir	94.9	66.7	74.4	56.5	0.66
5	Maharashtra	95.3	58.8	63	68.7	0.63
6	Himachal Pradesh	95.8	74.2	64.5	47.8	0.61
7	Andhra Pradesh	93.7	46	67.5	74.9	0.56
8	Karnataka	94.5	55	62.4	69.7	0.55
9	Haryana	94.8	65.3	60.4	48.9	0.53
10	West Bengal	94	64.3	61.3	47.6	0.5
11	Gujarat	93.9	45.2	55.4	63	0.43
12	Orissa	90.9	51.8	59.3	44	0.33
13	Chhattisgarh	90.9	48.7	52.9	41.6	0.26
14	Rajasthan	91.5	26.5	60.1	41	0.24
15	Assam	91.5	31.4	63.6	31	0.23
16	Madhya Pradesh	90.6	40.3	40	32.7	0.12
17	Uttar Pradesh	90.4	23	57.6	27.2	0.11
18	Bihar	91.5	32.8	44.1	29.3	0.1
19	Jharkhand	90.7	34.2	43.5	27.8	0.08
	India	92.6	43.5	57	46.6	0.34

Source: NFHS-3 (IIPS 2005–6)

Note: The index of child health is an unweighted average of normalised values of columns 3 to 6. To arrive at the index, the indicators have been normalised using the procedure applied by the UNDP for the HDI namely $Y_i = (X_i - X_{min}) / (X_{max} - X_{min})$, where Y_i is the normalised indicator for state i, X_i is the corresponding prenormalisation figure and X_{max} and X_{min} are the maximum and minimum values, respectively, of the same indicator across all states. The normalised indicator varies between 0 and 1 for all states, with 0 being the worst and 1 being the best. A simple average of the normalised values for the three indicators is the index of child health.

Age groups: '12–23 months' for immunisation; 'below three years' for nutrition.

of children who survive until the age of five[4]), immunisation coverage, nutritional status and safe deliveries (indicated by deliveries assisted by health personnel). A simple average of normalised values of these four indicators is calculated and shown here as the 'index of child health'.[5] Based on this index as well, Tamil Nadu ranks second, following Kerala. The other states that are amongst the top five are Jammu and Kashmir, Punjab, Maharashtra and Himachal Pradesh. The bottom five states are Assam, Madhya Pradesh, Uttar Pradesh, Bihar and Jharkhand.

Tamil Nadu is the state with highest immunisation coverage, according to the National Family Health Survey (NFHS) – 3. Further, the percentage of deliveries assisted by health personnel, while still lower than in Kerala, is much higher than all other states. While the percentage of deliveries assisted by health personnel is about 91 per cent in Tamil Nadu, it is only about 75 per cent in Andhra Pradesh, which is the state with the next highest presence of skilled attendance during birth. The gap is much wider when compared with the lower-ranking states, as the percentage of births delivered with skilled attendance is less than 30 per cent in Bihar, Jharkhand and Uttar Pradesh. Skilled attendance during delivery is seen as a proxy for maternal health; and immunisation and safe deliveries contribute in major ways to decreasing neonatal and infant mortality.

From these data, it is clear that there is a wide difference among Indian states in terms of health and education outcomes. States such as Kerala, Tamil Nadu, Himachal Pradesh and Maharashtra are consistently on the top, while Uttar Pradesh, Bihar, Jharkhand and Madhya Pradesh are not only in the bottom but also significantly worse than the higher-ranking states. What factors contribute to this difference?

Differences in economic conditions such as economic growth and per capita incomes do not adequately explain the difference in human development achievements across Indian states. On the other hand, women's status, particularly female literacy, emerges as a significant factor in explaining better health outcomes in the major states. Other aspects of women's status, such as women's paid employment and mobility, are seen to play an important social role. In this context, defining and measuring women's status and understanding women's status in the public and private spheres separately are seen as key issues for further study. Provision of public services is another factor that can generate differences in health outcomes across the states. Factors that are favourable for the effective provision of public services by the state are existence of social movements, collective action, mobilisation of backward castes and higher women's status.

Understanding each of these factors and their interplay is what this book attempts to do. The book is in two parts. The first part (Chapters 2 to 5) looks at relevant literature and analyses state-level data to understand the relationship between these factors and different aspects of human development at the state level, with a focus on indicators related to health status – particularly infant and child mortality rates. Infant and child mortality rates are widely considered the most sensitive indicators of not just health status but also overall development. Infant mortality is a generally accepted social indicator of a nation's health and quality of life. Inequality in IMRs is indicative of the inequality in the level of development, especially in the health status and living standards of the people (Reidpath and Allotey 2003; Chaurasia 2005).

The second part of this book looks at the same issues in greater depth by presenting the case of two contrasting states – Uttar Pradesh and Tamil Nadu. In this analysis, data from secondary sources as well as a field survey conducted in Tamil Nadu and Uttar Pradesh is used. Even though the field survey was based on a small sample from a single block in each state, it was extremely useful in clarifying the factors that need to be looked at in the larger study. Repeated visits to the survey villages in Tamil Nadu and Uttar Pradesh allowed me to gain an insight into the ways in which public services affect people's lives, how the quality of public services can be different even when they are broadly of the same design (like schools, anganwadi centres and ANMs), the difference in 'work culture' among public servants and so on. Each of these is difficult to measure and therefore not part of the quantitative analysis but nevertheless helps in understanding why there is a difference between the two states. The field observations also helped me choose the questions I should pursue through my secondary research and at the same time tie together the learning from the vast literature on this subject.

Notes

1 This is a broad regional pattern. In case of individual indicators, some states in other regions are better off than some of the southern states. The western region consisting of Maharashtra, Gujarat, Punjab, Haryana and Himachal Pradesh also has better human development indicators whereas the states in the East including Orissa and Assam are amongst those with the poorest indicators. In the analysis in the following chapters, data for individual states are examined in more detail. This broad categorisation is made currently for the convenience of explaining the main argument.

2 Out of these states, three new states of Jharkhand, Chhattisgarh and Uttarakhand were carved later.

3 School life expectancy (or expected years of schooling) is defined as the number of years of schooling that a child of school entrance age can expect to receive if prevailing patterns of age-specific enrolment rates were to stay the same throughout the child's life. Estimates for states in India are made taking into account age-specific enrolment rates for the age group 6 to 18 years (both inclusive). Estimates of school life expectancy are made based on the NSS unit record data on education in India (Suryanarayana et al. 2011).

4 While the under-five mortality rate is usually in terms of the number of child deaths per 1,000 live births, here it has been converted into percentage of child survival for the purposes of the index.

5 This index is adapted from the 'ABC Index' developed in the FOCUS Report (FOCUS 2006). While the ABC Index is an unweighted average of the four indicators related to child mortality, immunisation, nutrition and school attendance, in the index of child health presented here, we have replaced school attendance with skilled attendance during delivery. A normalised ABC Index was used in Drèze and Khera (2012). States are ranked in descending order of this index.

Chapter 2

Not just economic conditions

Economic conditions of living at the household and society level are important factors to be considered in studying the causes for the variation in human development outcomes between different states, regions, countries or social groups. Traditionally the focus has been on economic growth or per capita incomes as the ultimate objective of development. With the introduction of the human development approach, there has been some shift in economic analysis with greater attention being paid to outcomes such as better education or health as the end goals to be achieved and economic growth being one of the important instruments towards this. However, there is still no consensus on the exact relationship between economic growth and human development, especially when it is translated into recommendations on policy priorities.[1]

On the one hand it is argued that economic growth is central to the process of improving human development and therefore the priority of policy makers should be on enhancing growth *per se*. On the other hand many propose that while economic growth is an important (and maybe even necessary) factor for progress in human development, it is only one of many factors. In the second approach it is further argued that the *nature* of economic growth is critical in determining the relation between growth and human development (Ravallion 1997) and also that other factors such as female literacy, public expenditures and developments in health technology can be equally or at times even more significant. Therefore, public policy must balance its priorities with a focus on improving human development outcomes.

Economic growth can promote human development mainly in two ways. One is through improvement in personal incomes enabling people to spend more in ways that lead to better human development outcomes. These could be, for instance, expenditures on food, nutrition, health care and education. It is seen that within a population, the better-off invariably have better health outcomes than those who are poor. This is true in both rich and poor societies.[2] Many studies conducted in different countries across the world have shown that an increase in incomes of the poor invariably leads to an increase in such expenditures, especially an increase in spending on more and better quality foods (Ranis and Stewart 2000).

However, the extent to which this occurs depends on the way in which economic growth is distributed. If it is highly unequal growth that does not significantly increase the incomes of poor people, then such growth will not have a significant human development improving impact. On the other hand, equitable growth whereby per capita incomes of the poor are increasing can significantly contribute to enhanced human development.[3] Therefore, for any given level of economic performance (economic growth or per capita income) there can be very different human development performance. The way in which growth translates into income distribution or poverty reduction depends on the nature of the growth process (Preston 1975; Ranis and Stewart 2000).

Second, at the macro level, economic growth enables governments to spend more on services that enhance human development. Therefore, with more resources available governments are able to spend more on provision of health care or education. This can be seen through increases in government expenditure as a share of GNP, increase in social sector expenditure ratios and so on. This again is not an automatic process and depends on the nature of the government of the day. While economic growth creates an enabling environment for increased government intervention, whether this actually takes place depends on the political priorities of the government in power. What becomes an issue of political importance is in turn affected by many factors related to the historical and social context of the country or region in question (Anand and Ravallion 1993; Anand 1994; Ranis and Stewart 2000).

There is extensive literature that looks at the relation between economic growth and various human development outcomes. Drèze and Sen (1989) categorise the 10 best performing countries, among developing countries, in terms of the percentage decrease in under-five mortality achieved by them in the period 1960–85, according to the strategy used to provide social security. They find that five countries followed a 'growth-mediated' approach, which promotes economic growth and then utilises the enhanced income for increased public support. The other five followed a 'support-led security' approach, which promotes wide-ranging public support in areas such as employment provision, income redistribution, health care, education and social assistance in order to improve quality of life without waiting for a transformation of the level of general affluence.

Many cross-country studies that have looked at the relation between per capita incomes and human development outcomes find that income is a significant correlate with health outcomes (e.g. Filmer and Pritchett 1999; Thorbecke and Charumilind 2002; Wang 2003; Pritchett and Viarengo 2010). Preston (1980) attributes about half of the 50 per cent rise in life expectancy (17 years) in developing countries between 1940 and 1970 to increases in standards of living, a period when LDC income rose by roughly 250 per cent, while another study by Pritchett and Summers (1993) with cross-country time series data over the period 1960 to 1990 finds that differences in income growth rates explain roughly 40 per cent of the cross-country differences in mortality improvements. Based on cross-country regressions for data between 1960 and 1992, Ranis et al. (2000) find that there is a strong and significant positive relation between growth in per capita GDP and human development performance (measured in terms of shortfall in life expectancy from a maximum of 85 years)[4] (Ranis et al. 2000).

Country experiences show that while overall there is a significant positive relationship between the level of per capita income (or GDP/GNP) and indicators of human development such as life expectancy or infant mortality rates (and the HDI), there are significant outliers. There are examples of countries that show much lower levels of human development than would be predicted by their per capita income levels alone and vice versa. For example, countries such as UAE, Qatar, Kuwait and Turkey are ranked highly on the basis of their gross national income (GNI) per capita compared to their performance based on HDI.[5] On the other hand countries such as Ireland, Fiji, Ukraine and Tajikistan have a HDI rank, which is much higher than their rank on the basis of GNI per capita.

While New Zealand ranks 31 on the basis of GNI per capita (2011 PPP $), it ranks 7 on the basis of its HDI value. The per capita GNI of New Zealand (32,569 PPP $) is less than 60 per cent that of the UAE (58,068 PPP $), but New Zealand ranks much higher than the UAE on the basis of its HDI (UNDP 2014). This is quite a significant difference considering that per capita income contributes to one-third of the HDI. Therefore, just on the basis of nonincome human development indicators, the difference between New Zealand and UAE would be even more.

Table 2.1 compares India's per capita income and human development indicators with those of a few other developing countries. Although

Table 2.1 Human development indicators for select countries

Country	GNI per capita (PPP $ 2011)	HDI value	Life expectancy at birth (in years)	Mean years of schooling
Bangladesh	2,713 (164)	0.558 (142)	70.7	5.1
Cambodia	2,805 (161)	0.584 (136)	71.9	5.8
Vietnam	4,892 (142)	0.593 (128)	75.9	5.5
India	5,150 (139)	0.586 (135)	66.4	4.4
Indonesia	8,970 (113)	0.684 (108)	70.8	7.5
Philippines	6,381 (125)	0.660 (117)	68.7	8.9
Bolivia	5,552 (131)	0.667 (113)	67.3	9.2
Sri Lanka	9,250 (109)	0.750 (73)	74.3	10.8
Cuba	19,844 (57)	0.815 (44)	79.3	10.2

Source: HDR (UNDP 2014)

Cambodia has a much lower per capita income (2,805 PPP $ compared with 5,150 PPP $ for India), in terms of life expectancy and mean years of schooling, it is better as seen in Table 2.1. Bangladesh, which has an even lower per capita income (2,713 PPP $), has a higher life expectancy at birth (70.7 years vs. 66.4 years for India) and higher mean years of schooling (5.8 years vs. 4.4 years for India). Similar is the case with Vietnam, which also has a slightly lower per capita income (4,892 PPP $) but much higher life expectancy at birth (75.9 years) and mean years of schooling (5.5 years).

Even countries that have slightly higher per capita incomes such as Indonesia or the Philippines show greater difference in terms of HDI values, especially nonincome HDI. Sri Lanka, which is a neighbouring country, also has a much higher life expectancy (74.3) and mean years of schooling (10.8) than India. Sri Lanka, Cuba and Costa Rica are examples of countries whose ranking in terms of human development is much higher than their rank in terms of GNI per capita showing that while there is an overall positive relationship between levels of per capita income and HDI values, there are significant variations as well.

The evidence related to the relation between economic growth and health/human development outcomes among different states in India also points to the importance of factors other than just economic conditions. Guilmoto and Rajan (1998) find that for similar rates of economic progress the impact on fertility appears to be different. For instance, in Punjab and Haryana the impact of economic progress on fertility appears to be low, while on the other hand a faster rate of fertility decline is seen in the southern states for a similar improvement in the economic development levels. They conclude that this reflects the absence of a strong link between economic variables and birth rates in South India. Further, based on district-level analysis, they find that economic development has little measureable impact on fertility. On the other hand, variables depicting women's status and autonomy are systematically related to fertility decline. District-level analysis using Census data to study the role of different factors affecting fertility and child mortality by Murthi et al. (1997) also finds similar results where, along with income, other factors, particularly female education, have a strong influence on demographic outcomes.

Looking at malnutrition, Subramanian et al. (2007) find that there was no evidence that in high-growth states the risk of greater proportion of underweight children was lower than in states with considerably lower levels of economic growth. It is also interesting to note that the interstate variations in health-related indicators do not always correlate with poverty levels. Poverty, as measured by the head count ratio, is higher in the eastern states of Bihar and Orissa, but child death rates are much higher in the central and northern states of Uttar Pradesh, Madhya Pradesh and Rajasthan. 'Despite poverty being lower in Uttar Pradesh, child mortality is more than twice as high in the state as compared to Tamil Nadu' (Pal and Ghosh 2007: 15).

Subramanyam et al. (2011), in their analysis of the determinants of undernutrition in Indian states using data from three rounds of the NFHS, failed to find consistent evidence that economic growth leads to higher reduction in childhood undernutrition in India. There was also no statistically significant association between per capita state domestic product and mean levels of child undernutrition. They conclude that direct investments in appropriate health interventions may be necessary to reduce childhood undernutrition in India.

The results of Deolalikar's (2005) analysis indicate strong interstate differences in mortality even after controlling for household living standards, caste, maternal education and infrastructure access. Dholakia (2003), on the other hand, finds two-way causality between per capita incomes and human development based on an analysis of data related to major Indian states for the period 1981–2000 and concludes that the relationship of per capita incomes causing human development is more stable over time (with a two-year lag) than that of human development causing a rise in per capita incomes (with an eight-year lag).

An examination of recent state-level data for India shows that while it broadly holds true that there is a positive relation between economic conditions and human development, some states make for interesting exceptions. The causality is not clear either, in terms of whether rise in per capita incomes came first or better initial conditions in terms of human development led to faster economic progress.

Relation between current economic status and health outcomes across Indian states

Table 2.2 provides the ranks of the states based on different indicators related to economic conditions and IMR. The data show that it does not always hold true that better economic conditions mean a lower

Table 2.2 Relation between IMR and economic conditions

State	IMR rank	Poverty ratio rank	Per capita NSDP rank	MPCE rank
Kerala	1	2	4	1
Tamil Nadu	2	5	8	7
Maharashtra	3	11	2	8
West Bengal	4	10	11	12
Punjab	5	3	3	2
Karnataka	6	7	7	10
Jharkhand	7	15	17	15
Himachal Pradesh	8	1	6	3
Gujarat	9	9	5	9
Andhra Pradesh	10	6	9	5
Haryana	11	4	1	4
Bihar	12	17	18	18
Chhattisgarh	13	18	10	17
Rajasthan	14	8	13	6
Assam	15	14	14	11
Uttar Pradesh	16	13	15	14
Orissa	17	12	12	16
Madhya Pradesh	18	16	16	13

Source: Ranking done based on data from the following sources: *IMR* (infant mortality rate for 2009) from Sample Registration System (GoI 2011b); *poverty ratio* (headcount ratio of percentage of people below the poverty line in rural areas based on NSS data and official poverty lines for 2009–10) from Planning Commission (GoI 2012); *per capita NSDP* (per capita National State Domestic Product for 2009–10) from Central Statistical Office (CSO) data available on website http://mospi.nic.in; *MPCE* (average monthly per capita consumption expenditure based on mixed method recall period for rural areas for 2009–10) from NSS 66th round (GoI 2011c)

Notes: The columns present the ranks of the state in respect to each of the indicators. Rank 1 is the best state, so the ranking has been done in an ascending order of IMR and poverty ratio and descending order for the other indicators. The state with the least IMR has IMR rank 1, least poverty ratio has poverty ratio rank 1, highest NSDP has NSDP rank 1 and highest MPCE has MPCE rank 1.

IMR. Haryana is the state with the highest per capita NSDP among all states; however, it ranks 11th in terms of its IMR. Similarly, Gujarat is another state that has a high per capita NSDP (rank 5) but also a low IMR (rank 9). Tamil Nadu, which has a per capita NSDP that is less than 60 per cent of that of Haryana, has an IMR that is much lower than that of Haryana. On the other hand, Maharashtra, Punjab and Kerala are among the top five states in terms of both per capita NSDP and IMR.

As can be seen in the scatter plot in Figure 2.1, there is an overall negative relationship between the indicators of health outcomes and per capita NSDP, with IMR getting lower as per capita NSDP increases. However, the correlation between these two is not very high ($R^2 = 0.34$). The correlation between NSDP with under-five mortality rate (U5MR) and stunting rates amongst the major Indian states is even lower ($R^2 = 0.21$ and 0.23, respectively).

The relationship between average rural monthly per capita consumption expenditure (MPCE) and IMR is also seen to be along the same lines. Overall there is a negative relationship between the two, with

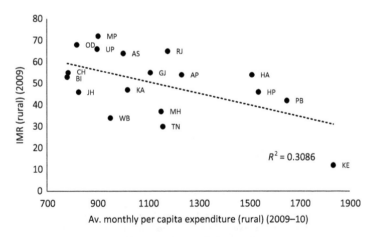

Figure 2.1 IMR and economic conditions among major Indian states

Source: Ranking done based on data from the following sources: *IMR* (infant mortality rate for 2009) from Sample Registration System (GoI 2011b); *poverty ratio* (headcount ratio of percentage of people below the poverty line in rural areas based on NSS data and official poverty lines for 2009–10) from Planning Commission (GoI 2012); *per capita NSDP* (per capita National State Domestic Product for 2009–10) from Central Statistical Office (CSO) data available on website http://mospi.nic.in; *MPCE* (average monthly per capita consumption expenditure based on mixed method recall period for rural areas for 2009–10) from NSS 66th round (GoI 2011c)

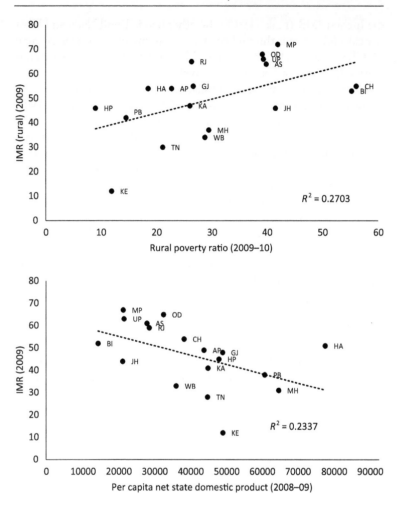

Figure 2.1 (Continued)

lower IMRs at higher levels of average MPCE. Even MPCE is not very highly correlated with IMR ($R^2 = 0.31$). The R^2 is 0.39 in the case of U5MR and a higher 0.6 in the case of stunting prevalence. Kerala is the state with the highest average rural MPCE as well as lowest IMR. Punjab and Himachal Pradesh also perform well on both counts. But once again it is seen that while Haryana has the fourth highest average rural MPCE, its rank on the basis of rural IMR is 11. Rajasthan is the state with the sixth highest average rural MPCE, but is also among the states with

the highest IMR (rank 14). On the other hand, Tamil Nadu and West
Bengal rank among the middle states in terms of their average rural
MPCE (ranks 7 and 12, respectively) but among the top states in terms
of rural IMR (ranks 2 and 4, respectively).

We would expect a higher correlation to be seen between the head
count ratio of poverty (poverty ratio, HCR) and the IMR (or U5MR/
stunting) levels in rural areas across different states. However, while
there is a positive relationship between IMR and HCR levels, it is seen
that the correlation between these two indicators is low with an R^2 of
0.27. Once again, Kerala, Punjab and Himachal Pradesh are good performers on the basis of both indicators. However, Haryana and Andhra
Pradesh have low rural poverty ratios but relatively high rural IMRs.
While Rajasthan and Maharashtra have a similar proportion of people
below the poverty line in rural areas, the IMR in Rajasthan is 28 points
higher than that in Maharashtra. West Bengal, on the other hand, has
a high rural poverty ratio (ranking 11th) but is among the five best performing states in terms of its rural IMR.[6]

Kerala, Punjab and Himachal Pradesh are consistently good performers on most indicators of economic conditions and health outcomes.
Tamil Nadu and West Bengal on the whole are in the middle range as far
as economic indicators are concerned but amongst the highest-ranking
states in terms of health outcomes.[7] While Maharashtra has a high per
capita income level and good indicators for health outcomes, its average rural MPCE is low and poverty ratios are high. On the other hand,
while Rajasthan has a high rural MPCE, its health indicators are poor.
Gujarat is another state that, on some health indicators, shows very poor
outcomes (particularly stunting) but is amongst the top states in terms of
economic conditions especially on the basis of per capita income.

While there is a lot of variation in the ranking in terms of indicators
of economic conditions and health outcomes for states that are top or
medium performing in any of these indicators, it is also seen that in the
case of low performing states, they consistently have poor indicators for
both. States such as Uttar Pradesh, Orissa, Madhya Pradesh, Jharkhand
and Chhattisgarh are amongst the worst in terms of both economic conditions and health outcomes.[8]

Figure 2.2 presents the relation between per capita NSDP and IMR
using panel data for the period 1980–2010 for all major states. This also
shows that link between these two indicators is not very strong (R^2 of
0.34).

While there is an overall positive relationship between economic
conditions and health outcomes across Indian states, this relationship is

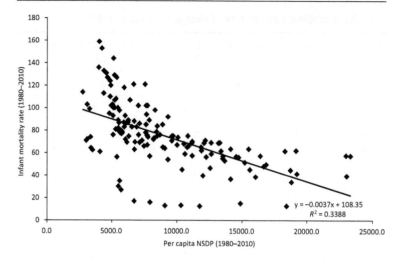

Figure 2.2 Health outcomes and per capita NSDP among major Indian states: panel data for the years 1980–2010

Source: CSO (for per capita NSDP) and SRS (for IMR) (various years)[9]

not enough to explain the variations among the states in terms of their human development outcomes. As seen in the previous paragraphs, there are significant examples of both: states with health indicators not as good as their economic performance and those with better health indicators than would be predicted by their income and expenditure levels.

I now briefly look at the relationship between change in economic conditions and change in IMR over the last two decades (Table 2.3).[10] Here again, it is seen that there is an overall positive relation between the rate of annual change in MPCE (rural) and the rate of annual change in IMR (rural) over the period 1983 to 2009–10. However, this relation is weak, even weaker than it is when considering the relation between the two at a point of time.[11] The correlation between the annual growth rates in IMR and MPCE for this entire period is −0.32.

Kerala shows one of the highest rates of growth in both MPCE and IMR. West Bengal and Tamil Nadu show higher annual rates of reduction in IMR than in their growth in MPCE. Both of these states are in the middle in terms of their increase in MPCE, but among the top when it comes to reduction in IMR. States such as Uttar Pradesh and Gujarat, which show low annual growth in MPCE, also have relatively faster rates of reduction in IMR. In fact, IMR in Uttar Pradesh has reduced

Table 2.3 Compound annual rate of change in MPCE and IMR

State	MPCE CAGR	IMR CAGR	MPCE CAGR	IMR CAGR	MPCE CAGR	IMR CAGR
	1983 to 1993–4		1993–4 to 2004–5		2004–5 to 2009–10	
Andhra Pradesh	1.1	−1.5	1.0	−1.0	2.4	−3.0
Assam	0.9	−2.1	2.0	−1.2	1.2	−2.0
Bihar	0.8	−3.7	1.2	−1.3	1.1	−3.2
Gujarat	0.3	−5.7	0.9	−0.8	1.7	−2.6
Haryana	1.7	−3.8	2.3	−0.8	−0.3	−3.2
Karnataka	0.2	−0.7	0.5	−2.9	0.2	−2.8
Kerala	1.2	−6.7	3.7	−0.8	5.1	−2.9
Madhya Pradesh	1.2	−2.4	−0.1	−2.5	2.7	−2.5
Maharashtra	1.1	−2.5	0.7	−4.0	2.1	−2.3
Orissa	2.1	−2.0	0.7	−3.1	2.0	−2.9
Punjab	1.4	−3.1	1.1	−1.7	1.2	−3.3
Rajasthan	−0.4	−2.9	0.6	−1.5	0.5	−2.6
Tamil Nadu	1.8	−4.0	0.9	−4.0	1.7	−6.3
Uttar Pradesh	0.4	−5.4	1.0	−1.9	0.2	−2.5
West Bengal	2.1	−4.4	1.4	−3.9	0.1	−3.3
All India	1.1	−3.4	1.1	−2.3	1.4	−2.7
Correlation	−0.04		0.45		0.01	

Note: CAGR = compound annual growth rate

Source: Estimated using MPCE data from NSSO (rounds 38, 50, 61 and 66) and IMR data from SRS Bulletins for respective years

almost at the same rate as it did in Kerala, in spite of much lower annual growth in MPCE.[12] On the other hand, Haryana, which shows the highest annual growth rate in MPCE during this period (after Kerala), has a low rate of reduction in IMR. The same is the case with Punjab, although the growth rate in MPCE in Punjab is not as high as in Haryana.

It is interesting to observe that when this period is broken up into three subperiods of 1983 to 1993–4, 1993–4 to 2004–5 and 2004–5 to 2009–10,[13] the direction of the relation between the annual rate of change in MPCE and the rate of change in IMR changes. During the decade of the 1990s (1993–4 to 2004–5), states that had lower MPCE growth actually had a faster reduction in IMR than those that had higher growth of MPCE. The direction of the relationship during this period is therefore reverse, with improvement in economic conditions going along with a deceleration in improvements in IMR.[14] At the All

India level, the change in IMR was more rapid during the earlier period than in the later periods. While IMR reduced at the rate of 3.4 per cent per annum during 1983 to 1993–4, it fell only at a rate of 2.3 per cent per annum during 1993–4 to 2004–5. The last five years have again witnessed a higher rate of decline in IMR of 2.7 per cent per annum. The rate of change in MPCE was more or less than same during the first two periods, slightly increasing in the last five years (1.11 per cent per annum, 1.12 per cent per annum and 1.4 per cent, respectively).

These observations from the data fit in well with the trend that is talked about in existing literature that while there seems to be some convergence in human development outcomes, there is a divergence as far as economic growth is concerned. For example, Kenny (2009), using cross-country data related to income and health indicators such as life expectancy and infant mortality for two different sets of countries (wealthy countries and developing countries) for two different time periods (1913–99 and 1975–2000), finds that while there is a strong cross-country link between income and health, the relationship between improvements in income and improvements in health is comparatively weak, even over the very long term. In fact, most of the studies find that while there might be a strong correlation between current *levels* of per capita incomes and current *levels* of health indicators, the relationship between changes in income and changes in other aspects of human development is even less significant (Kenny 2005, 2009; UNDP 2010). For example, as mentioned in HDR (2010), on average, countries with negative economic growth over 1970–2010 (e.g. Iran, Togo and Venezuela) experienced an increase of 11 years in life expectancy, 22 percentage points in gross enrolment and 40 percentage points in literacy (UNDP 2010).

Within India as well, the literature shows that while there has been divergence in economic growth among Indian states in the 1990s, in relation to human development there is some convergence, although this is debatable. In the 2000s, the backward states have slowed down with the better-off states, again showing an improved reduction in IMRs even in percentage terms. The growth experience in India in the 1980s was more evenly spread, whereas the 1990s saw most of the benefits of liberalisation going only to the more advanced states, with the traditionally backward states of North India remaining backward (Bhattacharya and Sakthivel 2004; Kar and Sakthivel 2007; Pal and Ghosh 2007; Ramaswamy 2007; Nayyar 2008[15]). For instance, Bhattacharya and Sakthivel (2004) find that the coefficient of variation of per capita SDP growth rates increased from 0.22 in the 1980s to 0.43 in the 1990s.

Another study by Purfield (2006) also finds that the gap in per capita income levels between the richer and poorer states has widened over the past three decades.[16]

There is also a variation among Indian states in the rates of change in poverty ratios over the last few decades. Datt and Ravallion (1997), analysing data from the 1960s onwards, show that there has been a remarkable change in the rankings of Indian states on the basis of poverty ratios between 1960 and 1990. For example, the southern state of Kerala moved from having the second highest incidence of rural poverty around 1960 to having the fifth lowest around 1990.[17] For the period 1957 to 1991, Kerala, followed by Andhra Pradesh, Tamil Nadu and Maharashtra, shows the highest trend rates of consumption growth. Estimates by Dev and Ravi (2007) reveal increasing concentration of poor in a few states. A group of six states comprising Bihar, Chhattisgarh, Jharkhand, Madhya Pradesh, Odisha and Uttar Pradesh had a share of 43.3 per cent in the rural poor of the country in 1993–4. This share increased to 49.1 per cent in 2004–5 and further to 54.9 per cent in 2009–10.[18]

The extent of decline in poverty in the postreform period was not faster compared to the prereform period, in spite of higher overall growth. Apart from other factors, an increase in inequality seems to have slowed down the rate of poverty reduction in the postreform period (Dev and Ravi 2007). There have been different explanations given for this variation in economic growth and poverty reduction. Adabar (2004) finds that per capita investment, population growth rate and human capital could explain around 93 per cent variation in the growth rate of per capita real income across 14 major states from 1976 to 2000. An inverse relation between economic growth and population growth among states is seen (Bhattacharya and Sakthivel 2004).

Datt and Ravallion (1997) argued that taking account of differences in initial conditions explains to a large extent the better performance of some states in the longer term. They find that starting endowments of physical infrastructure and human resources appear to have played a major role in explaining the trends in poverty reduction, and a sizable share of the variance among states in the trend rates of progress is attributable to 'differences in initial conditions of physical and human resource development – differences that may well reflect past public spending priorities' (Datt and Ravallion 1997).

There are a number of studies that have shown that while higher per capita income does have a positive impact on health and social indicators, this is only one measure among numerous sociocultural and other factors that influence it. Further, when these other factors, such as female literacy, state spending and provision of public services, are controlled for, the strength of the relation between economic indicators and health outcomes decreases (Anand 1994; Aturupane et al. 1994; Phillips and Verhasselt 1994; Ranis and Stewart 2000; Deaton 2004; Fay et al. 2005; Cutler et al. 2006; Soares 2007). In an influential article based on cross-country data, Preston (1975) found that, over time, the life expectancy associated with a given level of income rose rapidly. Preston argued that factors other than a country's current level of income account for around 75–90 per cent of the rise in life expectancy for the world as a whole between 1930s and 1960s. At the same time, this does not mean that mortality is disassociated with standard of living at a moment of time. Income distribution also plays a role, with more equitable distribution showing higher life expectancy.

Based on a weak relationship between economic growth and changes in health outcomes, some studies conclude that policies for progress in HDI must look beyond enhancing economic growth and in particular must look into spreading the use of available health technologies (Binder and Georgiadis 2010; Georgiadis et al. 2010). Cutler et al. (2006) argue that the fact that almost all of China's reduction in infant mortality happened prior to the acceleration in economic growth after 1980 shows that economic growth is not the only or most important factor explaining mortality reductions. The fact that the later period in China that saw higher growth actually saw slower progress in improving mortality status only reinforces this finding.[19] Bourguignon et al. (2008), in a paper assessing the progress in achieving the Millennium Development Goals (MDGs), find that the correlation between GDP per capita growth and nonincome MDGs is practically zero (during the period 1990–2006).

Based on a review of a number of recent studies, the HDR 2010 states that,

> One of the most surprising results of human development research in recent years, confirmed in this Report, is the lack of a significant correlation between economic growth and improvements in health and education. Our research shows that this relationship is particularly weak at low and medium levels of the HDI. Nor do our results negate the importance of higher income for increasing poor people's access to social services, a relationship supported by extensive microeconomic evidence. The strong correlation between socio-economic status and health often reflects wealthier people's relative advantage in gaining access to health services. But the analysis in

this Report sheds doubt on whether economy-wide income growth is sufficient to further health and education in low and medium HDI countries.

(UNDP 2010: 4)

Further, the relationship between economic development and human development is not unidirectional and works both ways, with one affecting the other.[20] Therefore, it is very difficult to establish causality. Human development can also contribute to economic growth (Suri et al. 2011). Economic growth provides opportunities to 'make sustained efforts towards improvements in human development' while better human development status of a population contributes to higher economic growth through improvements in 'quality of labour force' (Ranis et al. 2000). A more educated population leads to a more productive labour force. Studies have shown, for instance, that farmers with some education have higher productivity compared with illiterate farmers. Further, with improved education and a skilled labour force, many opportunities for economic development open up in an economy. Similarly, a well-nourished or healthy population is more productive than one in which there is a large section that is malnourished and prone to disease. In such different ways an expansion in human 'capital' has a positive effect on economic growth and development.[21]

To study this two-way relationship, Ranis et al. (2000) categorise country performance into four groups: virtuous, vicious and two types of lopsidedness, that is lopsided with strong human development/weak growth (called HD-lopsided) and lopsided with weak human development/strong growth (economic growth (EG)-lopsided).[22] They classify developing countries into these four groups for the period 1960–92 and find that most are in either the vicious or virtuous groups, a significant number in the HD-lopsided pattern and very few in the EG-lopsided pattern.

More interestingly, when they break up this classification into different subperiods they find that while HD-lopsidedness permitted movement towards a virtuous cycle (occurring in about a third of the cases), in the case of EG-lopsidedness, all the cases reverted to a vicious cycle. Very few countries managed to go directly from vicious to virtuous, but some succeeded in moving to HD-lopsided, from where it was possible to move into the virtuous category. The important policy conclusion that is drawn from this study is about the sequencing of policy change, that is that human development must be strengthened before a virtuous cycle can be attained. Policy reforms that focus only on economic growth are unlikely to succeed. Countries in a virtuous cycle category may well slip back into HD-lopsidedness, if for some reason growth slows down, but as long as human development stays high, such cases have a good chance of resuming their virtuous cycle pattern (Ranis et al. 2000). In this analysis (*ibid.*), India is seen to be in the vicious category during the first two periods and in the EG-lopsided category in the latest period, indicating that there is a need to shift focus in India towards policies that enhance human development.

The analysis of the data related to Indian states presented earlier in this chapter does indicate that there are other significant factors influencing health outcomes that need to be studied and that differences in economic conditions do not adequately explain variations in health outcomes across Indian states. Most studies show that good performance on many elements is needed simultaneously and there is no unique path for progress in human development. Based on the historical context and institutional framework, different countries follow different paths towards progress in human development and the role economic growth plays in each of these paths is also different[23] (Ranis and Stewart 2000). The same is the case when we look at each state within India, as will be seen in the rest of this book.

Notes

1 See for example the collection of articles in Mehta and Chatterjee (2011), which puts together various contributions to the debate, on the role of economic growth in poverty reduction, which was generated following a speech by Prof Jagdish Bhagwati in the Indian Parliament.

2 A vast literature shows that individuals with low income, low wealth, low education or low social status often die younger than those who are better off or better educated, and this is true for many countries and for many (if not all) periods (Cutler et al. 2006). If poor houses have additional income, they spend this on food and HD-related items (Ranis et al. 2000).

3 For a further debate on whether inequality causes ill-health, see for example Thorbecke and Charumilind (2002) and Deaton (2003).

4 They also find a similar significant and positive effect of HD on economic growth (Ranis et al. 2000; Ranis and Stewart 2010).

5 The HDI values and data on per capita incomes and a few human development indicators are presented in the Human Development Reports (HDR) brought out by the UNDP each year. Here, we use the rankings and values provided in the HDR (2014). The HDR (2014) provides complete information for 187 countries.

6 Maharashtra ranks high when it comes to per capita NSDP. But its MPCE is low and poverty is high. Distribution is clearly a problem.

7 In all the graphs in Figure 2.1 it can be seen that IMR in Tamil Nadu, West Bengal and Kerala is lower than what is predicted by the economic

indicators with 95 per cent confidence level. On the other hand, the IMR in Uttar Pradesh is above what is predicted.

8 All part of the BIMAROU group. Rajasthan, however, has better MPCE and poverty ratios. These states can be thought of as being the 'vicious' cycle of human development in the Ranis–Stewart framework. The other states are 'EG-lopsided', 'HD-lopsided' or in the 'virtuous cycle'. Based on the data on MPCE and poverty ratios, Tamil Nadu can be classified as being 'HD-lopsided' (Ranis and Stewart 2000).

9 Central Statistical Office (CSO) data available on website http://mospi.nic.in and Sample Registration System (SRS) data available at http://censusin dia.gov.in.

10 As mentioned earlier, a similar analysis cannot be conducted for U5MR and stunting/malnutrition prevalence because of lack of data for these indicators for earlier periods.

11 This is consistent with the literature that finds that correlation between change in economic conditions and change in human development is found to be weaker than the relation between these two at any one point of time (Kenny 2009; UNDP 2010).

12 It must be noted that these two states cannot be compared in these terms so much because reduction of IMR in Uttar Pradesh is easier as it is at a much higher level ('low hanging fruit'). Therefore the achievement of Kerala or Tamil Nadu is much more impressive. See related discussion on base effect in Chapter 1.

13 The periods are basically chosen to be co-terminus with NSS survey years, as MPCE data are available for these years. IMR data on the other hand are available annually. Real MPCE (at 1993–94) prices are used for the analysis. Further because, Jharkhand, Chhattisgarh and Uttarakhand were formed only in 2001 the data presented in Table 3.2 are for the regions corresponding to the older states of Bihar, Madhya Pradesh and Uttar Pradesh, respectively. This is also the reason that this analysis includes only 15 states.

14 This is a probably a reflection on the nature of economic growth in the latter decade.

15 He uses data from 1978–79 to 2002–03.

16 Also see Ahluwalia (2000).

17 Tamil Nadu had the highest incidence of rural poverty around 1960 according to the figures presented by Dev and Ravi (2007).

18 Based on official poverty estimates on the basis of poverty lines recommended by the Expert Group under the Chairpersonship of Prof S. D. Tendulkar (Planning Commission Press Note on Poverty Ratios, GoI 2012).

19 For further evidence on the weak relationship between economic growth and levels of infant mortality or life expectancy, also see Szretzer (1997), Easterly (1999), McGuire (2001), Younger (2001), Deaton (2004) and Bourguignon et al. (2008).

20 Economic development is also a component of human development. However, in this context we are talking about the relationship between economic development and nonincome aspects of human development, such as health and education.

21 For a discussion on human capital, health, education and their contribution to economic growth, see for example Barro (1991), Benhabib and Spiegel

(1994), Rosenzweig (1995), Commission on Macroeconomics and Health (2001), Wilson and Briscoe (2004), Government of India (2005a), Bloom and Canning (2005), Huffman and Orazem (2007) and Whalley and Zhao (2010).

22 In the virtuous cycle case, good HD enhances growth, which in turn promotes HD, and so on. In the vicious cycle case, poor performance on HD tends to lead to poor growth performance, which in turn depresses HD achievements, and so on. The stronger the linkages in the two chains described earlier, the more pronounced the cycle of economic growth and HD, either in a positive or dampening direction. Where linkages are weak, cases of lop-sided development may occur.

23 Ranis and Stewart (2000) find that one necessary condition for progress in human development seems to be a high female enrolment ratio. Beyond that they mention relatively important combinations of elements for success in HD performance. 'One is good growth, if accompanied by reasonably good distribution and social expenditure ratios; the second is moderate growth combined with good distribution and supportive social sector performance; and the third is a strong emphasis on social expenditures (well prioritized) that can even be combined with poor economic growth when accompanied by relatively good distribution' (ibid.: 65).

Chapter 3

Women's status is key

One of the factors that contribute favourably to human development outcomes (especially health status) of the entire population is what is roughly described as 'women's status'. Women's status measured in terms of women's education or women's paid employment is seen to play a major role in determining human development outcomes. It is argued that both women's education and gainful employment increase the decision-making power of women, thereby giving them access to resources and knowledge. Women being the primary caregivers in most societies, increased access to resources through wage earning among women translates into better decisions regarding children's health, education and fertility preferences.[1] Similarly, an educated woman can take informed decisions, has a greater role in decisions of the household and is able to access available public services better. In this manner and other ways, increased maternal education is seen to have a major influence on reduced child mortality.

A direct way in which women's status affects health outcomes is through biological mechanisms. For instance, in the context of child health, one of the most obvious ways in which women's status affects children is through the impact of the mother's health on the child she bears. It is well established that a malnourished mother gives birth to a low-birthweight baby. A low-birthweight baby has greater chances of being a malnourished adult and in case of girls will in turn give birth to malnourished children. Therefore the poor nutrition status of women results in an intergenerational cycle of malnutrition (Martorell et al. 1998; Ramakrishnan et al. 1999). Malnutrition, further, is one of the leading causes of child death and illness in developing countries like India (Pelletier et al. 1995; UNICEF 1998; WHO 1998).

In fact the low status of women in South Asia is one of the most influential explanations given for poor child health, especially high levels of malnutrition among children in these countries. The 'South Asian Enigma'[2] is explained by the role of gender relations and poor social and economic status of women, which impact on women's health, and through intergenerational effects, on child health. The poor status of women has been seen as one of the main reasons for the poor status of child nutrition in India compared to even sub-Saharan African countries (Ramalingaswami et al. 1996; Osmani 1997; Haddad 1999; Smith et al. 2003).

On women's status

Different terms such as women's 'status', women's 'autonomy', women's 'empowerment', 'bargaining power' and 'agency' are often used to indicate the position of women in society. Most often, these terms refer to women's position in relation to men and to some aspect of gender inequality (Mason 1986). They are based on the idea that there is gender inequality in the society, thereby resulting in an overall lower status or position of women. Most also focus on either prestige or power or access to or control over resources (Acharya and Bennett 1981; Sen 1993; Batliwala 1994; Kabeer 2001; Malhotra et al. 2002). Along with control or access over resources, the other concept that is often talked about is 'agency', that is the ability and control to make choices (Sen 1999; Kabeer 2001). Often there is an overlap between these different concepts, and some authors use these terms interchangeably. Of these different terms 'women's status' is the more general one and that is what I use in this study.

Whatever the terminology used, it is difficult to arrive at any single measure that reflects gender relations or women's position in society because gender inequality is empirically as well as conceptually a multidimensional problem. It is difficult to talk about the 'status' of women in any society. The nature of gender inequality is different in different contexts or cultures. Further, within each society women may be better off in terms of one aspect of 'status' while not so in other aspects. Women's 'status' may vary between the private sphere of the household and the public sphere of the community. Moreover, within each community there are differences among women depending on other socioeconomic characteristics such as whether they belong to a rich or poor family, whether they are of an upper caste household or *dalit* household, whether they are married or unmarried, young or old and so on (Acharya and Bennett 1981; Mason 1986; Kishor 1995; Malhotra and Mather 1997; Kishor 2000).

While studying the relation of women's 'status' with fertility or mortality decline or health status in general, the conclusions can therefore depend to a large extent on how 'status' of women is conceptualised and measured. It is difficult to come up with a single measure for even one dimension of women's status.[3] Additional information is usually needed to interpret data on any given indicator (Malhotra et al. 2002). Different aspects of women's status such as education, employment or autonomy also influence each other. Women's status is seen to be primarily determined by levels of education and employment among women. Cultural and social norms, including kinship systems, are also seen to have an influence on women's status (Caldwell 1986).

Definitions of autonomy and empowerment are mostly focussed on the 'control' women have over their own lives – on the decisions they can make, their access and control over resources and so on (Dyson and Moore 1983; Batliwala 1994;[4] Jeejeebhoy 2000). Many agree that empowerment is more a process whereas autonomy is related to a point of time. In studies looking at causal relationships, 'autonomy' is often used (Jeejeebhoy 2000; Kabeer 2001; Malhotra et al. 2002). Since 'empowerment' is a process, it is also difficult to measure. Again, as with regard to 'status' there cannot be a single indicator of autonomy and usually multiple indicators are used. Since there are no direct measures of 'autonomy' available, for a long time many proxies were used, such as women's education, economic activity, age at marriage, postmarital residence without in-laws and proximity to natal home.[5] Later studies have used some direct indicators of autonomy such as economic decision making, mobility, access and control over resources (Jeejeebhoy 2000). The Demographic and Health Surveys (DHS) (NFHS in India) also collect information on many of these direct indicators. Therefore, along with education and employment, I also include 'autonomy' as one of the aspects studied in relation to health outcomes.

As mentioned earlier, 'women's status' is the generic term used in this study when discussing the role of women's position and gender relations in explaining differences in health outcomes. However, in the detailed analysis there is a focus on different aspects of women's status separately. For instance, I look at how female education, female employment and a few direct indicators of women's autonomy such as mobility and decision making are each associated with health outcomes. It is shown how different aspects of women's status operate differently. Many of the aspects of women's status are also very difficult to measure. At the conceptual level, therefore some questions are raised on how these indicators are measured. While the different indicators of 'status' might not all vary in the exact same manner across states, there are some broad patterns that allow us to rank states when comparing them. In this sense one is able to say that women's status is largely better in southern states when compared to some of the states in the northern belt. 'Status' is used as a convenient term to communicate such an understanding.

One other clarification before getting into the details of the relationships – all of these aspects of women's status are also desirable ends in themselves. By focussing attention on how better status of women can influence improved health outcomes, it is not being argued that this should be the only reason for improving women's status or removing gender inequality. Even if there is no relation between the two, there is reason enough to proactively intervene to improve women's lives (in absolute terms and also in relation to men). Having said this, in the present chapter, I focus mainly on the instrumental role of women's status, particularly with reference to health outcomes.

Women's education

Female education is one of the most commonly used indicators to explain differences in levels of human development across countries and regions. A number of cross-country studies have established the positive association between female education and health outcomes such as IMRs, even after controlling for differences in economic growth, per capita incomes and so on. Studies have looked at the influence of female education both at the 'macro' level and at the individual/household ('micro') level. Therefore one aspect is to look at the relation between the level of female education (such as female literacy rate) in a country, state or district and the level of health outcome (such as IMR) in the same unit. The other is to compare the outcomes at the individual/household level (e.g. probability of a child dying or probability of a child being malnourished) with the status of female education at the household level (e.g. mother's education level). As seen in the case of the relation between economic conditions and health outcomes, the relation between female education and health outcomes could also be different at the macro and the individual levels.

Across different studies it has been seen that female education, even more than male education, has a positive effect on the well-being of the entire family, especially of children (Caldwell 1979; Das Gupta 1987; Jejeebhoy 1995; Hobcraft 2000; Miller and Rodgers 2009). Higher levels of mother's education have been seen to be associated with a wide range of positive health outcomes for children including decrease in child and infant mortality, better immunisation, less stunting and better weight for age (Hobcraft 2000; Mishra and Retherford 2000). High female-to-male primary enrolment ratios is one of the factors that have been seen to be necessary, if not sufficient, conditions for success in improving human development (Ranis and Stewart 2010). Another study by Ranis et al. (2000) found that the higher the social expenditure, adult literacy and female education enrolment for a given level of GNP per capita of a country, the larger the improvement in HD.

Martin (1995) in a cross-country study of data from DHSs of 26 countries finds that higher female education is consistently associated with lower fertility and that education enhances women's ability to make reproductive choices. However, the strength of this relationship varies depending on the context – the level of socioeconomic development, social structure and cultural context as well as the society's stage in the fertility transition.

Many studies in the Indian context also find maternal characteristics to be strongly associated with the risk of child mortality. Controlling for other factors, the U5MR decreases by about four deaths per 1,000 live births for each additional year that the mother delays having a child. Likewise, children of literate mothers have an U5MR that is 14 deaths per 1,000 live births lower than that of children of illiterate mothers. The corresponding number for the literacy status of the household head is 8½, indicating that mother's literacy is far more important to children's survival than literacy of the household head (Deolalikar 2005).

A study of the determinants of health and education outcomes in Indian states during the period 1980 to 2000, using data from NSS and NFHS, found that higher levels of educational attainment, especially among females, are strongly and consistently correlated with lower IMRs (Bhalla et al. 2003). Caldwell et al.'s (1982) study in Karnataka found that the largest differentials in infant mortality were related to mother's education, with a level of 130 per 1,000 where the mother had not been to school, 80 where she had only primary schooling, and 70 where she had some secondary schooling. A study by Jain (1985) found that adult women's literacy has a significant impact on infant mortality. Further, this was seen to affect infant mortality primarily through its association with indicators such as better medical care at birth and better preventive and medical care during the postnatal period.

Based on a study on the links between child mortality and maternal education, Caldwell (1979) argues that three factors resulting from increased education are important. These are (1) a reduction in fatalism in the face of children's ill health; (2) a greater capability in manipulating the world (e.g. in knowing where facilities are, and in securing the attention of doctors and nurses); and (3) a change in the traditional balance of family relationships that shifts the focus of power away from the patriarch and the mother-in-law and ensures that a greater share of available resources is devoted to children.[6] Hobcraft (1993) talks about pathways including increase in direct child health knowledge and ability to access such information, increased autonomy or agency that enables the mother to take her own decisions and access medical care and potential health benefits from delayed and lower fertility among educated women, enabling greater investment per child.

Research has also shown that women's education has a positive impact on reducing fertility. More education contributes to reduced fertility by delaying marriage; by reducing desired family size by stimulating aspirations for a higher standard of living and increased investments in fewer children and by preparing women for employment and exposing women to new knowledge, attitudes and practices, related to contraceptive use (Mahmud and Johnston 1994). Cleland and Wilson (1987) have argued that education lowers fertility mainly by changing women's 'perceptions, ideas and aspirations' rather than by affecting such objective realities such as work opportunities or the costs of children. Drèze and Murthi (2001) find that women's education is the most important factor explaining fertility differences across the country and over time. Low levels of child mortality and son preference also contribute to lower fertility. By contrast, general indicators of modernisation and development such as urbanisation, poverty reduction and male literacy bear no significant association with fertility.

In a lot of the literature, increased female 'autonomy' is seen to be the pathway through which female education has a positive effect on fertility rates. However, this relationship between female education and autonomy is somewhat contentious (Jeffery and Basu 1996). Nevertheless, the strong association between female education levels and low fertility rates is well established. This apparent inconsistency is probably because of the way 'autonomy' is defined and also because there are different pathways through which female education impacts fertility rate – autonomy as measured in these studies may not be one of them.

Female education is seen to have an impact not only through the characteristics of the individual mother but also through the educational level of the society as a whole (Ware 1984). According to a model based on NFHS-2 data, the average education among women (but not men) in the census enumeration area has a strong impact on child mortality, net of the mother's own education. The relatively low child mortality associated with women's autonomy explains some of this community education effect (Kravdal 2003; Moursund and Kravdal 2003; Arokias-wamy et al. 2004; Parashar 2005; Moestue and Huttly 2008).

Female literacy in Indian states

Data show that there is a large variation in the level of female literacy among Indian states, with states such as Kerala, Himachal Pradesh, Tamil Nadu and Maharashtra having high levels of female literacy and states such as Uttar Pradesh, Bihar, Jharkhand and Madhya Pradesh having substantially lower female literacy rates. There has been a significant increase in the literacy rate in all states between 2001 and 2011, bringing down the gap between the states. However, a large gap still remains with the female literacy rate in Bihar, for instance, being a little over 70 per cent of that in Tamil Nadu and even less than 60 per cent the female literacy rate in Kerala according to Census 2011.

The gender gap in literacy (difference in the percentage of literates among men and percentage of literates among women) is one basic indicator of the relative status of women in terms of education, which varies widely. Based on the 2011 Census, the state with the highest gender gap in literacy rates is Madhya Pradesh (20.5 percentage points) and the state with the lowest gender gap is Kerala (4 percentage points). In terms of the overall literacy rate in the state, Madhya Pradesh is better than five other states (Andhra Pradesh, Bihar, Jharkhand, Rajasthan and Uttar Pradesh), indicating that female literacy has been particularly ignored in Madhya Pradesh. Incidentally Madhya Pradesh is also the worst performing state in terms of some indicators of health outcomes such as child mortality rate, IMR and child malnutrition. After Kerala, the other states that have a low gender gap in literacy rates are Punjab, Assam, Tamil Nadu and West Bengal. Of these, Tamil Nadu, West Bengal and Punjab (along with Kerala) are among the top performing states in terms of most health outcome indicators.

Looking further at the relation between female literacy rates and health outcomes, we plot health outcomes such as IMR, U5MR and stunting against female literacy rates. As seen in Figure 3.1, there is a clear relation between the two factors. States with higher female literacy are more likely to have lower IMRs. Moreover, the correlation between female literacy and IMR is higher than what was seen in the case of the relation between IMR and indicators of economic well-being such as per capita income, MPCE or poverty ratios. The R^2 is between 0.56 and 0.58. A similar relationship is also seen with U5MRs and stunting. The female literacy rate in a state is negatively related to the U5MR and stunting prevalence in the state.

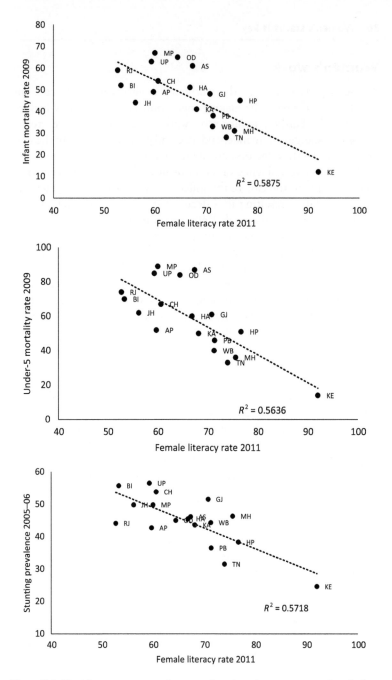

Figure 3.1 Health outcomes and women's education among major Indian states

Source: Female Literacy Rate from Census 2011; IMR and U5MR from SRS Bulletins, Stunting from NFHS-3

Women's work

Women's participation in the workforce is also seen to increase the social status of women by making their contribution to family income more visible. Further, women who work for an income have greater access to resources, more independence and greater exposure to the outside world. All these factors contribute to women's agency, thereby also having a positive influence on child health. This has been seen to be especially true in the case of the influence of women's employment on female mortality, resulting in a decrease in the gender differential in child mortality (Murthi et al. 1997; Durrant and Sathar 2000; Nurul Alam 2006). Where women control cash income, it is seen that expenditures are more geared towards human development-related expenditures such as on food and health (Ranis et al. 2000;[7] Duflo 2011).

However, the positive impact of women's increased control over resources has to be considered along with the possibility of the negative effect of mother's employment on child health, due to decreased availability of time for childcare. When the mother is employed, particularly when she works away from home, children are left either without a caregiver or in the care of siblings or grandparents. These children may not be fed appropriate food or may be more vulnerable to other health hazards such as accidents. This is particularly true when the alternate care provider is another child, such as an older sister.

Studies focussing on the conflict between women's participation in the workforce and the time they have for childcare suggest that children of employed mothers face greater health risks than children whose mothers are not employed. It is argued that for mothers of young children, participation in income-generating activities diminishes the time available for childcare, which in turn results in poor health outcomes and higher mortality for children. A study based on the data of NFHS-1 concludes that the mother's employment is associated with higher infant and child mortality. Controlling for relevant biodemographic, socioeconomic, and individual background characteristics, Kishor and Parasuram find that the odds of dying at ages 12–47 months are significantly higher when mothers are employed (Kishor and Parasuram 1998).[8]

Zachariah et al. (1994) found that in Kerala if a woman was working, the mortality risk for her child during infancy and childhood was higher than if she was not working, because the working woman had a shorter duration of breastfeeding and less time with the child. In a study of a slum population in Delhi, Basu and Basu (1991) also found a higher risk of child mortality for working mothers at least in the poorest section of the population. Similarly a study by Sivakami (1997) in a village in Tamil Nadu found that morbidity rates were higher for the children of working women than for the children of nonworking women. Logistic regression analysis showed that the children of working women are at significantly greater risk of morbidity even when socioeconomic factors are controlled for.[9]

The extent of influence of women's employment on child health may be dependent on the quality of work that women are involved in and overall socioeconomic status of women (Desai 1994;[10] Desai and Jain 1994; Swaminathan 1997; Nakkeeran 2003). Women's economic activities are strongly correlated with family income and socioeconomic status. Hence, the apparent negative correlation between mother's wage work and child health is seen to be caused by the family's socioeconomic circumstances and may have little to do with maternal work status. Looking at the causal role of women's work on child mortality, Krishnaji (1983) argued that working mothers in rural areas generally belong to poor labour or peasant families, and it is the extreme poverty in such families that may indeed explain the higher death rate. In effect, the extent of both female work participation and child mortality is perhaps independently determined by the economic status of the family.[11]

The effects of mother's work on childcare need to be seen differently for women who work out of the necessity to bring in additional income to the family and those who work out of interest and for a higher standard of living. In either case, it needs to be seen whether childcare is compatible with the nature of women's work. Ware (1984) mentions three factors that are relevant to understanding the effects of women's engagement in economic activities on child rearing: the compatibility of the task itself with childcare, the availability of relatives to provide substitute childcare and the distance between the workplace and the home. Related to the economic status of the household is also the ability to hire others to do some of the care work allowing mothers to work in outside jobs.

While the nature and conditions of work that women are engaged in might be an important determining factor, another issue that has received little attention is the amount of time available for childcare for women who are not engaged in paid work outside the household. It is well known that even women who are not 'gainfully employed' do a lot of work, which includes unpaid but 'economic' work, for instance on the family farm or tending to the cattle and domestic work including fetching firewood and water. Implicit in this argument is the assumption that mothers who are not involved in economic work are available for childcare. The above-mentioned study in rural Karnataka (Desai and Jain 1994) finds that regardless of their level of economic participation, most women spend a great deal of time in domestic activities that are not necessarily compatible with caring for their young children. As a result, almost all women rely substantially on older children, older women in the family and even neighbours to look after their children.

The relationship between gainful employment and greater reproductive and sexual choices is also dependent on a myriad factors, such as type of occupation, income, motivation, whether the woman works for someone or is self-employed, duration and continuity of work and whether the work is full or part time (Mahmud and Johnston 1994).

While reduced availability of time at home and difficulty in the provision of childcare are ways in which women's work may have a negative impact on child's health, the positive effect of control over income, increased access to information and resources, enhanced social contact, increased capabilities and so on could result in improved health practices within the household and hence better health outcomes. It is also thought that the benefits of working such as increased control over income or greater say in decision making are higher when the woman is working for cash. Working for an income increases the woman's perceived contribution to the household's economic status and also gives her greater bargaining power as she has a fallback option (Smith et al. 2003). In either case, it is therefore important to understand the impact of women's work based on the context and conditions under which women are living, the kind of work they are engaged in and so on.

Further, while these divergent factors might have a certain effect at the individual/household level, how women's work affects outcomes at the societal level might be different. At the individual/household level, there is a conflict between the positive effect of women's working leading to, for example, increased decision-making power and the negative effect of women having less time for childcare (especially because poorer women are more likely to be working out of economic compulsion and do not have proper alternate childcare arrangements). As seen in the studies mentioned earlier, the resulting effects on child health and mortality vary depending on context, nature of work and so on.

On the other hand, at the societal level, one can think of ways in which higher female employment has a positive effect on health outcomes. A society where more women are working might also be one that is more accepting of women in decision-making roles. Higher levels of women's participation in the workforce indicate greater possibilities for women being part of public life, greater social networks for women and a society in which women have greater 'freedoms'. This could have a positive impact on health outcomes in spite of the negative impact of women's work on childcare at the household level. A cross-country study by Smith et al. (2003) finds that the role of societal gender equality on child malnutrition is positive and significant in South Asian countries. In a study on determinants of child labour and school attendance, Jayachandran (2008) finds that a child is less likely to go to school if his or her mother participates in the workforce but more likely to go to school if he or she lives in a society with high levels of female labour force participation. Therefore, women's workforce participation has important societal effects that might not be captured in individual or household-level analysis.

Women's workforce participation in Indian states

Data on women's work are not as easy to get as measuring women's work is complicated. The two major sources of workforce statistics in India are the Census of India and the National Sample Surveys. It is well known that both of these surveys tend to underestimate women's work. One of the reasons for the underestimation is problem with the understanding of what 'work' is on the part of both women respondents and the Census and NSS investigators. Women who contribute to productive activity often do not believe that they are doing so because it is unpaid. Therefore neither do they report themselves as workers, nor are they seen as 'workers' by the investigators.

There are also empirical problems associated with the measurement of work in a subsistence economy where much work is unpaid and is undertaken at home or on a person's own premises. Although the 1993 UN Systems of National Accounts (SNA)[12] includes production of goods for self-consumption (i.e. subsistence sector) under the purview of national income, the workers (and sometimes output) of this sector are excluded from the official workforce data. In the same way, workers in the informal sector and home-based workers are also sometimes excluded from conventional estimates of the workforce. In addition, activities like collection of fuel wood and fetching water, which are recognised as a part of a national accounts system and are now included in the NSS definition of work, are frequently excluded from the official data on the workforce (Hirway 2002, 2012).

There is also a tendency to consider only paid employment as being 'productive'. However, a significant share of women in rural and urban areas belongs to the category of unpaid workers. For instance Neetha (2006), in a paper based on the analysis of the NSS 55th round (1999–2000) data, showed that in rural areas unpaid family workers constituted about 37 per cent of women while the proportion was 17 per cent in urban areas in the category of principal status workers. Even if one looks at male–female share of unpaid workers, irrespective of the fact that the work participation rate is almost double for male workers, women's share in total unpaid workers was 58 per cent (Neetha 2006). In activities that are recognised to be directly contributing to the national income, that is activities listed under the SNA, over 50 per cent of women's contribution is unpaid (Bhatia 2002).

The workforce in the difficult-to-measure sectors, such as subsistence work, home-based work or informal work, can be better captured through time-use surveys. A pilot study of time use conducted by the NSS in six states of India showed that the WPRs for women as per the time-use data were 58 and 31 per cent for rural and urban areas, respectively, against 25 and 13 per cent according to current weekly status in the closest NSSO employment survey (CSO 1999; Hirway 2005; Mazumdar and Neetha 2011). Analysing such time-use data, Hirway finds that on average, within the extended SNA activities, men spend maximum time on community services (7.9 hours), followed by household maintenance and management (6.7 hours) and on care of children, the old and the sick (6.6 hours). In the case of women, the maximum time is spent on household management (34.4 hours in a week), followed by care activities (12.4 hours) and community services (9.3 hours). Therefore, women spend double the time men do on care activities and five times the time men do on household management (Hirway 2000).[13]

While keeping these constraints in mind, in this section we use workforce participation rates among women as given by NSSO data for 2009–10 and Census 2011 data. The workforce participation rate includes the percentage of women usually employed in principal as well as subsidiary status. In the subsequent household-level analysis, data from NFHS and the field survey are used. This aspect has not been looked at in great detail at this stage, because there is no significant bivariate relationship between women's workforce participation and any of the health outcomes such as IMR at the state level.

Based on data from Census 2011, states with workforce participation rates among women that are higher than 40 per cent are Andhra Pradesh, Chhattisgarh, Himachal Pradesh, Madhya Pradesh, Maharashtra, Odisha, Rajasthan and Tamil Nadu. This list includes states like Himachal Pradesh, Tamil Nadu and Maharashtra with higher levels of human development as well as states like Madhya Pradesh, Chhattis-garh and Rajasthan with poor health outcomes. On the other hand, Kerala, with the best health outcomes, is one of the states with the low-est female workforce participation among the major states. The female workforce participation rate in Uttar Pradesh (35 per cent) is close to that in Kerala (33 per cent). The NSS data for 2009–10 also show a similar ranking. Himachal Pradesh (47 per cent), Andhra Pradesh (44 per cent) and Tamil Nadu (40 per cent) are the states with the highest level of female workforce participation rates in rural areas. Chhattisgarh is the next highest with 37 per cent female WPR. The states with the lowest rural female WPRs are Bihar (6 per cent), West Bengal (15 per cent), Jharkhand (16 per cent) and Uttar Pradesh (17 per cent).

As seen in Figure 3.2 there is no clear relation between female work-force participation and the IMR, among Indian states. There is a posi-tive relationship with higher IMR at higher levels of female workforce participation, but this relationship is very weak, with many exceptions. However, nothing much can be said on the relation between workforce participation and health outcomes at this stage. All we can say is that based on the simple bivariate relationship, these two factors do not seem to be highly correlated.

Female workforce participation is normally seen to have a positive impact on women's autonomy, and such increased autonomy is in turn

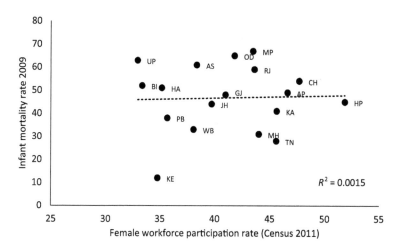

Figure 3.2 Female workforce participation and health outcomes

Source: Female Workforce Participation Rate from Census 2011; IMR from SRS Bulletins

expected to result in better health outcomes, especially for children. On the other hand, studies have also shown that the context in which women are working needs to be considered before arriving at any such conclusion. For example, while female labour force participation is low in Kerala, women in Kerala account for 40 per cent of organised sector employment (34 per cent in Tamil Nadu) while women form only 11 per cent of the organised sector in Uttar Pradesh (GoI 2011e).

The entry of women into paid employment is not necessarily an indicator of well-being because in many cases women enter the labour force as an act of desperation. Therefore more women participating in paid employment may even indicate pauperisation, impoverishment and greater levels of vulnerability for many of those doing so. There is also the question of what kind of work women are entering into. It has been seen that a large majority of women are employed in jobs that are low paid and with poor conditions of work. In many settings, where the norm is for women not to be involved in wage work, it is only under circumstances of extreme poverty that women choose to work outside the house for a wage. In such a context, it is quite likely that poverty might override any positive effect that women's work participation might have on child health outcomes. Further, the absence of supportive social institutions that decrease women's burden of care and domestic responsibilities means that their entry into paid employment results in the double burden of work inside and outside the home (Kak 1994; Kingdon and Unni 2001; Ghosh 2009; Mazumdar and Neetha 2011).

Under these conditions of work, whether being employed in any way contributes to women's status is debatable. Even when women work, in many cases they have no control over their earnings and so the fact that they are working might not change their position in the household. However, it is also true that employment gives women access to the outer world, delays their age of marriage and child-bearing and so on, and therefore can be empowering.[14]

Autonomy and kinship systems

Many studies that have looked at reasons for the wide interstate variations within India have identified low status of women in North India compared to more open societies in the South as an important determining factor for North India's continuing backwardness, especially in comparison with the southern states (Malhotra et al. 1995; Drèze and Gazdar 1997; Ramachandran 1997; Drèze and Sen 2002). Women's status has been seen as an explanatory factor, especially in the context of differences in fertility levels in North and South India and the fertility transition in states like Kerala and Tamil Nadu (Dyson and Moore 1983; Jejeebhoy 1991).

In a comparative study on women's autonomy in Tamil Nadu (Tamil Nadu) and Uttar Pradesh (Uttar Pradesh), Jejeebhoy (2000) found that while generally levels of autonomy were low in most aspects in both places, there was a clear difference between the two states, with women in Tamil Nadu having more autonomy than those in Uttar Pradesh in terms of most indicators. She looked at various indicators related to decision making, mobility, work, child-related decisions and so on. While studying factors that affect autonomy, she found that these are quite different in the two states, with factors such as education levels playing a greater role in Tamil Nadu while in Uttar Pradesh more traditional factors such as co-residence with mother-in-law and size of dowry were more likely to be prominent determinants. She also found that the influence of community-level indicators is notable. Even after controlling for individual and household factors, region plays a significant role in influencing all indicators of autonomy, with Tamilian women experiencing significantly greater autonomy than women from Uttar Pradesh.[15]

Based on a study of Indian states, Guilmoto and Rajan (1998) found that among the relatively better-off states in terms of human development, the pattern of development in South India has relied more on women's involvement and position in society.

Kinship systems and family structure play a role in determining gender relations especially within the household. Rules related to marriage practices, inheritance and so on influence the bargaining power women have within the family. This in turn has an effect on the decisions that are taken in relation to child health and education, thereby affecting health and education outcomes (Miller 1981; Agarwal 1994, 1997). Bargaining power of women is lower in patrilocal and patrilineal societies compared with matrilineal and matrilocal societies. Women who live farther away from their natal homes tend to have less support of their natal family (Agarwal 1994; Chakraborty and Kim 2010). Women's bargaining power is therefore higher in societies where cross-cousin marriages are allowed than in societies that restrict marriages to nonkin. Women have a greater say in the marital home in the case of cross-cousin marriages because they go into a familiar environment.

In India, kinship systems vary by region and within each region by caste, language and religion (Karve 1965). In general, southern kinship systems are considered to be more favourable to women's autonomy than northern kinship systems. Northern systems are patrilineal and patrilocal where marriage between relatives is prohibited, village exogamy is strictly followed and women are not expected to be in close contact with their natal kin after getting married. On the other hand, in South India, cross-cousin marriages are dominant, women are not expected to lose touch with their natal kin, males are likely to form associations with men from the bride's family, dowry is not so important, there is no seclusion and so on, making these systems relatively more consistent with female autonomy than northern kinship systems.[16]

Among higher castes in North India, the *gotra* system disallows marriage within the *Sapinda* kin (which prohibits marriage of two persons who have a common ancestor not more than six degrees removed on the male side or four degrees removed on the female side). Because relatives were likely to be in closer proximity, this *Sapinda* rule increases the distance of marriage for brides. For lower castes, the rules are less restrictive, but cross-cousin marriages are not allowed. These and other features of the northern kinship system such as restrictions on daughters marrying into same families, hypergamy, restrictions on widow remarriage, the 'purdah' system and severance of the relationship between the woman and her natal family contribute to weakening the position of women in society (Karve 1965; Miller 1981; Dyson and Moore 1983; Kolenda 1987; Agarwal 1994; Chakraborty and Kim 2010).

Southern kinship systems on the other hand are more favourable to women. Although even in the South a patrilineal and patrilocal system is followed generally, the practice of close-kin marriages contributes towards enhancing the position of women. Married women live close to their natal homes and continue to have deep ties with the natal family. Further, widow remarriage was generally allowed in the South except amongst Brahmins. Inheritance practices in the South provide greater access to property for women than in the North and the East. Dowry in the South is usually considered to be the woman's property, whereas this is not the case in the North (Karve 1965; Miller 1981; Dyson and Moore 1983; Kolenda 1987; Agarwal 1994; Chakraborty and Kim 2010). It has also been noted that although dowry is now a common practice in both the North and the South, there is greater reciprocity in the South and the burdens of wedding expenses are more equally shared in the South than in the North (Agarwal 1986).

Dyson and Moore (1983) see kinship systems as a close proxy for female autonomy. They argue that this difference in kinship systems predates Muslim influence, reflecting instead basic differences between northern 'Aryan' and southern 'Dravidian' culture. One of the pathways through which the kinship system influences fertility is that the northern kinship system favours early age at marriage. Agarwala (1957) concluded that the states that had consistently high mean age at marriage were Travancore-Cochin, Madras, Mysore (all in the South) and Punjab based on his study of Census data for the period 1891–1951 (Agarwala 1957 cited in Dyson and Moore 1983). Further after marriage, woman's standing improves once she has children, especially male children. Also in the North, women are less educated and have less access to information and health services.[17] For instance, poor acceptance of contraception in the North and greater contraception acceptance in the South might be because women have greater autonomy, they are less likely to be constrained by the influence of senior wives in a joint family situation and there is better interspouse communication. These reasons can also be seen as the link between female autonomy and child mortality. All this does not mean that female autonomy in South is very high but only that it is relatively better despite being low by international standards (Dyson and Moore 1983).[18]

Data related to kinship systems are not available through large-scale surveys. Since kinship is believed to basically influence women's autonomy and bargaining power within the household, for recent periods data available on more direct indicators of autonomy from DHSs have been used in analyses.

Data on women's autonomy in India

Table 3.1 looks at some further indicators of women's autonomy and decision-making power. It is seen that while women in Tamil Nadu seem to have more mobility and say in making household decisions, the situation is quite regressive when it comes to opinions on domestic violence or control over money. Surprisingly, even in Kerala while women seem to have a greater say in household decision making, the proportion of women having the mobility to go out alone or those who think that domestic violence is not justified is quite low and below the national average. There is no clear pattern as far as these indicators of women's autonomy are concerned in relation to human development or economic status of different states. This requires further in-depth analysis.

This apparent lack of relationship between the decision-making indicators might also have to do with the way these questions are asked, especially in large-scale surveys. As we will see some of these indicators in Chapter 7, the field survey data show a significant difference between the sample women in the two states (Tamil Nadu and Uttar Pradesh). This therefore raises questions about these particular indicators and the

Table 3.1 Some indicators of women's autonomy from NFHS-3

S. No	State	Percentage who agree that husband is justified in beating his wife with at least one specified reason*	Percentage of women allowed to go to three specified places alone**	Percentage who know of a microcredit programme	Percentage who have money that they can decide how to use	Percentage who participate in specific household decisions***
1	Andhra Pradesh	75.3 (19)	37.3 (9)	59.6 (4)	48.6 (7)	40.4 (7)
2	Bihar	56.9 (11)	25.2 (16)	27 (13)	58.6 (4)	32.7 (14)
3	Chhattisgarh	33 (2)	17.8 (19)	29.1 (12)	34.3 (14)	26.8 (16)
4	Gujarat	57.2 (12)	47.3 (4)	45 (6)	57.8 (5)	36.6 (10)
5	Haryana	46.1 (4)	40.7 (6)	36.8 (9)	35.5 (13)	41.7 (6)
6	Himachal Pradesh	28.3 (1)	64 (1)	20.2 (15)	28.8 (16)	39.2 (8)
7	J & K	64 (15)	51 (3)	13.1 (18)	55.4 (6)	25.2 (17)
8	Jharkhand	50.4 (7)	36.6 (10)	25.5 (14)	60.2 (2)	41.8 (4)
9	Karnataka	65.7 (17)	30.6 (14)	55 (5)	60.3 (1)	35.2 (12)
10	Kerala	65.7 (17)	34.7 (11)	82.6 (1)	20.7 (19)	47.2 (2)
11	Madhya Pradesh	51.4 (10)	25.7 (15)	30.6 (11)	36.8 (10)	29.4 (15)
12	Maharashtra	50.9 (8)	40.2 (7)	35.5 (10)	40.8 (8)	45.4 (3)
13	Orissa	61.2 (14)	18.7 (18)	69.4 (3)	36.2 (11)	41.8 (5)
14	Punjab	51.3 (9)	39 (8)	40.8 (8)	26.5 (17)	37.4 (9)
15	Rajasthan	57.6 (13)	31.6 (13)	12.3 (19)	32.7 (15)	22.8 (19)
16	Tamil Nadu	65.5 (16)	54.2 (2)	79 (2)	25.4 (18)	48.8 (1)
17	Uttar Pradesh	47 (5)	23.4 (17)	14.1 (16)	59.9 (3)	33.7 (13)
18	Uttaranchal	49.8 (6)	42.8 (5)	13.7 (17)	36.1 (12)	36 (11)
19	West Bengal	42.2 (3)	32.3 (12)	41.4 (7)	37.4 (9)	23.9 (18)
	India	**54.4**	**33.4**	**38.6**	**44.6**	**36.7**

Source: NFHS-3

Notes: Ranks in parenthesis.

* Percentage who agree that a husband is justified in hitting or beating his wife for any of the following reasons: if she goes out without telling him, she neglects the house or children, she argues with him, she refuses to have sexual intercourse with him, she doesn't cook properly, he suspects she is unfaithful, she shows disrespect for in-laws.

** To the market, to the health facility and to places outside the village/community.

*** Percentage of women who usually make specific decisions alone or jointly with their husband regarding own health care, making major household purchases, making purchases for daily household needs and visits to her family or relatives.

way in which these data are collected in large surveys. Further, it is perhaps misleading to use any one of these autonomy indicators independently as representing women's 'status' in society.

Exposure to media

One of the pathways through which education and workforce participation are supposed to have positive impacts on health outcomes is
through increasing women's access to knowledge and information. An
indicator that is a direct measure of women's access to information is
exposure to media. In NFHS-3, respondents' media exposure was measured by asking women and men about the frequency (almost every day;
at least once a week; less than once a week or not at all) with which they
read a newspaper or magazine, watch television or listen to the radio.
Individuals who do not read a newspaper or magazine, watch television
or listen to the radio at least once a week or see a movie at least once a
month are considered to not be regularly exposed to any media.

It is true that exposure to media would also depend on the household's
economic status (whether a TV or a radio is available in the house or
not) and on more macrolevel factors (such as whether there is electricity supply in the village) and therefore any relation we see between
exposure to media and health outcomes might indeed be due to other
correlated factors. While the effect of media exposure (as of other factors) controlling such factors will be studied in Chapter 5, to get a better sense of the bivariate relationship, along with women's exposure to
media, we also look at the relation between the gender gap in media
access (gap between percentage of men who are regularly exposed to any
media and women who are regularly exposed to any media in each state)
and its relation to health outcomes.

In the southern states of Kerala, Tamil Nadu, Andhra Pradesh and
Karnataka, women have high exposure to media. This is also true
for Jammu & Kashmir, Himachal Pradesh and Maharashtra. In the
North Indian states of Madhya Pradesh, Chhattisgarh, Uttar Pradesh,
Rajasthan, Bihar and Jharkhand, the exposure to media among women
is the lowest and also much lower than the all India average of 65.4 per
cent. Not only are one in three women not regularly exposed to media
in the country, but there is a large gender differential in media exposure
evident from these data. However, the extent of this difference is not
the same amongst all the states. In the states of Tamil Nadu, Jammu
and Kashmir, Punjab and Kerala where there is high exposure to media,
it is seen that the gender gap in the exposure to media is low. In other

words, in the states that showed higher levels of human development, women have relatively higher exposure to media and the gender gap in the exposure to media is lower.

As seen in Table 3.2, the correlation coefficients between women's exposure to media with all the three indicators considered are quite high and negative. Therefore, there is a pattern whereby states with higher women's exposure to media are also states with lower IMR, U5MR and stunting prevalence. Similarly, a correlation with gender gap in exposure to media is also evident. The positive coefficients indicate that states that have a higher gender gap in exposure to media are also the ones that have higher IMR, stunting and U5MRs. However, the correlation coefficients in relation to the gender gap indicator are slightly lower for all the indicators, compared to that for absolute level of female exposure to media.

The state-level data presented in this chapter clearly show a positive relation between female literacy and health outcomes across the different states in the country. On the other hand, the effect of female workforce participation and also certain direct measures of autonomy are not as straightforward. Further, at the household/individual level as well, it is seen both from the primary and NFHS data that female literacy seems to have a strong positive relationship with health outcomes. In the case of women's work status, NFHS data show women who are unemployed having healthier children. In the case of both education and employment, the effects that they have on health outcomes will be further studied in later chapters by controlling for other factors such as income and availability of public services.

As far as autonomy and decision-making indicators are concerned, it has been seen that some of the data are counterintuitive. A distinction that can be made while understanding women's status is between women's status in the public sphere and private sphere. Within each state and among different states, women's status in the public (outside the family) and private (within the family) spheres differs. For example, even though the prevalence of domestic violence is similar in Tamil

Table 3.2 Women's exposure to media and health outcomes

Correlation coefficients	IMR	Stunting	U5MR
Women's exposure to media	−0.65	−0.79	−0.74
Gender gap in exposure to media	0.54	0.70	0.62

Source: Estimated from NFHS-3

Nadu and Uttar Pradesh, the participation of women in public spaces is much greater in Tamil Nadu than in Uttar Pradesh. Within Tamil Nadu, although women may not have much voice within the household in relation to their husbands or mothers-in-law regarding issues such as decision making over household budgets, they are quite mobile and able to access markets, health centres, ration shops and so on on their own when compared to other Indian states. Both of these aspects of women's status can influence human development outcomes. Higher women's status in the private sphere influences intrahousehold decision making in favour of better human development outcomes. Better women's status in the public sphere allows women to access services and information, and their needs can become part of public action.

A similar distinction can also be made between the household effect of women's status and its social effect. While children of women who are working outside the house might be at a disadvantage due to the absence of alternate childcare arrangements, an area or region where more women work places greater value on women, allows for collective action by women, makes women's voices public and so on. All of this contributes to better human development outcomes. Therefore, some aspects of women's status may have an important 'social' effect even though this might not show up in individual-level analysis. These issues related to the pathways of how women's status affects human development outcomes are discussed further in the chapters ahead.

Notes

1 See for example Murthi et al. (1997), Haddad (1999), Smith and Haddad (2000) and Smith et al. (2003).
2 The 'Asian Enigma' is discussed in the context of the high levels of malnutrition in South Asia even when compared with sub-Saharan Africa. Here, the lower level of child mortality in South Asia is explained by the better state of child health care services in these countries (Sundararaman and Prasad 2006).
3 For example if decision making within the family were to be measured, this would usually require a number of indicators related to decision making around different aspects. The NFHS for instance collects information on whether women play a role in decision making related to buying assets, children' schooling, children's health, family meals and so on.
4 'The most conspicuous feature of the word empowerment is the word power,' which, to sidestep philosophical debate, may be broadly defined as control over material assets, intellectual resources and ideology. . . . Empowerment is a process and also the result of a process' (Batliwala 1994).
5 Other proxy indicators used include age, marital duration, number of children/sons, marriage within kin and the size of dowry.

6 Also see Helen Ware (1984).

7 They quote studies from Gambia, Philippines and Cote d'Ivoire.

8 Jatrana (1999), based on a study in Haryana, finds that combining work and childcare does decrease the time spent on childcare, especially for girl children, in terms of breastfeeding duration and adequate care.

9 This study however had a small sample size and the author cautions that the two groups studied, working women and nonworking women could represent two classes in the society and coefficients from pooled regressions may not reflect true effects in individual classes.

10 Desai also points out that focus on individual behaviour change is not right and even while we talk of women's education and work, larger socioeconomic conditions under which women live must be focus of policy. The resulting policy recommendations cannot overburden women.

11 It is noted here that the Kishor and Parasuraman (1998) study did control for socioeconomic factors and found that women's employment is positively correlated with child mortality but not infant mortality.

12 Human activities carried out in any society can be divided into three broad groups: market oriented and nonmarket-oriented economic activities falling within the SNA production boundary, which could be termed as 'SNA activities'; nonmarket-oriented 'noneconomic activities', which essentially generate services (and some goods), which are produced by households without undergoing monetary transactions. These activities fall outside the SNA Production Boundary, but within the General Production Boundary. These activities can be termed as 'extended SNA activities' and personal activities, as defined by the third-person criterion, that is activities that cannot be delegated to others and need to be performed by a person himself or herself. These activities are usually known as non-SNA activities (Hirway 2000).

13 About 62.8 per cent of men and 62.8 per cent of women participate in SNA activities, while 88.7 per cent of women and 46.6 per cent of men participate in extended SNA activities.

14 Later in this book I argue that there is a difference in the way employment contributes to women's status and in turn health outcomes at the individual level and the social level. Even in the case of quality of work and working conditions one can say that while at the individual level this might not benefit a woman much when the conditions of work are so poor, at the societal level the fact that a large number of women are going out of the house and participating in work can contribute to women's status and position. It is also easier for women to organise themselves for collective action when they are working together outside the home.

15 Also interesting is that she finds no such influence of religion. Jejeebhoy and Sathar (2001) conclude that their findings confirm that extent to which women enjoy autonomy in terms of decision making, mobility, threatening relations with husband and access to and control over economic resources is powerfully shaped by social institutions of gender within each community, as defined here by region. Further similar results are found when, along with Tamil Nadu and Uttar Pradesh, they include data from Punjab province in Pakistan.

16 Southern kinship system predominates in Kerala, Tamil Nadu, Andhra Pradesh and Karnataka. The northern system prevails in the northwestern states including Rajasthan, Gujarat, Punjab, Haryana and Uttar Pradesh. Maharashtra and Madhya Pradesh are intermediate between the two. West Bengal is closer to southern kinship system, seen by lower median distance between natal and marital homes. Orissa and Bihar are difficult to categorise and can at best be described as being intermediate (Dyson and Moore 1983).

17 The poor access is also because of the unavailability of female workers in these services.

18 See Karve (1965), Kolenda (2003) and Jejeebhoy and Halli (2006) on kinship systems in South India.

Chapter 4

Public provisioning matters

There are compelling reasons to justify the role of states in health provision.[1] First, there are equity and social justice considerations – the poor cannot always afford health care. Health is a basic need and access to health care is a fundamental right. Any democratic government therefore has the responsibility to ensure that its people have access to health care. Support can be provided to the poor through health insurance or direct provision of health services. The health system in a country can be one that provides universal access or targeted support. While there are debates on the form in which health care should be provided (public vs. private, state funding vs. state provision), it is well accepted there is a need for governments to spend on the health care of the population and that out of pocket health care expenditure must be minimised (CSDH 2008).

Second, even from an economic point of view, health care is a commodity that is not always produced efficiently by the markets. Health care is unlike other commodities, and therefore the principles of competitive markets resulting in efficient outcomes do not always apply. There are multiple market failures in the provision of health care that necessitate state action (Arrow 1963). Some actions that promote health care are public goods or have large positive externalities. Externalities are considered to be causes of inefficiency in the market because private markets would not produce them at all or would produce too little (in the case of positive externalities). In the field of health care, the prevention of communicable diseases is an example of positive externalities. It is advantageous to the entire community, and not just to the people affected by the disease. Left to the market, immunisation against such diseases would not be universal, as it is not profitable to do so at an individual level. Goods and services with positive (or negative) externalities can therefore not be left to the free market and there is a need for some kind of collective action (provision or regulation) or state intervention for the same.

A related argument in favour of state intervention in provision of health care is that health care is a merit good. Merit goods have two characteristics: The net private benefit to the consumer is not fully recognised at the time of consumption and the goods also have positive externalities associated with them. For instance, individuals do not know exactly when and if the benefits of inoculation will arise and therefore underestimate the private benefit. At the same time, being immunised also protects others from getting the disease and hence has positive externalities. Therefore, while markets may form for the provision of merit goods the supply is unlikely to be at the level that is socially efficient. This therefore warrants government intervention (Dasgupta 1993).

Moreover, there are other market failures involved because of asymmetric information in markets for health care, generating problems like 'adverse selection' and 'moral hazard', thereby requiring government intervention (World Bank 1993; Peabody 1999). Adverse selection is a market failure due to asymmetric information between the buyer and the seller before a transaction takes place (Akerlof 1970). In the field of health care, adverse selection arises, for example, when unhealthy people seek insurance coverage more than healthy people. One of the reasons for this is that people are better informed of their health conditions than insurance companies.

Another issue in health discussed widely in literature as leading to market failure is the moral hazard problem. Moral hazard is a tendency to be more willing to take a risk, knowing that the potential costs or burdens of taking such risk will be borne, in whole or in part, by others. An example of moral hazard is the claim that people with a health insurance tend to be less careful about their own health (by indulging in unhealthy practices such as smoking) in spite of knowing the ill effects because they are insured for any illness that may occur. Patients not responding to the true cost of care and asking for additional diagnostic testing and treatment because they are insured is also an example of moral hazard (Kurian 2006).

In their book, *Poor Economics*, Banerjee and Duflo (2011) argue that people's health seeking behaviour (of the poor as well as the rich) is often influenced by their beliefs and theories. For example, the poor in many countries believe that injectables are more effective than oral medicines. The belief might be a result of overmedication by doctors who prescribe medicines even when the disease is self-limiting. However, because the patient feels better after visiting the doctor, he or she attributes it to the injection unaware that it probably had nothing to do with it. In a private unregulated market, where there is a nexus between doctors, pharmacists and pathologists, such overmedication and overdiagnosis can be quite common. Similar maybe the case with immunisation where no direct benefit is seen and when it is not understood what exactly is being prevented, falling ill in spite of immunisation might be attributed to the failure of immunisation even though the vaccine might have been for something completely different. Banerjee and Duflo (2011) argue that there is a need for a system of incentives, along with provision of services, for people to take the 'right' health care decisions. This is another example of how market failures arise in health care, warranting the need for public intervention.[2]

These different market failures that are seen in the provision of health/medical care along with equity and social justice considerations make a strong case for state intervention.

Role of public expenditure in health outcomes

Many studies look at public expenditure as one of the explanatory factors in determining health outcomes such as IMR, U5MR or life expectancy. The evidence from these studies is mixed. While most find a significant and expected negative relationship when looking at a bivariate model between spending and IMR, once other factors are controlled for in a multivariate analysis, the relationship is not always significant. Some studies find the level of public expenditure plays a significant role while controlling for other factors such as income levels, while others find that it is insignificant. The difference in results could be because of differences in the datasets used, time periods under study, countries included, methodology of analysis and so on.

A cross-country study by Anand and Ravallion (1993) found that public health expenditure raises life expectancy and that, conditional upon this, income has no effect. The route through which increased income results in better human development outcomes is through increased public expenditures. They find that life expectancy has a significantly positive correlation with GNP per capita, but this relationship works mainly through the impact of GNP on incomes of the poor and public expenditure in health care. Based on this study they state,

> If social expenditures and the reduction in income poverty are the main forces driving human development, rather than economic growth per se, then policy intervention can play a role in promoting

human development independently of the promotion of aggregate affluence. Some countries have followed this route, and achieved impressive social outcomes for their income level (p. 144).

Conley and Springer (2001) study the relationship between welfare spending on health and IMRs across rich countries and find that there is a significant relationship between the two. This association is stronger when they look at the cumulative effect of state spending over three or five years, with a 1 per cent increase in per capita public health spending (average per year) over a period of five years being associated with a 0.348 per cent reduction in IMR. They find that state spending affects infant mortality both through social and medical mechanisms.

Wang (2003) using cross-country data from across 60 developing countries finds that among the factors that can significantly reduce child mortality are access to electricity, vaccination in the first year and public health expenditure. Caldwell's (1986) study looking at the reasons behind improved human development in Sri Lanka, Costa Rica and Kerala finds that public provisioning by the state of health and education services for all is a significant contributor. This is also true of China and Vietnam, where although there was no open democracy the commitment of the state to the human development of its population saw tremendous improvements in health and education outcomes even without commensurate rise in incomes.

Based on cross-sectional data for developing countries, Gupta et al. (2002) and Baldacci et al. (2003) also find that social spending is an important determinant of education and health outcomes. Gupta et al. (2003) argue that public spending on health may matter more to the poor, because they rely more on public health resources while the non-poor are able to substitute private spending for public spending.[3] They argue that along with higher public spending on health, additional complementary policies are needed to make sure the health interventions reach the intended beneficiaries.

Dholakia and Dholakia (2004) develop a model to study the welfare returns of public expenditure allocation. Applying this model to data from 14 Indian states for the period 1971 to 1991, they find that the role of government expenditure in accelerating basic welfare (using indices for health, education and nutrition) is important, even while controlling for average annual real per capita income. In another study comparing Indian states, it is seen that infant mortality in rural India is significantly affected by variations in state health expenditure while controlling for state income and allowing for a lagged effect (Bhalotra 2007).

Bokhari et al. (2006) in their study comparing data across 127 countries find that government health expenditure is an important factor in determining the U5MR and MMR, along with other factors such as economic growth, quality of public spending, levels of corruption, sanitation and road network. Deolalikar's (2005) paper points to the importance of household living standards and infrastructure – access to piped water, toilets, all-weather roads, and regular electricity – in bringing about mortality reduction. In addition, he finds that immunisation coverage in a district has a significant (inverse) association with both U5MR and infant mortality.

On the other hand, a study by Bhalla et al. (2003) found no role for public expenditures at all and concluded that it is simply girls' education that can explain most of the improvement in human development outcomes. Some earlier studies (summarised in Musgrove 1996) also found no evidence that public spending on health has any impact on child mortality.[4]

In a study looking at the effect of government health expenditure on infant and under-five mortality using cross-sectional data on 98 developing countries in 1992–3, Filmer and Pritchett (1999) find that while public expenditures on health do reduce under-five mortality, empirically this is a very small and statistically insignificant effect. Using data for 50 developing and transition countries observed in 1994, Gupta et al. (2002) find some evidence that government health expenditure is negatively correlated with childhood mortality, but they show that this relationship is not robust. Using a state panel for 1980–99, the Deolalikar (2005) study finds no effect of current health expenditure on mortality rates once state-fixed effects and a linear time trend are included in the model.

It is argued that what needs to be looked at is not just the scale of public expenditure but its composition, for instance what is the share of public expenditure that is reaching the poor; how much of the expenditure on education is on primary education and how much on higher education; the 'efficiency' with which public services are delivered and so on. International comparisons on health spending and outcomes across lower income countries find rather weak links, suggesting that how well money is spent is at least as important as how much is spent (Berman and Ahuja 2008).

For example, using data across 120 countries for the period 1975 to 2004, Baldacci et al. (2004) find that health spending has a positive and significant effect on health outcomes. An increase in health spending of 1 percentage point of GDP is associated with a rise in the under-five child survival rate of 0.2 percentage points, on average, in developing countries. They further find that governance has a significant effect on the relation between social spending and social indicators, with health spending being particularly sensitive to governance. In their study, health spending is seen to have no effect on health indicators in countries suffering from poor governance. Therefore, the lack of control for governance could account for the weak relationship between spending, social indicators, and growth found in some previous studies.

This reiterates the point that instead of looking at public expenditures *per se*, it is more relevant to examine the actual availability and quality of services for the people utilising them. However, such data are more difficult to get.

Public health expenditure across states in India

In India most health expenditure is out of pocket, with public health expenditure being amongst the lowest in the world relative to GDP or in per capita terms. In terms of proportion of GDP spent on health (government expenditure), India ranks amongst the bottom five across all the countries included in the Human Development Report. However, there are large variations in what different states spend on health. Health is a state subject, and so analysis of health budgets at the state level is essential. Eighty-five per cent of public health expenditure in India is by state governments. While the share of state governments' expenditure in overall public health expenditure is decreasing, especially after the introduction of the National Rural Health Mission (NRHM), it constitutes the major part.

Studies have found that social sector spending in India reduced in the 1990s, after the introduction of economic reforms. However, in the following decade there was a reversal in this trend with increased expenditures being seen in many sectors.[5] Mooij and Dev (2002) for example, find that in the postreform period (1990s), in most of the states, the proportion of GSDP spent on social services (including health and education) and rural development declined.

Bhat and Jain (2006) find that there was a decline in public health care expenditures in the period between 1990 and 1996 across all major Indian states, which then increased in the period 1996 to 2002 in most states. Bihar and Uttar Pradesh have the lowest levels of expenditure. Further, these states show a lot of fluctuation. On the other hand states such as Tamil Nadu, Maharashtra and Rajasthan do not show much fluctuation in public health care expenditure. Taking the entire period from 1990 to 2002 together it is seen that there was an increase in the public health care expenditure in all states except for Uttar Pradesh, Orissa, Gujarat and Assam, which saw a decline.

Studies have also found that there is a difference in the composition of spending and use of public services across states. Mahal et al. (2001) find that

> Overall, Southern and Western states had a more equitable use pattern for public services than states in the North and North East parts of the country. . . . Kerala was the only state that showed a pro-poor concentration index while Gujarat, Tamil Nadu and Maharashtra had concentration indices not statistically different from 0. Bihar, Himachal Pradesh, Rajasthan, Uttar Pradesh, Orissa and the North East states had a pro-rich orientation for public spending on curative care (p. 18).

Public provisioning data across states and their relation to health outcomes

One of the common indicators of public expenditure used in human development analysis is the ratio of social sector expenditure to total public expenditure. This could be seen as an indication of the priority given by the governments to the social sector among various expenditure commitments. The data on government expenditures for Indian states have been accessed from the RBI Bulletins on state finances.[6] Social sector expenditure (SSE) as given by the RBI includes expenditure on social services,[7] rural development and food storage and warehousing under revenue expenditure, capital outlay and loans and advances by the state governments. Health expenditure on the other hand includes expenditure under the heads 'Medical and Public Health' and 'Family Welfare'.

Table 4.1 presents the average, for a period of three years, of the proportion of social sector expenditure to total expenditure by the state governments from 1990 to 2011 for the major states in the country. Throughout all these periods (except for 2002–5) on average around 35 per cent of total public expenditure was on the social sector at the All India level. While the proportion of social sector expenditure to total expenditure for southern states (also those with better human development outcomes) such as Kerala, Tamil Nadu and Andhra Pradesh is consistently higher than the All India average, this is also true of Bihar and Madhya Pradesh, which have very low human development indicators.

Table 4.1 Proportion of social sector expenditure to total expenditure

S. No	State	Proportion of social sector expenditure to total expenditure						
		1990–93	1993–6	1996–9	1999– 2002	2002–5	2005–8	2008– 11
1	Andhra Pradesh	40.9	36.6	39.1	36.5	31.7	33.4	38.4
2	Assam	37.1	39.5	39.7	37.7	34.5	39.2	37.6
3	Bihar	41.4	40.7	43.2	41.8	34.5	40.0	42.4
4	Chhattisgarh	–	–	–	–	38.4	46.9	52.9
5	Gujarat	33.7	34.1	33.4	35.4	28.9	33.3	37.8
6	Haryana	31.1	24.4	24.3	34.0	23.1	31.5	39.7
7	Himachal Pradesh	33.6	36.9	37.0	35.6	29.3	33.4	36.1
8	Jharkhand	–	–	–	–	46.2	45.5	46.1
9	Karnataka	36.6	38.4	38.6	37.1	29.4	34.3	39.2
10	Kerala	41.5	39.7	42.5	39.9	34.5	33.1	34.0
11	Madhya Pradesh	40.3	40.9	40.9	39.7	30.3	34.9	37.2
12	Maharashtra	37.7	37.2	37.6	35.5	30.8	37.0	39.9
13	Orissa	36.9	38.6	38.4	39.8	29.5	33.3	41.7
14	Punjab	25.0	23.9	22.6	24.7	17.4	19.8	24.6
15	Rajasthan	37.4	37.5	39.3	40.4	35.7	39.7	44.2
16	Tamil Nadu	40.4	41.0	39.9	38.5	33.0	35.5	40.2
17	Uttar Pradesh	35.5	30.6	33.6	33.0	26.1	33.8	38.3
18	West Bengal	44.0	40.6	38.4	37.1	27.7	31.8	38.2
	All states	**37.4**	**36.0**	**36.7**	**36.3**	**30.2**	**34.6**	**38.8**

Source: Estimated from State Finances: A Study of Budgets, RBI (2011)

A cursory look at Table 4.1 suggests that there is no significant relation between states that have a higher proportion of social sector expenditure to total expenditure and those that have better social sector outcomes. This indicator is not very useful as the absolute amounts of total public expenditure vary to a large extent between states and therefore even though the proportion of social sector expenditure may be higher in some states, in terms of the absolute amount spent or the per capita benefit it might be very low.

Per capita public spending on health and health outcomes

Per capita spending is therefore a better indicator to compare the extent of public spending on human development across the states. The data related to the average per capita expenditure on health during the last decade are presented in Table 4.2. The states that spent the highest amount on health (public spending) on average during the period 2000–5 are Kerala, Maharashtra, Punjab and Tamil Nadu – all states that are also amongst the top five in terms of health outcomes. In the latter period too (2005–10), these states are the highest spenders in terms of per capita public spending on health. However, the states where the spending increased most in absolute terms between the two periods are the poorer and backward states of Assam, Chhattisgarh, Jharkhand and Uttar Pradesh.[8]

Table 4.3 (reproduced from Prabhu and Selvaraju 2006) shows the average per capita public spending on health, for four different time periods, between the years 1980 and 2003. These time periods were chosen by the authors to indicate pre- and post-reform periods. The figures in this table show the real average per capita public spending on health. Here it is clearly seen that states with better human development outcomes such as Kerala, Maharashtra, Punjab and Tamil Nadu have spent higher amounts on health than average in all the time periods. In the periods 1992–3 to 1997–8 and 1998–9 to 2002–3, the per capita average

Table 4.2 Average per capita public spending on health, 2000–10 (in rupees)

State	Period	
	2000–5	2005–10
Andhra Pradesh	182	323
Bihar	89	155
Chhattisgarh	110	245
Goa	722	1,236
Gujarat	167	255
Haryana	159	275
Jharkhand	117	334
Karnataka	190	300
Kerala	251	403
Madhya Pradesh	91	122
Maharashtra	272	466
Orissa	135	222
Punjab	248	346
Rajasthan	167	261
Tamil Nadu	200	332
Uttar Pradesh	98	249
West Bengal	173	249

Source: Estimated from RBI (2011)

public expenditure in Tamil Nadu was second only to Punjab. This is significant considering that Punjab is a richer state. Even in the earlier time periods of 1980–1 to 1987–8 and 1988–9 to 1991–2, the average per capita public spending on health in Tamil Nadu was the fourth highest among the major states, with Kerala and Gujarat spending more in the latter period and Maharashtra, Kerala, Gujarat and Haryana spending more in the former period. Again all of these are states that are economically better off than Tamil Nadu.

Other states such as Haryana and Gujarat, which have lower human development outcomes, have had higher social spending. These two states, while among the richer states in terms of economic status, are not amongst the better performers in human development. However, it is also true that states with the lowest human development outcomes such as Bihar, Uttar Pradesh, Madhya Pradesh and Orissa have consistently spent lower amounts per capita on health.

By the last period for which data are provided in Table 4.3, the per capita public health spending in Uttar Pradesh was less than half of what it was in Tamil Nadu. Bihar is the only other state that spent such a low amount on health. Other poor states such as Orissa and Madhya

Table 4.3 Average per capita public spending on health

S. No	State	1980–81 to 1987–8	1988–9 to 1991–2	1992–3 to 1997–8	1998–9 to 2002–3
1	Andhra Pradesh	62.57	73.22	75.30	102.61
2	Bihar	33.70	44.01	46.90	56.54
3	Gujarat	74.99	86.70	89.33	120.71
4	Haryana	74.90	73.86	71.32	90.40
5	Karnataka	65.07	77.24	86.02	118.41
6	Kerala	74.65	90.07	96.78	116.22
7	Madhya Pradesh	50.68	57.11	57.49	74.49
8	Maharashtra	76.25	82.71	84.74	100.76
9	Orissa	54.48	60.42	57.80	76.91
10	Punjab	92.22	117.22	107.01	161.90
11	Rajasthan	62.38	77.94	88.04	106.81
12	**Tamil Nadu**	**70.73**	**89.80**	**101.33**	**124.04**
13	Uttar Pradesh	40.61	59.19	57.64	56.76
14	West Bengal	58.39	66.56	70.73	104.18
	Average spending	**63.97**	**75.43**	**77.89**	**100.77**

Source: Reproduced from Seeta Prabhu and Selvaraju (2006)

Note: Per capita expenditure in 1993–4 prices

Pradesh while being amongst the low spenders still had per capita public health spending that was considerably higher than these two states. On the other hand, Haryana, which is amongst the richest states spent a lower amount per capita on health than did Tamil Nadu, Kerala or West Bengal.

Per capita health spending and IMR/U5MR

There is a broad relationship between per capita public health spending and health outcomes. While some states that spent higher amounts did not show the best health outcomes (Haryana, Rajasthan), it is clear that those that had the lowest health outcomes such as Bihar, Uttar Pradesh, Orissa or Madhya Pradesh were also amongst the lowest spenders on health. Figure 4.1 shows a clear negative relationship, with the IMR (and U5MR) being lower at higher levels of per capita spending on public health. Fitting a trend line into these scatter plots suggests that the correlation is high, with the R^2 value being around 0.52 when we look at the relationship between the average per capita public expenditure on health with the U5MR and IMR.

In fact, looking at the same relationship, but taking into consideration the average per capita public expenditure for a previous period (2000–5), we find a stronger relationship. Figure 4.1 also shows the

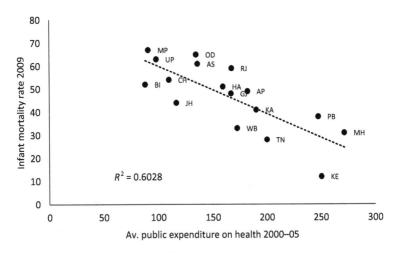

Figure 4.1 Health outcomes and public spending on health

Source: SRS for IMR and U5MR; pub. health exp estimated from RBI (2011)

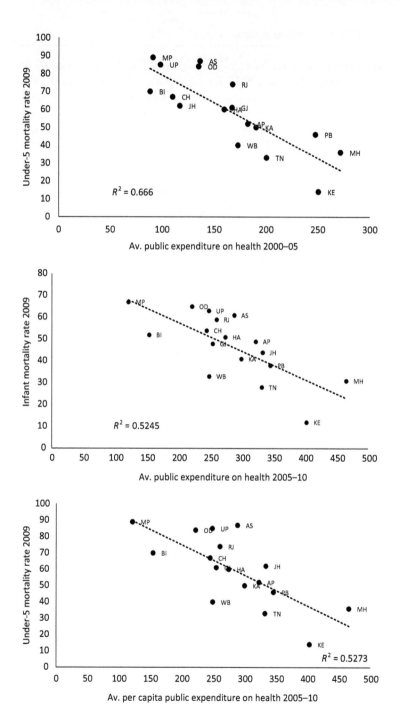

Figure 4.1 Continued

relationship between average per capita public health spending in 2000–5 with IMR and U5MR for 2009. As can be seen from the two graphs, the R^2 is higher in this case than when the average per capita public health spending for the current period is considered. This could be because there is a lag for the effect of public spending to be seen in the health outcomes. This adds weight to the argument that the direction of the relationship (at least to some extent) is mainly from public spending to IMR/U5MR and not only the other way round.[9]

As noted in the literature, it is not just the public expenditure on health that matters but the efficiency with which this amount is spent and the way the spending is distributed across different sectors and groups of population. In the following sections, I present some of these aspects of health availability and access across the different states by looking at some indicators of health infrastructure and access to health services.

Health infrastructure and human resources

Primary- and secondary-level health care in the public health system are provided through a network of subcentres (SCs), primary health centres (PHCs) and community health centres (CHCs). The norms for these centres are that there should be an SC for every 5,000 population, a PHC for every 30,000 population and a CHC for every 100,000 population. Table 4.4 shows the shortfall in the availability of these health centres across Indian states with reference to these norms. It also gives the average rural population covered by each of these health centres.

As can be seen from Table 4.4, the southern states of Andhra Pradesh, Karnataka, Kerala and Tamil Nadu, along with Himachal Pradesh, Orissa, Chhattisgarh and Assam, have a greater number of PHCs than is required by the norms. Of these, all the states except Orissa, Chhattisgarh and Assam are also those that rank high in terms of their health outcomes such as IMR or U5MRs. In relation to CHCs, while there is a shortfall in all states, the extent of the shortfall varies across states. In some states such as Tamil Nadu and Kerala where there is a shortfall in CHCs, it is probably not such an issue because of the surplus SCs and PHCs, which are also well-staffed with good infrastructure when compared with other states. The northern states of Uttar Pradesh, Madhya Pradesh and Bihar have shortages at all levels, such as SCs, PHCs and CHCs. Even in terms of the average rural population served by each health centre, there is a vast difference between different states.

Table 4.4 Availability of health centres in rural areas

S. No.	State	Percentage of shortfall			Average rural population covered by		
		SC	PHC	CHC	SC	PHC	CHC
1	Andhra Pradesh	S	18.4	65.3	4,424	35,287	331,743
2	Assam	9.3	S	50.0	5,056	27,507	225,401
3	Bihar	40.8	34.1	88.7	8,390	45,287	1,061,667
4	Chhattisgarh	S	S	17.1	3,512	23,090	122,412
5	Gujarat	S	8.4	6.8	4,364	29,581	116,267
6	Haryana	19.0	16.0	31.2	6,177	35,784	174,759
7	Himachal Pradesh	S	S	S	2,647	12,210	75,100
8	Jharkhand	21.7	59.1	3.5	5,294	63,491	108,000
9	Karnataka	S	S	S	4,285	15,895	108,016
10	Kerala	S	S	45.7	4,628	25,934	220,322
11	Madhya Pradesh	15.1	31.2	35.3	5,024	38,626	164,374
12	Maharashtra	13.0	8.5	17.9	5,272	30,715	137,046
13	Orissa	8.2	S	20.9	4,678	24,462	135,443
14	Punjab	11.2	9.7	6.0	5,632	33,257	127,750
15	Rajasthan	S	3.3	10.1	4,030	28,804	124,048
16	Tamil Nadu	S	S	29.7	4,011	28,742	169,523
17	Uttar Pradesh	22.1	15.9	53.1	6,416	35,680	255,647
18	West Bengal	14.4	53.6	29.9	5,576	62,499	165,470
	India	**12.9**	**17.2**	**36.0**	**5,084**	**31,652**	**173,641**

Source: Health Bulletin (2008)

Note: S – surplus, SC – subcentre, PHC – primary health centre, CHC – community health centre.

In terms of human resources in the public health sector as well, there is a big difference across states. Of the various indicators seen in Table 4.5 such as population served per doctor, per government hospital or hospital bed and per government doctor or ANM in rural areas, Tamil Nadu ranks in the top five in all of them. The other states that appear in the top five positions are Himachal Pradesh, Orissa, Kerala and Karnataka. The states in the bottom are Bihar, Uttar Pradesh and Madhya Pradesh. Surprisingly, Maharashtra too is a state that seems to have too few human resources in health in relation to its population, in spite of it being among the richest states in the country. Further, the gap between the better states and the poor states is wide. For instance, while population served per government hospital bed is 1,391 in Tamil Nadu, it is four times higher at 5,646 in Uttar Pradesh (Table 4.5).

Table 4.5 Availability of health personnel and hospital beds in rural areas

State	Population served/ government doctor	Population served per government hospital	Population served per government hospital bed	Population served per government doctor (PHC + CHC specialists) in rural areas	Population served per ANM in rural areas
Andhra Pradesh	17,988	224,825	2,351	23,278	4,617
Assam	13,066	278,780	9,293	NA	NA
Bihar	23,174	54,533	4,163	38,033	8,346
Chhattisgarh	19,585	105,202	2,433	13,839	4,540
Gujarat	15,550	145,943	1,896	28,442	4,489
Haryana	13,165	162,221	3,131	38,636	7,873
Himachal Pradesh	NA	44,262	813	NA	2,986
Jammu & Kashmir	5,152	120,641	2,813	9,716	4,803
Jharkhand	17,486	59,490	5,494	8,510	4,792
Karnataka	11,457	64,518	1,163	12,771	4,816
Kerala	10,116	134,140	1,217	14,091	4,184
Madhya Pradesh	18,451	179,228	3,392	32,348	5,167
Maharashtra	16,472	219,455	3,563	34,032	5,811
Orissa	7,808	23,231	2,725	NA	4,623
Punjab	7,256	114,247	2,485	30,544	6,400
Rajasthan	10,268	133,491	1,977	22,572	3,528
Tamil Nadu	9,234	112,959	1,391	12,891	3,374
Uttar Pradesh	23,986	198,143	5,646	NA	6,012
West Bengal	14,089	224,869	1,734	40,243	5,833

Source: National Health Profile (2008)

Access to health services

An even more direct indicator of the state of government health services comes from data on how many people actually use these services. This could also be seen as a proxy for the quality of government health services in relation to the private sector. In this section I look at data from two sources – the NSS and NFHS. The NSS in its 60th round (2004) had a special section on health care where respondents were asked about the kind of health care they accessed, the costs involved and so on. Similarly the NFHS also gathered data on the place of delivery, usual preference of respondents when in need of health care and so on.

From Table 4.6, it is seen that overall most people in India in both rural and urban areas use private health facilities. This is especially true in relation to outpatient services. While only 20 per cent of households opted for a public hospital for outpatient services, around 40 per cent did so in cases of hospitalisation. Himachal Pradesh, Rajasthan and Orissa are three states where a high percentage of people accessed a public facility for inpatient and outpatient services. On the other hand in states such as Assam, Jharkhand, Gujarat, Madhya Pradesh and West Bengal, while a high percentage of people utilised public facilities for hospitalisation cases, in terms of outpatient services a lower proportion went to public facilities. Tamil Nadu and Kerala also show higher-than-average utilisation of public facilities for both hospitalisation and outpatient services, while in Bihar and Uttar Pradesh a very small percentage of the people reported using public health facilities. This indicates the poor state of health facilities in these two states, which also have some of the lowest health indicators.

While the NSS data show actual utilisation (over the last one year for hospitalisation and last 15 days for outpatients), the NFHS asks women about which health facility they generally prefer when somebody in the household falls sick. In response to this about one-third of women across the country reported a preference for public health facilities (ranging from anganwadi centres and subcentres to district and state-level hospitals). The states where a large number of women reported that they generally go to a public facility were again Himachal Pradesh, Rajasthan, Orissa and Assam. In Kerala and Tamil Nadu as well, more than 50 per cent of the women said that they generally go to a public health facility. On the other hand, in Bihar and Uttar Pradesh very few women said they go to a public health facility (6.7 and 15.3 per cent).

Table 4.6 Utilisation of public health facilities

S. No.	State	% hospitalised treatment in a public hospital*		% outpatient treatment in a public hospital*		% of households that generally use government health facilities**
		Rural	Urban	Rural	Urban	
1	Andhra Pradesh	27.2	35.8	21	20	25.7
2	Assam	74.2	55.4	27	24	65.2
3	Bihar	14.4	21.5	5	11	6.7
4	Chhattisgarh	53.5	49.3	15	20	36.3
5	Gujarat	31.3	26.1	21	18	27.5
6	Haryana	20.6	29	12	20	27.7
7	Himachal Pradesh	78.1	89.5	68	86	82.7
8	Jharkhand	46.6	31.2	13	24	22.3
9	Karnataka	40	28.9	34	16	36
10	Kerala	35.6	34.6	37	22	50
11	Madhya Pradesh	58.5	48.5	23	23	37.4
12	Maharashtra	28.7	28	16	11	29.7
13	Orissa	79.1	73.1	51	54	76
14	Punjab	29.4	26.4	16	18	19.2
15	Rajasthan	52.1	63.7	44	53	70.2
16	Tamil Nadu	40.8	37.2	29	22	53
17	Uttar Pradesh	26.9	31.4	10	13	15.3
18	West Bengal	78.6	65.4	19	20	28.8
	India	**41.7**	**38.2**	**22**	**19**	**34.4**

* NSS, 60th round (2004)
** NFHS-3 (2005–6)

Figure 4.2 plots the data on infant and child mortality rates along with the percentage of deliveries taking place in a public health facility. The data for all these indicators are taken from the NFHS-3. Percentage of deliveries in a public health facility is chosen, because it is a good proxy for maternal and childcare facilities. The scatter plots show a strong negative relationship between the percentage of deliveries in a public health facility and IMR (or U5MR). States where a higher proportion of deliveries take place in a public health facility tend to have low IMR and U5MR. However, a similar strong relationship was not found between child mortality rates and the indicators of general utilisation of public health facilities (such as those reported in Table 4.6). This could be because the percentage of deliveries in a public facility is a better indicator of the access to maternal and child health services. With the increased focus on these services in government programmes such as the NRHM (and also the earlier RCH programmes) it is possible that in many states these services are available at reasonable quality in the public sector even if people use private facilities for other health services.

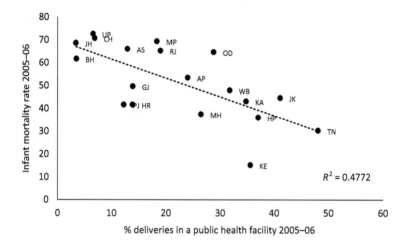

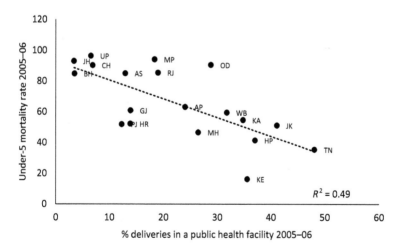

Figure 4.2 Utilisation of public facilities and health outcomes

Source: NFHS-3 (2005–6)

Expenditure on health services in public facilities can also be seen as an indicator of the quality of health care, since the objective of public facilities is to provide free or cheap medical care. The NSS survey on health expenditure (data in Table 4.7) shows that Tamil Nadu is the only state where people responded as having no expenditure on outpatient care in a government hospital. It is also the state where, on average, people spend the least on hospitalisation for child birth in a government hospital, as well as lowest in terms of the loss of household income due to hospitalisation. Bihar, Chhattisgarh, Jharkhand, Orissa

Table 4.7 Health expenditure in rural areas

S. No	State	Average medical expenditure for treatment in a government hospital (outpatient) in the last 15 days	Average medical expenditure due to hospitalisation in a government hospital	Average expenditure per childbirth (Rs.) in a government hospital	Loss of household income due to hospitalisation per treated person
1	Andhra Pradesh	6	2,176	885	805
2	Assam	14	3,157	1,252	1,025
3	Bihar	42	4,998	2,327	1,008
4	Chhattisgarh	37	4,038	678	711
5	Gujarat	1	2,253	1,415	442
6	Haryana	1	11,665	2,786	654
7	Himachal Pradesh	4	6,035	3,437	1,893
8	Jharkhand	36	2,961	660	1,357
9	Karnataka	4	2,610	340	530
10	Kerala	3	2,174	2,088	431
11	Madhya Pradesh	4	3,238	1,626	836
12	Maharashtra	12	2,243	633	535
13	Orissa	25	3,096	1,603	582
14	Punjab	3	9,774	3,342	589
15	Rajasthan	4	5,464	1,714	846
16	Tamil Nadu	0	637	482	369
17	Uttar Pradesh	10	7,648	1,725	920
18	West Bengal	20	2,464	827	386
	India	11	3,238	1,165	636

Source: NSS, 60th round (2004–5)

and West Bengal report high expenditure for outpatient care in public health facilities. The remaining states show low or nominal expenditure in case of outpatient care.

In case of hospitalisation very high average expenditure is seen in Punjab and Haryana, which are also states that show low utilisation of public health care facilities. On the other hand, high average expenditure for hospitalisation is also reported in states where there is high utilisation of public health facilities such as Rajasthan and Himachal Pradesh. Uttar Pradesh also has high average cost of hospitalisation in public health facilities.

In the case of expenditure due to hospitalisation in a government hospital, the average expenditure in Tamil Nadu is the lowest, and the gap with other states where the expenditure is low is quite significant. For instance, the state with the second lowest average levels of expenditure due to hospitalisation in a government hospital is Kerala, where the average expenditure at Rs. 2,174 is more than three times that in Tamil Nadu (Rs. 637). The expenditure in other states such as Andhra Pradesh, Maharashtra, Karnataka, Gujarat and West Bengal is in a range closer to Kerala. Further, the states that were seen to be poor performers in terms of health outcomes are also the ones that show very high levels of average expenditures in public facilities. For instance, the average expenditure due to hospitalisation in a government hospital in Uttar Pradesh is Rs. 7,648, which is more than 10 times what an average person in Tamil Nadu spends.

What is important is not just public spending but also the effectiveness of the public spending with respect to the composition of spending (reflecting political priorities), as well as to what extent the services are actually reaching the people. These in turn are seen to depend on both political will and how accountable the government is to the people, whether there is 'public action' on these issues and so on. While these aspects are difficult to measure, they can be very important. Many studies that look at the factors behind Kerala's success in improving human development of the people in the state emphasise the role of public action by both the state and people's organisations from the pre-Independence period onwards (Mencher 1980; Panikar 1985; Nag 1989; Sen 1992; Ramachandran 1997). On the other hand the absence of public action is seen as one of the central reasons for continued backwardness in states like Uttar Pradesh and Bihar (Drèze and Gazdar 1997; Mehrotra 2006).

The evidence based on literature is inconclusive about the impact of public expenditure on health outcomes. However, the studies suggest that what matters, along with levels of public expenditure, is the quality of the spending. Quality of public health spending includes the way the public spending is divided amongst different subheads, the efficiency of spending, the public health strategies undertaken, level of corruption and so on.

Data across Indian states on per capita public health expenditure and health outcomes show a significant positive relationship where in most cases states with higher per capita public health expenditures also show better health outcomes. It is also seen that health outcomes are positively correlated with the extent of usage of public health facilities in a state.

Data across Indian states on per capita public health expenditure and health outcomes also show a significant positive relationship, whereby in most cases states with higher per capita public health expenditures also show better health outcomes. This is also reflected in more direct indicators of health access such as public health infrastructure and availability of health providers. Health outcomes are also positively correlated with the extent of usage of public health facilities in a state. This also illustrates that it is important to look beyond crude indicators of public health input like public health expenditure. Such an exercise leads to showing those indicators of public health intervention do correlate quite clearly with health outcomes.

Notes

1 Governments being interested in the health of the population do not automatically mean they are involved in provision. Government role in health provision can be justified on grounds of equity and efficiency.

2 Behavioural economics, which combines economics and psychology, acknowledges that people do not always act rationally in the economic sense (as is often assumed in traditional economic theory) and also offers an explanation for market failures in health care. People often make decisions that are not in the best interests of their health such as eating junk food and not completing immunisation schedules. Behavioural economics offers tools to understand and influence such behaviour (Rice 2013). While there is no space to go into the details here, this is another field of study that can be used to argue for public intervention in health.

3 See references in this paper for examples of other studies that find such a result where public expenditure has a greater impact on the health status of the poor.

4 Musgrove (1996) summarises: 'multivariate estimates of the determinants of child mortality give much the same answer: income is always significant, but the health share in GDP, the public share in health spending, and the share of public spending on health in GDP never are'.

5 Joshi (2006) and Prabhu (2001).
6 The RBI puts together the data generated by the CSO National Account Statistics, RBI (2011).
7 Social services include education and related items; medical and public health; family welfare; water and sanitation; housing; urban development; welfare of SCs, STs and OBCs; labour and labour welfare; social security and welfare; nutrition and expenditure on natural calamities.
8 This can be attributed to some extent to the National Rural Health Mission (NRHM) that was launched by the central government in 2005. The NRHM provided for additional funds for health, with the amount being larger for the poorer states ('High Focus States'). While the NRHM funds went directly to the Society and therefore is not reflected in the state budget, the NRHM also stipulated that 15 per cent of the contributions must be made by the state government.
9 Similar results were found when I plotted data related to average public expenditure on health for a single year (2004–05 and 2008–09) and IMR and U5MR for 2009.

Chapter 5

Putting the puzzle together

While the simple bivariate analysis presented till now gives an idea of how the major states differ from each other and provides some clues on what factors need to be looked into further, the strength of each of these indicators and how they affect the health outcomes can be better understood through a multivariate analysis. Some simple multivariate analysis was conducted at the state, district and household levels to understand how significant these factors remain. Table 5.1 puts together the correlation coefficients for the relation between the indicators of influencing factors as seen in previous chapters with the health outcomes. Both female literacy and public health spending have very high correlations with the IMR and U5MR in a state. Indicators of economic conditions are also correlated with these health outcomes, but the coefficients are lower. While the details of each of the models, variables used and tables showing the results are available in Appendix A, here I just discuss the main findings.

Factors affecting infant and child mortality at the state level

Simple OLS regression was used to determine how the different factors affect health outcomes. Data related to 18 major states were used, and the outcome variables studied included IMR, child mortality rate (CMR) and malnutrition indicators. In the independent variables, indicators for economic conditions, women's status and public services such as poverty ratios, average MPCE, female literacy, female workforce participation and average public health expenditure are included. Decision making[1] and extent of mobility were included as indicators of women's autonomy. The proportion of respondents in the NFHS survey who said that people in their households usually use a government health facility

Table 5.1 Determinants of health outcomes: correlation coefficients

Indicator	Per capita NSDP 2009–10	Average MPCE (MMRP) rural 2009–10	Poverty ratio rural 2009–10	Female literacy 2011	Gender gap in literacy 2011	Per capita public health spending 2000–5	Per capita public health spending 2005–10
IMR 2009	−0.48	−0.56	0.52	−0.8	0.72	−0.78	−0.46
U5MR 2009	−0.58	−0.63	0.64	−0.79	0.71	−0.81	−0.52

Source: Estimated on the basis of data presented in Chapters 2, 3 and 4

in the event of sickness is alternatively used as an indicator of public services.[2] From the supply side, the average rural population covered by a PHC has been included as a variable to capture the spread of health facilities. All the other indicators included in the models are listed in Table A1. In the regression equations, the log values of the dependent and independent variables have been used. These regressions explain two-thirds to three-fourths of variation in child mortality and infant mortality across Indian states (see Tables A2 and A3 for results).

The analysis of factors affecting child and infant mortality across the different states shows that the most important factor that is significant in explaining the variation in these health outcomes is female literacy. In all the models, female literacy rate is significantly and negatively related to the dependent variables used, that is the higher the female literacy rate the lower is the mortality/malnutrition rates. This remains true even if we use the measure of gender gap in literacy or female literacy rate among women in the reproductive age from NFHS.

In the case of female workforce participation rates the results are not as strong. While the female workforce participation does have a negative relation with the dependent variables as far as infant mortality and child mortality are concerned, this is not always significant. The women's autonomy indicators used in these models, that is women's decision-making power within the household and mobility, are not significantly related to mortality and malnutrition rates.

While indicators of overall economic conditions such as the poverty ratio have a positive relation with child mortality and malnutrition, this is not always significant in case of IMR. Other indicators such as real MPCE and *pucca* house are seen to be significantly and negatively related to mortality and malnutrition indicators, in most cases.

Indicators of public provisioning also do not always show a significant effect in these models. Average public health expenditure is highly correlated with other variables in the model and therefore difficult to interpret. However, a supply side variable such as spread of PHC provisioning has a significant effect on the mortality/malnutrition rates. This can be interpreted to mean that public provisioning does have an effect on the dependent variables.

The limitations of these models are first that the number of observations is very few. Further, the state as an administrative unit is very large and not homogenous across districts. Some of the independent variables are highly correlated with each other at the state level, making it difficult to single out the effect of each. It is possible that some of the variations across districts within states, particularly large states with high variations across districts, make it difficult to capture the effect of some of the variables. Because of these limitations, these state regressions are only indicative. The district analysis in the next section throws more light on how these different determinants affect health outcomes.

Factors affecting infant and child mortality at the district level

In India, districts are fairly large units (with an average population of about 1.8 million). Using district-level data also gives us the advantage of a larger sample, there being about 600 districts in India. However, there are limitations to the data available at the district level. At the time of writing, the relevant data from Census 2011 were still not released and therefore the analysis is conducted for 2001. The dependent variables analysed in this exercise are the IMR and CMR, available from Census 2001. Since the focus of this study is on rural areas, rural IMR and rural CMR rates are used.[3] The data are from a report by the Population Foundation of India, published in 2008 (Rajan et al. 2008).

As in the case of the state-level analysis, the explanatory variables have been chosen to represent the factors studied in the previous chapters – economic conditions, women's status and availability of services in a simple OLS regression model. Some results are shown in Tables A5 to A8; many more equations were tried out using alternate specifications, but the main results remained the same.

First, it is seen that the strong and significant relationship between female literacy rate and IMR/CMR that was found at the state level continues to hold true at the district level as well, even after controlling for other explanatory variables such as poverty ratio, SC/ST population and availability of health facilities. Districts that have a higher female literacy rate tend to have a lower IMR/CMR controlling other factors.

Second, in contrast to our findings based on bivariate analysis at the household level, it is seen that female workforce participation rate is also significantly (though not highly) and negatively associated with IMR and CMR. Earlier studies do not find the relationship between IMR and CMR and female workforce participation rate to be negative and significant. Kapoor (2010) does find the relationship in a district-level regression as significant and negative but only in the presence of variables such as male workforce participation and percentage of agricultural workers. However, these three measures of employment are highly correlated. On the other hand, Drèze et al. (1997) do not find the relationship to be significant in a district-level regression in relation to child mortality even though it is found to be significant and negative as far as fertility and female disadvantage is concerned. Their analysis is based on the 1981 Census data that are well known for underestimating female workforce participation rates. Subsequently there have been efforts by the Census to enumerate women workers through intensive training and use of female investigators. It is generally agreed that the measure of female workforce participation rate does not suffer from the same problems in 1991 and 2001 as was the case in 1981 Census.

Nonetheless, there has been a valid concern that the measurement of female workforce participation rate does suffer from various problems including underestimation in the measurement of home-based work and participation in domestic activities. Further, there is a problem of endogeneity, since mortality, fertility and work participation tend to be simultaneously determined. Moreover, as seen in the following text, this relationship is in the opposite direction when the analysis is conducted at the individual/household level. This suggests that the 'social' effect of female workforce participation is different from that of the 'individual' effect.

Both of our indicators of women's 'status' – female literacy and work participation – therefore turn out to be fairly robust factors in explaining the variation in IMR (and CMR), lending strength to the argument that women's improved position in society leads to improved human development outcomes. Since this is the case even when other factors are controlled for, it can be said that there is some direct link between these indicators of women's status and IMR (CMR).

What the pathways of influence are – whether it is through increased bargaining position of women within the household, greater awareness/

exposure among women, better access to health services, impact of women's status on public policies or a combination of some or all of these – needs to be studied further. What is indicated however is that while female literacy works as both an 'individual' and 'social' factor, in the case of female workforce participation rate, the 'social' role seems to be stronger.

Third, this analysis at the district level shows that economic indicators like poverty ratios and standard of living index (SLI) continue to be important, albeit to a smaller extent than female literacy.[4] The relation with the availability of health facilities is negative, with more villages having health facilities resulting in lower mortality rates. However, the indicator used is not a very strong one. As seen in Chapter 4, even more than the availability of public services, the quality of the services is what is important. Further, even in relation to availability, multiple indicators related to availability of infrastructure, personnel and so on have to be looked at, which is not possible using Census data.

What this district-level analysis shows is that all the factors discussed in the previous chapters do have an effect on IMR/CMR even when we conduct a multivariate analysis, even though the size of the effect of the different indicators may vary. Our results are also broadly on the same lines as those found by Drèze and Murthi (2001), based on the analysis of data from the Census rounds of 1981 and 1991.

Finally it is seen that these models explain about 40 per cent variation in IMRs between districts, suggesting that there are other factors that are not captured by available district-level data that are also significant. These could be factors such as differences in culture, women's status (e.g. kinship) and political priorities (a result of public action).

Factors affecting infant and child mortality at the individual/household level

To understand how these factors play out the individual level, analysis of the NFHS-3 unit level data is conducted. Logistic regression is done with the dependent variable being whether the child is alive or dead (mortality in the period 0–11 months, to capture infant mortality). The data related to births and deaths in the last five years are considered (43,560 births). To get a large sample, in one of the models the period of the last 10 years is considered.[5] The dependent variable is infant death (=0, if child is alive and =1, if it is a case of infant death). Information related to 91,865 births for which complete data are available is used in this analysis.

The results of these models are presented in Table A9. At the individual level, once again female literacy has a positive effect on the chances of child survival. The odds of a child dying during infancy are lower for mothers who have had some education than for mothers who have had no education. Further, as the level of education increases, the odds of the child dying in comparison to mothers who are not educated at all decrease further. Therefore, whether the mother is educated and also how much education she has received are both important factors.

In the case of the mother's employment status, the relationship is inverse.[6] A child of an employed mother has higher odds of dying during infancy than a child of a mother who is unemployed. This is true and significant even after controlling for wealth and other factors. However, it is also seen that once we introduce the indicator of percentage of women in the PSU (primary sampling unit) who are employed, then whether the individual mother is employed or not becomes an insignificant indicator (the odds are still higher than 1). It is also interesting that in relation to the PSU-level indicator on the percentage of mothers employed, higher women's employment means lower chances of infant death (however this is not significant).

This suggests that the 'individual effect' and 'social effect' of women's employment on child mortality are in opposite directions. A child born in a village or area that has more women working has greater chances of survival than a child born in a community where fewer women work outside the home. This is consistent with our results based on the analysis at the district and state level. On the other hand, a child born to a working mother has smaller chances of survival than a child born to a nonworking mother.

The 'social effect' can be interpreted to mean that a society where more women get out and work is one where greater value is placed on women and this has a positive effect on child survival. On the other hand in individual cases, it is poorer women who are working and the conflict between getting higher incomes (and thereby being more aware and able to make decisions) and having less time for childcare has ill effects on the child. Although poverty is controlled for, it is the 'childcare' effect of women working that shows a negative relationship.[7]

Other indicators of women's status, such as mobility, decision making and exposure to the media, do not show any significant effects on the probability of child survival. A child of an anaemic mother has significantly higher odds of dying than children of mothers who are not anaemic. In the case of mothers with low BMI, however, the odds are not significant.

When all the other competing factors are controlled for, the social group to which the household belongs still significantly affects the odds of child survival. Whether the household resides in an urban or rural area does not make a significant difference. On the other hand how wealthy the household is does affect the odds of whether the child will die during infancy. While there is no significant difference between households in the lowest two quintiles ('poorest' and 'poor'), as the wealth quintile increases further, the odds of the child surviving in relation to the poorest quintile increase and do so significantly.

While looking at the sex of the child, after controlling for all the other socioeconomic factors, the odds of a female child dying are lower compared to a male child. A study by Kishor and Parasuraman (1998) based on data from NFHS-1 also finds that being female reduces the odds of dying between age 0 and 11 months (by 12 per cent in their study and by about 10 per cent here). They find that in the age 12–47 months the odds of dying almost double for females. This, they suggest, could be because the effects of gender discrimination begin to outweigh the effects of girls' biological advantage some time before the first birthday.

Assuming that the indicator on how many people are using public health services is a better indicator of public provisioning than looking at where people usually go for health care on an individual basis, we introduce a dummy that takes the value of 0 if the percentage of households in the state usually accessing government health services is less than the national average, and 1 otherwise. Children living in states that have a higher percentage of people normally accessing government health services have lower risk of dying than children in states where people use private services more.

Once I introduce regional dummies, I find that children in the southern states have significantly lower risk of dying than children in the eastern states, even after controlling so many other variables. On the other hand, children in the central states have significantly higher odds of dying than children in the reference region. Therefore, the regions with some of the best health outcome indicators namely South and that with the worst indicators namely Central both have strong region-specific factors affecting the outcomes, which are not captured by the socioeconomic, maternal and child characteristics that have been included in the analysis as controls.

Conclusion

In this chapter a multivariate analysis of the factors affecting health outcomes – infant and child mortality – was conducted at the state, district and individual/household levels. Through this analysis, I tested how the different factors that were analysed in the previous chapters contribute to health outcomes when competing variables are controlled for. Many of the findings based on the bivariate analysis in the previous chapters were reinforced.

Economic conditions come out as being more significant at the individual level than at the social level. At the state level, poverty ratios or percentage of population in the lowest wealth quintile are not always significant predictors of the health outcome measures. At the individual level, however, belonging to a higher wealth quintile or having a higher SLI significantly reduces the odds of an infant dying or a child being malnourished. Therefore, within a community economic conditions of a household matter with children in richer households being better off compared to other children in the same area. However, when we are comparing two districts or states or regions, other factors are equally or more important.

Female literacy, on the other hand, is a highly significant variable associated with positive health outcomes at all levels. Both the levels of female literacy at the district or state level and the mother's education levels have a positive impact on child's health outcomes even after controlling many other socioeconomic variables.

Female workforce participation has opposite effects at the individual level and community level. While higher female workforce participation has a positive 'social' effect on child health outcomes, when it comes to individuals, children of working mothers are worse off. It could be inferred that while at the household level the mother working can mean having less time for care of children, at the societal level more women moving out of the home and working is a reflection of women's status in that society. A society that has a large number of women working could be seen as one having a higher status for women, thereby on an average having a positive effect even on women who do not work. This could be because higher female workforce participation in an area indicates better women's status in that place, therefore, having a positive effect on child outcomes. At the societal level, a higher female workforce participation provides women better control over social resources and freedom in social interaction (Agnihotri 1997). On the other hand, at the individual level while women's involvement in paid work increases the economic worth of the female members within the household, resulting in their having a greater bargaining power, there is also a negative effect of childcare suffering when women work due to absence of adequate alternatives for childcare.[8]

As seen in the bivariate analysis, other variables representing women's status such as autonomy- or mobility-related indicators are not significantly related to the child health outcomes. This could be because they are highly correlated to female education. It also means that more work is needed in understanding how these aspects are measured and whether it is possible to quantify such subjective indicators through large-scale questionnaire-based surveys.

The results with regard to public provisioning are also positive. Per capita health expenditure and access to health services are significant but not as much as the women's status-related indicators are. However, when a dummy is introduced in relation to whether a state has a high proportion of persons accessing public health facilities or not, it turns out to be significant with children in states with higher access to public health facilities having better health outcomes than children in states where most people go to private facilities. At the district level, districts that have more villages with a PHC have better health outcomes and at the individual level children living in a PSU with an established angan-wadi centre have lower risks of being stunted.

This is an interesting result of these regressions as it shows that the access to public services has a role in influencing the health outcomes. While at the district and state levels, the indicators of availability of public services had a positive impact (although not always statistically significant) at the individual level as well, the access to public health services in the area seems to have a significant influence. This is a note-worthy finding in itself since there are very few studies in the past that show this significant positive relationship between availability of ser-vices in an area and the impact on health outcomes at the individual level. However, we also need to keep in mind that the placement of these facilities may themselves be influenced by the other factors such as economic status, area of residence and female literacy. Therefore there could be a problem of endogeneity. Nevertheless this is a positive finding and it remains significant in various equations in spite of changing the combination of other variables included.

The analysis also shows that regional effects are very important in determining what the health outcomes will be. Controlling for differ-ent socioeconomic and women-related indicators, it is seen that health outcomes in some regions are better than in others. Children at a similar standard of living and with similar maternal indicators but living in the southern states have better health outcomes than children in the poorer states of the eastern and central India. Similar regressions were carried out at all levels using indicators of child malnutrition as the dependent variables, and the results were mostly similar.

Notes

1 While there are different indicators of women's autonomy available from the NFHS, I choose to include 'decision making within the household' in the regression equations, as it is least correlated with female literacy among the different indicators (mobility, media exposure, access to money, having a bank account). There is otherwise a high degree of correlation between female literacy and these other indicators of women's autonomy. Female literacy and each of the other indicators mentioned earlier (mobility, media exposure, access to money, having a bank account), except decision making, are highly correlated at a significance level of less than 0.05. The decision-making indicator represents the percentage of women in a state who have a say with regard to making decisions on all of the following four issues – own health care, major household purchases, purchases for daily household needs and visits to her family or relatives.

2 As discussed earlier, it is difficult to capture the effectiveness of public services in any one indicator. While per capita public health expenditure is included in a few models, the problem is that this is very highly correlated with female literacy and poverty ratio, resulting in the problem of multicollinearity.

3 Throughout this section when we say 'IMR' or 'CMR' we mean rural IMR or rural CMR. The results are not very different even when IMR or CMR for urban and rural areas put together are used.

4 While there is a significant and positive relationship indicating that economic conditions do matter, it is also interesting to find that when we estimate the elasticity of poverty ratio and female literacy rate with respect to IMR/CMR, the elasticity of female literacy is much higher. For example, in one of the equations related to IMR the elasticity of the poverty ratio is 0.086 whereas the elasticity of female literacy is −1.18. This indicates that an increase in 1 percentage point in female literacy has a much greater effect on IMR than a decrease in poverty by 1 per cent.

5 The NFHS in its statewise reports uses a 10-year time period, when reporting disaggregated data on IMR. So we use a 10-year period.

6 It must be noted that the data have the disadvantage that the employment status of the mother is current while the births and deaths could have occurred in the past when the situation was different.

7 This also adds weight to the need for improving childcare facilities for working mothers.

8 It is also possible that the poverty controls used are not entirely capturing the poverty effect of women in poorer families tending to work more.

Chapter 6

The contrasting cases of Tamil Nadu and Uttar Pradesh

While the analysis presented until now across Indian states makes it clear that there is wide regional variation in human development outcomes and that women's status and public services are important factors explaining this variation, the case study of two states provides insights on the processes through which these different factors interact with each other. From this chapter onwards, this book focusses on two states – Tamil Nadu and Uttar Pradesh.

Tamil Nadu is chosen because among the South Indian states, it is the one that in the recent period seems to be moving ahead of the rest of the country. Most human development indicators related to education and health in Tamil Nadu are much better than the Indian average; and definitely ahead of the North Indian states. Tamil Nadu stands out as a state that has considerably improved the health and education outcomes for its people over the last few decades. As Figure 6.1 shows, in the last decade Tamil Nadu experienced the largest fall in IMRs. This experience of Tamil Nadu could hold important lessons for the states that are still lagging behind.

While Kerala is known for its achievements in the field of human development with health and education indicators comparable to some high income countries, the Kerala model of development has been widely studied. The improvements in Kerala have also had a longer history, while Tamil Nadu is relatively recent. Scholars have attributed Kerala's achievement to different factors including public action by both the state and the people, the presence of strong and active left parties, land reforms, reformist rulers even pre-Independence, matrilineal societies, social reform movements and so on (e.g. see Ramachandran 1997). It would be interesting to see how relevant these are in the case of Tamil Nadu.

To further study why backwardness persists in some regions while others are moving ahead, especially within the same country, Uttar Pradesh

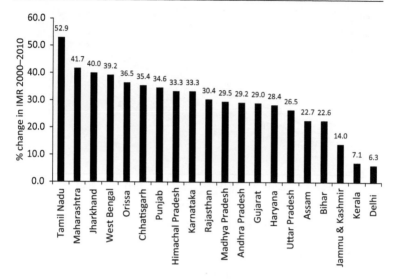

Figure 6.1 Percentage decline in IMRs, 2000–10

Source: Estimated from Government of India (2001, 2011a)

is chosen as the contrast state as it ranks amongst the bottom states in most of the indicators. Further, even in terms of change in IMR in the last decade, it shows very slow change compared to Tamil Nadu. In addition, the choice of states was also influenced by researcher-specific considerations: an interest in the 'north–south divide', my ability to speak Tamil (spoken in Tamil Nadu) and Hindi (spoken in Uttar Pradesh) fluently and easy access to Uttar Pradesh from Delhi.

Human development in Uttar Pradesh and Tamil Nadu: 1970s to present

Literacy

The literacy rate in Tamil Nadu was higher than the all India average even in 1951 (see Figure 6.2). Kerala, Tamil Nadu and West Bengal were among the top states in 1961, 1971 and 1981, both in terms of overall literacy as well as female literacy. These states seem to have continued to focus on female literacy since then. In terms of the overall literacy rate, Uttar Pradesh is clearly catching up with Tamil Nadu and even more so with the all India average. There is still a 10 percentage point

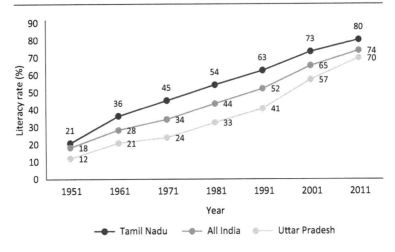

Figure 6.2 Literacy rates, 1951–2011

Source: Census of India (various years)

Note: The literacy rates for 1951 and 1961 pertain to population aged five years and above; for the rest of the years the literacy rates are related to population aged seven years and above.

difference between Uttar Pradesh and Tamil Nadu but the gap between Uttar Pradesh and All India has narrowed down to about 4 percentage points based on the results of Census 2011.

To illustrate this further, Figure 6.3 looks at the (absolute) gender gap in literacy rates for Tamil Nadu and compares it with Uttar Pradesh over time. Here, it is seen that the gender gap in literacy was in fact lower in Uttar Pradesh in 1961 and 1971, and only marginally higher in the year 1981 compared to Tamil Nadu. However, from 1981 onwards the gender gap in literacy in Uttar Pradesh has been higher than in Tamil Nadu. This is of course also a reflection of the very low overall literacy rates in Uttar Pradesh. In 1961 the male literacy in Uttar Pradesh was 31.9 per cent and female literacy rate was 8.3 per cent whereas it was 51.6 per cent and 21.1 per cent, respectively in Tamil Nadu.

What is relevant is the fact that while the gender gap in literacy rates has been constantly falling in Tamil Nadu, in Uttar Pradesh until the 1990s it was actually increasing. Therefore, while in Uttar Pradesh the increase in literacy rates for men was higher than that for women in the initial periods, in Tamil Nadu the increase in literacy rate was higher among women when compared to that for men. It is only in the decade of the 1990s that women in Uttar Pradesh began to catch up with men in the state in terms

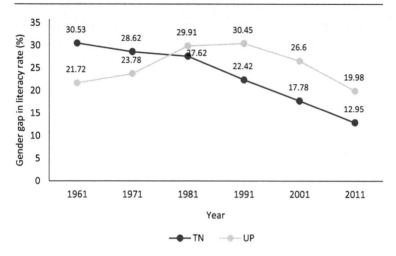

Figure 6.3 Gender gaps in literacy rate

Source: Census of India (various years)

Notes: The 1961 literacy rate is for population aged five years and above. Rest of the years, the literacy rate is for population aged seven years and above.

Gender gap in literacy rate is defined as the difference between the male literacy rate and the female literacy rate. Therefore, the gender gap is in terms of percentage points.

of literacy, with more convergence occurring in the 2000s. However, the difference in the gender gap in the two states is high even now, at 13 percentage points in Tamil Nadu compared to 19 percentage points in Uttar Pradesh.

Literacy rate in Tamil Nadu, even among women, has been much higher than in Uttar Pradesh since many decades. There was an early and decisive push for education in Tamil Nadu, which, in fact, started even before Independence. The Justice Party that formed the Provincial Government in 1923 considered education as a priority. Post-independence during Kamaraj's tenure (1954–63) as chief minister (CM), education was once again of great priority. Kamaraj reopened 6,000 schools that were closed down due to lack of funds during the tenure of the previous CM and set up additional 12,000 schools. The percentage of school-going children in the age group between 6 and 11 increased from 45 to 75 per cent within a span of 7 years after Kamaraj became the CM. He expanded the number of government schools to ensure that every village had a primary school and every panchayat a high school. Almost every village within a radius of 1 mile with a population of 300 and above inhabitants was provided with a school. He introduced the

Midday Meal Scheme to provide at least one meal per day to millions of poor school children (first time in the country). He also introduced free school uniforms to weed out caste, creed and class distinctions among school children (Kumaradoss 2004; Venkatesan and Sivakumar 2012).

Figure 6.4 looking at age-wise literacy rate in 1961 shows that early improvement in female literacy in Tamil Nadu resulted in a widening gap between Tamil Nadu and Uttar Pradesh. The difference in the female literacy between Tamil Nadu and Uttar Pradesh among lower age groups is much higher than that among higher age groups. It can therefore be concluded that in the period just prior to Independence and immediately after, there was a significant spurt in female education in Tamil Nadu with no corresponding take-off in Uttar Pradesh.

Infant mortality

The data provided by Datt and Ravallion (1997) show that in terms of IMR, Tamil Nadu ranked 11th among 15 states around 1960 and Uttar Pradesh was the worst-ranking state (IMR in Tamil Nadu was 104.5 and in Uttar Pradesh it was 187.7). SRS data are available for major states from 1971 onwards (for Bihar and West Bengal only from 1981). Based on SRS data for rural areas for 1971–3,[1] Tamil Nadu ranked seventh among 13 states with an IMR below the national average (rural IMR of 127), whereas Uttar Pradesh was the worst (rural IMR of 189). In 1981–3, Tamil Nadu ranked seventh among 15 states (rural IMR of 100) and Uttar Pradesh continued to be the lowest-ranking state (rural IMR of 159). By 1991–3, Tamil Nadu ranked third (rural IMR of 66) behind Kerala and Punjab, and Uttar Pradesh's rank improved only slightly, with it being the second lowest state (rural IMR of 100), Madhya Pradesh ranked the worst among 15 states in terms of rural IMR.[2] This shows that Tamil Nadu did not start off being one of the best states in terms of IMR, and its ranking improved over the years.

Compared to Uttar Pradesh, however, as seen in Figure 6.5, the IMR in Tamil Nadu was much lower in 1971. Further, over the last 40 years, the gap between the two states (seen in terms of the ratio of IMRs) has worsened. While IMR in Uttar Pradesh was about 1.6 times that in Tamil Nadu in 1971, it is almost double Tamil Nadu's IMR in 2010.

Life expectancy

Even in the case of life expectancy at birth, Tamil Nadu has had a lead over Uttar Pradesh since the 1970s. Further, the gap in the life

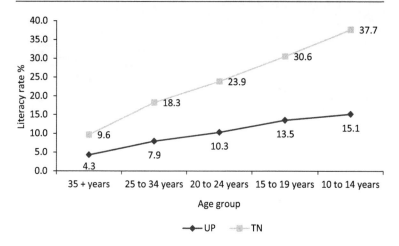

Figure 6.4 Age-wise female literacy rate, 1961 (Uttar Pradesh and Tamil Nadu)
Source: Census of India (1961)

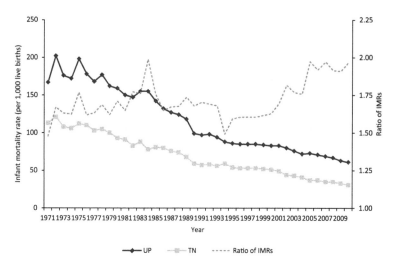

Figure 6.5 Infant mortality rates
Source: Sample Registration System (various years)

expectancy between the two states has also been increasing over the years as shown in Figure 6.6.

It is generally the case that the life expectancy of females is higher than that of males. This being the other way round indicates female

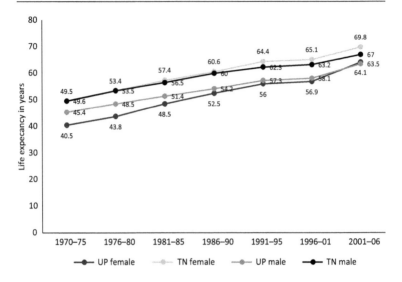

Figure 6.6 Life expectancy at birth

Source: Economic Survey (various years)

disadvantage in access to health in such societies. In Tamil Nadu, life expectancy at birth has been higher for females than for males right from the 1970s onwards and has also seen rapid increase over the years, with life expectancy currently being 2.8 years higher for women than men in Tamil Nadu. On the other hand, in Uttar Pradesh, life expectancy of males was higher than that for females until very recently. However, the gap has been reducing over the years and in the last period for which data are available (2001–6), life expectancy of females in Uttar Pradesh is slightly higher than that for males.

Trends in human development

The data presented in this section show that Tamil Nadu's position in terms of human development indicators has been better than Uttar Pradesh for a long time. However, Tamil Nadu has also considerably improved its ranking among all major Indian states during the last 30-year period while improvements in Uttar Pradesh have not kept pace. While Uttar Pradesh seems to be 'catching up' in relation to literacy and life expectancy, its IMR remains far behind.

Table 6.1 gives the Improvement Index for each of the indicators for each decade from 1971 to 2011. This improvement index is based on the formula $(X_2 - X_1)/(X_{max} - X_1)$, where X_1 and X_2 are the indicator

Table 6.1 Improvement index

Indicator	State	1971–81	1981–91	1991–2001	2001–11
Literacy rate	Tamil Nadu	0.16	0.18	0.29	0.26
	Uttar Pradesh	0.11	0.12	0.28	0.29
IMR	Tamil Nadu	0.22	0.43	0.18	0.51
	Uttar Pradesh	0.11	0.38	0.16	0.31
Life expectancy*	Tamil Nadu	0.11	0.12	0.03	0.24
	Uttar Pradesh	0.07	0.11	0.03	0.26

Source: Census of India; Sample Registration System and Economic Survey (various years)

Note: For literacy rate best is 100 per cent, for IMR best is 12 per cent and for life expectancy 85 per cent.

*The last period is 2001–6 since the life expectancy data after 2006 are not available.

values in the initial year and the final year, respectively, and X_{max} is the chosen upper bound (lower bound in the case of IMR). This is based on Sen (1981) where he takes the absolute shortfall of actual longevity (or literacy) from some chosen upper bound and then examines the percentage decline of this shortfall. This formula reflects the view that as, say, longevity becomes high or IMR becomes low, it becomes more of an achievement to improve it further (Chakraborty 2011).[3]

The improvement index shows a greater improvement in Tamil Nadu compared to Uttar Pradesh in relation to all the indicators in the 1970s, 1980s and 1990s. In the 2000s, the improvement in literacy and life expectancy in Uttar Pradesh was marginally higher than in Tamil Nadu.[4]

Economic conditions in Tamil Nadu and Uttar Pradesh

While the human development outcomes in Tamil Nadu have been better than Uttar Pradesh since almost the beginning of the twentieth century, the same is not true in case of economic conditions. Currently, the state of Tamil Nadu has much higher per capita income, lower rural poverty ratios and also higher rural MPCE compared to Uttar Pradesh. While Tamil Nadu is among the middle-to-high-income states showing a relatively high rate of economic growth, Uttar Pradesh is amongst the poorest states in the country with a low growth rate.

As seen in Table 6.2, the difference in per capita SDP between Tamil Nadu and Uttar Pradesh was not so high in the 1970s. While the per capita SDP of Uttar Pradesh in 1973–4 was Rs. 793, in Tamil Nadu it was Rs. 669 (in current prices). In fact, going back even further, the data for various years in the 1960s show that the per capita SDP at current prices for Uttar Pradesh and Tamil Nadu were almost the same. For instance, the average per capita SDP for Tamil Nadu for 1965–70 was Rs. 476, while that for Uttar Pradesh was Rs. 447.[5] In fact, up to the 1980s, Tamil Nadu's per capita SDP was below the national average. It crossed the all India national average marginally only in 1991–2. Since the 1990s, per capita income has risen consistently taking Tamil Nadu among the top five states in the country, in terms of per capita income (GoTamil Nadu 2003).

On the other hand, throughout the period since Independence, Uttar Pradesh has had a per capita income lower than the national average, with the gap increasing over time. Figure 6.7 shows that since the early 1980s, the gap in the real per capita income (per capita SDP in 1993–4 prices) between the two states has been rising. While the per capita income of Tamil Nadu was about 1.3 times that of Uttar Pradesh in the period 1982–4, it became two times by 1997–9 and is now 2.6 times higher than the per capita income for Uttar Pradesh.[6]

Although the gap has been growing between the two states, the difference is not as stark when we look at the data related to the average MPCE in rural areas in Figure 6.8.[7] It is interesting to note that Uttar Pradesh had a slightly higher average rural MPCE in 1983 and in 1987–8 compared to Tamil Nadu. It is only since the 1990s that the average MPCE in rural Tamil Nadu has risen consistently. Even in terms of poverty ratios, Tamil Nadu had a higher rural poverty ratio compared

Table 6.2 Per capita NSDP in Uttar Pradesh and Tamil Nadu (current prices)

Per capita NSDP (Rs.)		
Year	Uttar Pradesh	Tamil Nadu
1973–4	669	793
1978–9	935	1,069
1983–4	1,658	2,024
1987–8	2,360	3,374
1993–4	4,794	8,051
1999–2000	9,719	19,378
2004–5	12,023	27,137
2009–10	21,874	45,058

Source: SDP data, Central Statistics Organisation (various years)

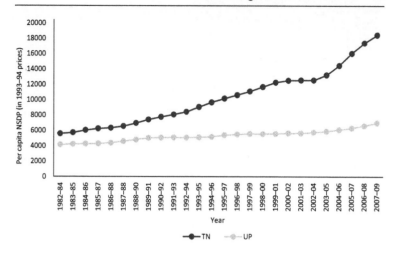

Figure 6.7 Per capita NSDP (in 1993–4 prices)

Source: SDP data, CSO (various years)

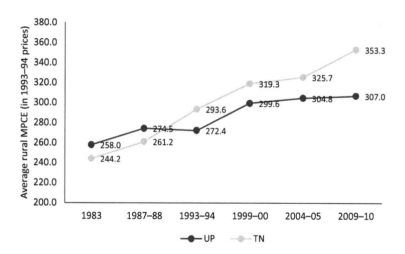

Figure 6.8 Average rural MPCE (in 1993–4 prices)

Source: NSSO (various years)

to Uttar Pradesh until the late 1980s, with a large reduction in poverty seen from the 1990s onwards. (There are problems with the poverty ratios for 1999–2000, and therefore, these are best ignored for our purposes.[8])

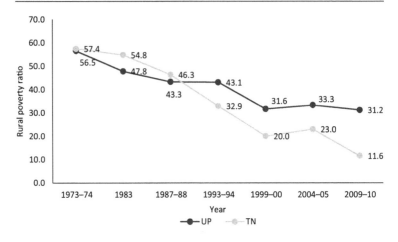

Figure 6.9 Rural poverty ratios

Source: NSSO (various years)

Note: All the poverty ratios are based on the official poverty lines that were in use prior to 2009, prior to change in poverty lines more recently based on the Recommendations of new expert group (Tendulkar Committee) of the Planning Commission.

Poverty ratios, based on the revised poverty lines[9] which are available for 1993–4 and 2004–5, show that Tamil Nadu still has a high poverty ratio. While Tamil Nadu had a rural poverty ratio that was slightly higher than the national average (and also slightly higher than Uttar Pradesh) in 1993–4, rural poverty in the state declined in this decade, with Tamil Nadu now having a poverty ratio that is below the national average and Uttar Pradesh's poverty ratio being slightly above the national average (shown in Figure 6.9).

Datt and Ravallion (1997)[10] in their paper on regional disparities in India provide comparable poverty ratios for two periods – around 1960 and around 1990. They find that Tamil Nadu and Kerala had the highest poverty ratios around 1960 (around 70 per cent), while the poverty ratio in Uttar Pradesh was a little less than 50 per cent. While the poverty ratio in Uttar Pradesh decreased by only about 10 percentage points by around 1990, Tamil Nadu saw a drastic fall in poverty by about 25 percentage points.

So until a few decades ago, Tamil Nadu was amongst the poorer states in the country, with per capita incomes below national average. However, on the basis of per capita incomes it is now one of the richest states. In terms of rural MPCE and poverty ratios although there is an improvement, Tamil Nadu still is not amongst the top performers in the country and would fall in the 'middle' category. Uttar Pradesh, on the other hand, has been consistently among the poorer states in the country, resulting in a rising economic gap between Uttar Pradesh and Tamil Nadu. In terms of health indicators, however, it seems that conditions in Tamil Nadu improved much before the 1990s, which is when we see the increasing economic growth rates in the state. It may be recalled (see e.g. Table 7.1) that the higher improvement in health indicators was seen in Tamil Nadu in all the decades from the 1970s onwards.

This overview of data for the last 30 years for the two states under study reaffirms our conclusion on the basis of data for all Indian states and the literature review that while economic growth is one of the important factors for progress in human development (here, health indicators), there are other factors that need to be studied as well. Further, the data for Tamil Nadu show that it is quite possible for progress in human development to precede improvement in economic conditions at the macro level. It can therefore be argued that better human development in Tamil Nadu contributed to the high economic growth that the state witnessed in later periods.

Therefore, the factors other than economic conditions responsible for the improvements in human development in Tamil Nadu become important. To study these, I use sources from literature and large-scale surveys as well as data from a field survey.

Field survey in Uttar Pradesh and Tamil Nadu

As the study is on human development outcomes, especially health outcomes, the field survey focussed on child health and nutrition. Further, since women's status is seen as one of the important contributing factors to child health outcomes, the field survey also tries to look at some such indicators. Therefore, the respondents to the survey were women with young children.

The field survey was conducted (during the period January 2009 to April 2010) in one district in each of the states – Moradabad district in Uttar Pradesh and Villupuram district in Tamil Nadu. One of the considerations for the selection of districts was to pick a district from a 'better-off' region in Uttar Pradesh and a 'worse-off' region in Tamil Nadu, so that they are broadly comparable in terms of the level of economic development. Therefore, districts from coastal northern Tamil Nadu and western Uttar Pradesh were chosen.[11] One district and within the district one block was then selected from these regions. Since the purpose of the field survey was to get a deeper understanding of how things actually work on the ground, with secondary data analysis providing the main quantitative evidence for testing the hypotheses, the districts and blocks for the field survey were chosen based on availability of baseline data and scope for further field work.

Uttar Pradesh and Tamil Nadu both have a history of 'village' studies conducted by economists and anthropologists (Jayaraman and Lanjouw 1999). A resurvey was being conducted in one village where village studies have been conducted in the past in both the states around the time when I was planning my field work. The London School of Economics was planning a survey of the village Palanpur in Moradabad district and the Madras Institute of Development Studies was doing the same in Iruvelpattu in Villupuram district.

In each district, a survey was conducted in five villages, including the resurvey village, in both the states. The four other villages were selected from the same block – Thiruvennainalur (in Villupuram, Tamil Nadu) and Baniakhera (in Moradabad, Uttar Pradesh). In each village, 25 women with at least one living child under the age of three years were randomly selected for the interview. In this manner, 125 women (total 250) were interviewed in each state.[12] In cases where the respondent had more than one child under the age of three years, information was collected for both children. A structured questionnaire was used to interview the women included in the survey.

During the survey, heights and weights of all the children under three years of age were also collected. The z-scores for height-for-weight, height-for-age and weight-for-age for all the children who had valid data were calculated using the new WHO references.[13] In a small sample survey such as this, it is impossible to get any reliable mortality estimates. Although some questions related to morbidity were asked, such as incidence of diarrhoea and pneumonia, these were based on a two-week recall period and therefore not reliable enough to be used as outcome indicators. Therefore, of the data available from the field survey, such anthropometric data are the most suitable to be used as the outcome (dependent) variable for all analysis related to factors affecting child health.

During the field work, I also visited schools, anganwadi centres and PHCs. I visited all the government schools (six in Uttar Pradesh and eight in Tamil Nadu) and anganwadi centres (seven in Uttar Pradesh and eight in Tamil Nadu) in each of the sample villages. In each of these institutions I observed what was going on, interviewed the service providers (teachers, ANMs, anganwadi workers), examined their regis-ters and spoke to the beneficiaries (children, patients, etc.). Although there was no questionnaire or formal 'interview', I maintained detailed notes of what I saw and learnt from the people in each of these places, which adds value to what the quantitative data tell us and provides some insight into the reasons why things are so different between these two states.

Further I visited four PHCs in Tamil Nadu and four in Uttar Pradesh. While I made one visit to each of these PHCs, there was a PHC just outside Iruvelpattu village (one of the sample villages) in Tamil Nadu, which I had a chance to observe many times, as this was one of the vil-lages where I conducted the survey. In each village, during the survey I also met with some 'key informants'. This group consisted of the pan-chayat president/sarpanch, secretary/village assistant, the school head-master, members of the Gram Panchayat, anganwadi workers, ASHAs, ANMs (where available) and so on. These conversations also informed many of my findings.

The districts chosen for field work were suitable for this study as they are broadly comparable in terms of economic conditions. Villupuram has similar levels of poverty and population with low SLI compared to Moradabad. Moradabad is located in western Uttar Pradesh, which is the most prosperous region in the state in economic terms. This region is close to Delhi and has benefitted greatly from the Green Revolution. Moradabad has a large urban population (33 per cent) with the district headquarters being a centre for trade in brass ware. Villupuram, on the other hand, is one of the poorest districts in Tamil Nadu located in the less developed northern region of the state.

While overall Tamil Nadu has a high proportion of urban population (48 per cent), in Villupuram district only 15 per cent of the population live in urban areas (Census 2011). Moradabad, on the other hand, is 33 per cent urbanised. In terms of most social indicators, Villupuram is better than Moradabad. The gap in female workforce participation rate between the two districts is very high. Female workforce participation rate in Villupuram as per Census 2011 is 40 per cent whereas it is only 10 per cent in Moradabad. It is seen that the male workforce participa-tion rate in Villupuram (58 per cent) district is much higher than in Moradabad (48 per cent). The literacy rate in Villupuram at 72 per cent is significantly higher than in Moradabad district (59 per cent). A simi-lar difference of almost 14 percentage points is seen in female literacy rates as well (Census 2011).

In terms of access to public facilities such as roads, water and electricity, Villupuram is way ahead of Moradabad, as seen in Table 6.3. This was also experienced during the field visits, where it was easy to reach any village in Villupuram using bus services whereas in Moradabad accessing villages was always a problem. According to the Census 2001, 84 per cent villages in Villupuram had access to bus services whereas this was as low as 13 per cent in Moradabad. With respect to the HDI rank, both the districts rank low among the districts within the respective states, with Moradabad ranking 54 out of 70 districts and Villupuram 28 out of 29 districts. The IMRs in the two districts vary widely, with the IMR in Villupuram being 46 and in Moradabad 73 (as per Census 2001).

However, in terms of economic indicators, gap between the two districts is not so wide. The DLHS-3 survey classified a high number of households as being in the category of low SLI in both the districts (76 per cent in Moradabad and 72 per cent in Villupuram) with a slightly higher percentage of households in the 'High' SLI group in Moradabad (7 per cent as against 5 per cent in Villupuram). In terms of ownership of land as well it is seen that while 66 per cent of rural households own some land in Moradabad only 44 per cent do so in Villupuram. The poverty ratios estimated for 1999–2000 based on consumption expenditure data from NSS show that the poverty ratio in Villupuram is marginally higher than in Moradabad. Moradabad also has a slightly higher percentage of irrigated land area than Villupuram. According to the data from Agricultural Wages in India for 2009–10, the average daily wage for agricultural labourers in Villupuram was Rs. 104 per day and in Agra (which is the district closest to Moradabad for which data are available) Rs. 103 per day.[14] Although Tamil Nadu has a high proportion of urban population, Villupuram is one of the districts in the states with the lowest proportion of urban population.

Therefore, the data in Table 6.3 show that while with regard to human development indicators related to education, health and social amenities there is a vast difference between the two sample districts, they are at similar levels when it comes to some economic indicators such as poverty ratios, SLI or irrigated area under cultivation.

The field survey also collected some basic information in relation to the economic conditions of living of people in both the states, such as ownership of assets and livestock. Based on the data collected, 24 per cent in Uttar Pradesh and 33 per cent in Tamil Nadu lived in kachcha houses. The rest lived in semi-*pakka* or *pakka* houses. In terms of

Table 6.3 Characteristics of sample districts

	Moradabad	Villupuram
Indicators from Census 2011		
Population (total)	4.8 million	3.5 million
Population (rural)	3.2 million	3 million
Av. household size	6.1	2.3
Literacy rate (all) (ages 7 & above)	58.7	72.1
Literacy rate (female) (ages 7 & above)	49.6	63.5
Sex ratio (number of females per 1,000 males)	903	985
Male work participation rate	47.7	58.4
Female work participation rate	9.9	39.9
Percentage of SC population	15.3	29.4
Percentage of ST population	0.01	2.2
Percentage of of households with		
Electricity as main source of lighting	35.9	93.0
Latrine facility within the household	63.2	21.1
Main source of drinking water as 'tap water from treated source'	26.2	41.5
Percentage of urban population	33.1	14.7
Indicators from DLHS-3 (2007–8): Percentage of rural households		
Have electricity connection	25.3	92.4
Live in a pakka house	13.8	24.4
Use piped drinking water	1	91.2
Own agriculture land	66.6	44.0
Standard of living index (rural)		
Low %	76.4	71.7
Medium %	16.6	23.5
High %	7	4.9
Other indicators		
Percentage of population below poverty line 1999–2000[15]	18.2	23.3
Net domestic product at constant (1999–2000) prices	Rs. 14,475[16]	Rs. 14,914[17]
Percentage of net irrigated area to net sown area	79.8[18] (2005–6)	70.8[19] (2009)
Human Development Index Rank (within the state)	54 out of 70[20] (2005)	28 out of 29[21] (2003)
Infant mortality rate[22]	73 (2001)	46 (2001)

Source: Dubey (2003); based on NSS data for 1999–2000 and official poverty lines; GoUP (2003, 2006, 2008, 2011); http://www.tnstat.gov.in/nddp-constant-percapita.pdf; Rajan et al. (2008) based on Census 2001

Table 6.4 Housing and land ownership

Percentage of respondents who	Uttar Pradesh sample villages	Tamil Nadu sample villages	Total
Own house	98.4	89.6	94
Own agricultural land	76.8	41.6	59.2
Kachcha house	24	33.1	28.5
Ownership of any livestock	81.6	43.2	62.4
Total number of respondents	125	125	250

Source: Author's field survey

Table 6.5 Ownership of consumer durables

Percentage of respondents owning:	Uttar Pradesh sample villages	Tamil Nadu sample villages	Total	Percentage of respondents owning:	Uttar Pradesh sample villages	Tamil Nadu sample villages	Total
Gas stove	17.9	44	31.1	Refrigerator	0.8	8	4.4
Electric fan	38.2	88	63.3	Television	42.3	92	67.3
Bicycle	71.2	48	59.6	Motorcycle/ scooter	17.9	22.4	20.2
Radio	38.2	28	33.1	Tractor	5.7	4	4.8
Sewing machine	27.4	9.6	18.5	Phone/ mobile	45.5	61.6	53.6

Source: Author's field survey

Note: *N* = 125 in Uttar Pradesh and Tamil Nadu sample villages; 250 Total.

ownership of the house they lived in, in Tamil Nadu,[23] 90 per cent of the respondents said that they owned the house they lived in while this was 98 per cent in Uttar Pradesh. A total of 102 (82 per cent) households in the Uttar Pradesh sample and 54 (43 per cent) households in the Tamil Nadu sample owned some livestock (cow/buffalo, goat or chicken).

In terms of some of the consumer durables on which data were collected, a greater percentage of households in Uttar Pradesh owned these goods compared to Tamil Nadu. For instance while 71, 38 and 27 per cent owned bicycles, radios and sewing machines, respectively, in Uttar Pradesh, 48, 28 and 10 per cent owned these goods in Tamil Nadu. It is the other way round when we look at other goods such as TV, gas stove, electric fan, refrigerator and phone. In some of the goods where the gap is very large, like TVs and gas stoves for instance, there is a direct relationship with government programmes that distributed these goods for free in Tamil Nadu.[24]

A SLI was developed using a methodology similar to the one in DLHS-2, with some minor changes based on data available.[25] Based on this SLI, there are more houses in the 'low' group in Uttar Pradesh than in Tamil Nadu, while Uttar Pradesh also had more houses in the 'high' group. Tamil Nadu had no family that fell in the 'high' group and most of the respondents' families could be classified as being 'medium'. Although there is a difference in the figures, a similar pattern is seen based on the DLHS-3 data for rural Moradabad and rural Villupuram, where Tamil Nadu has fewer households than Uttar Pradesh in the 'high' group and also in the 'low' group with most households being classified as having a 'medium' SLI.[26]

Based on observation as well, it was seen that while in some aspects there was not much of a difference in terms of the economic conditions of living, in others there was. For instance, most houses in Uttar Pradesh had *pakka* walls and *pakka* roofs, had at least one bed while in Tamil Nadu many houses even though had *pakka* walls but they had thatched roofs. Further, the Uttar Pradesh houses had more space than the ones in Tamil Nadu.

On the other hand, the internal roads in the villages were well developed in most Tamil Nadu villages, there were very few open drains and the general level of cleanliness was much higher. This was not the case in Uttar Pradesh, which made the villages look less 'prosperous'. The overall impression I got was that there was not so much difference in personal incomes, but that there was still a difference in the quality of life because of the public/common resources. In Tamil Nadu, all the villages had tap water supply (none in Uttar Pradesh), public bus services up to the village (none in Uttar Pradesh), separate public buildings for

Table 6.6 Standard of living index

Standard of living index (% of households that have):	Uttar Pradesh sample villages	Tamil Nadu sample villages	Total
Low SLI	44.8	35.2	40.0
Medium SLI	52.8	64.8	58.8
High SLI	2.4	0	1.2
Total N	125	125	250

Source: Author's field survey

a ration shop, an anganwadi centre and a panchayat office, which were absent in Uttar Pradesh. The only common public building that both states had, of comparable quality, was the school.

In terms of occupation, among the women interviewed, 48 per cent in Tamil Nadu and 93 per cent in Uttar Pradesh reported that their main occupation was domestic work. In Tamil Nadu, one woman said she did 'nothing in particular'. Among those who did not say that domestic work was their main occupation, in Tamil Nadu, 42 per cent of women were engaged in casual agricultural labour, 6 per cent in cultivation, 2 per cent in self-employment, one woman in salaried employment and one in nonagricultural labour. In Uttar Pradesh, there were only nine women who said their main occupation was something other than domestic work – of these there were four in cultivation, two each in casual agricultural labour and salaried employment, and one in nonagricultural labour.

In the case of the husbands of the respondents in Uttar Pradesh, most of them were in nonagricultural labour and cultivation on their own farms, in Tamil Nadu almost half of them said casual agricultural labour was their main occupation. In terms of land ownership also it is seen

Table 6.7 Occupation

Occupation	Mother's main occupation (%)			Father's main occupation (%)		
	Uttar Pradesh sample villages	Tamil Nadu sample villages	Total	Uttar Pradesh sample villages	Tamil Nadu sample villages	Total
Casual agricultural labour	1.6	41.6	21.6	16.4	48.8	32.5
Nonagricultural labour	0.8	0.8	0.8	32	11.6	21.8
Cultivation	3.2	5.6	4.4	26.2	12.4	19.3
Salaried employment	1.6	0.8	1.2	13.9	10.7	12.3
Domestic work	92.8	48	70.4	1.6	1.6	1.6
Other self-employment	0	2.4	1.2	9	13.2	11.1
Nothing in particular	0	0.8	0.4	0.8	1.6	1.2
Total N	125	125	250	122	121	243

Source: Author's field survey

Table 6.8 Malnutrition and immunisation

Number and % of children who are:	Uttar Pradesh sample villages	Tamil Nadu sample villages	Total
Stunted	89 (66.4)	57 (39.3)	146 (52.3)
Underweight	70 (51.5)	30 (20.8)	100 (35.7)
Wasted	24 (17.9)	9 (6.4)	33 (12)
Fully immunised*	22 (24.2)	69 (69.0)	91 (47.6)

Source: Author's field survey

Note: Figures in brackets are percentages.

*All those children above 12 months of age who have received doses of at least I BCG, 3 DPT, 3 Polio and I Measles (based on verifying records on the immunisation card, if not available then mother's recall).

that while only 42 per cent of the respondents in Tamil Nadu said that their family owned any agricultural land, in Uttar Pradesh 77 per cent of the families of the respondents owned agricultural land.

As far as health indicators are concerned, the sample in the survey also shows a large difference in the malnutrition rates and immunisation coverage between the two states. While 69 per cent of children covered in the survey in Tamil Nadu were reported to be fully immunised, only 24 per cent were fully immunised in Uttar Pradesh. About 40 per cent of the children weighed in Tamil Nadu are stunted compared to about two-thirds in Uttar Pradesh. Similarly, there is a gap in the percentage of children underweight and wasted. Therefore, the difference between the two states in terms of outcomes is huge. Such a large difference is not seen when we compare some of the indicators of living standards.

Notes

1 Moving average of three years.
2 From 1971–3 onwards, data from SRS, Registrar General of India (2008) Vital Rates of India 1971–96 based on the Sample Registration System (SRS).
3 Chakraborty (2011) calls this the principle of 'increasing marginal difficulty'.
4 In Chakraborty's analysis Tamil Nadu's rank based on improvement index of HDI between 1999–2000 and 2007–8 is 3rd following Kerala and Uttarakhand, whereas Uttar Pradesh ranks 20th.
5 This is based on annual data available from CSO. A simple average of the five years data at current prices was taken. During some individual years, Uttar Pradesh has a slightly higher per capita SDP than Tamil Nadu.
6 This graph takes three-year moving averages, to account for fluctuations in the data. For 2007–9, the real per capita SDP for Uttar Pradesh is Rs. 6,972

and for Tamil Nadu is Rs. 18,454. In current prices, it is Rs. 40,757 for Tamil Nadu and Rs. 16,060 for Uttar Pradesh.

7 The NCAER IHDS survey also has data on income. The median annual per capita income in Tamil Nadu is Rs. 7,000 and in Uttar Pradesh is 4,300. In rural areas it is Rs. 5,297 in Tamil Nadu and Rs. 3,605 in Uttar Pradesh. According to IHDS HCR of population below poverty line is 18.3 per cent in Tamil Nadu and 33.2 per cent in Uttar Pradesh (using official poverty lines).

8 The 55th Round of NSSO conducted in 1999–2000 is considered to be 'contaminated' because there was a change in the recall period for consumption expenditure.

9 The Expert Group to Review the Methodology for Estimation of Poverty set up by the Planning Commission under the Chairpersonship of Prof S. D. Tendulkar submitted its report in 2009. This report provides the revised poverty lines for 2004–5 and 1993–4. After 2004–5, the official poverty estimates released by the Planning Commission are based on these new poverty lines.

10 The paper does not have exact numbers but only a figure from which this is inferred.

11 Based on NSS data (2004–5) it is seen that Coastal Northern region in Tamil Nadu has the lowest MPCE and highest poverty ratios amongst all the regions in Tamil Nadu. Western Uttar Pradesh has the highest MPCE and lowest poverty ratios amongst all the regions in Uttar Pradesh.

12 Of the 250 respondents, about 40 per cent of the respondents belonged to SC community. While in Tamil Nadu 61 per cent were from OBC community, in Uttar Pradesh 31.2 per cent belonged to the General category and 28 per cent belonged to OBC groups. Most of the respondents belonged to the Hindu community. The average household size in Uttar Pradesh among the sample households is 6.4 and in Tamil Nadu it is lower at 5.9.

> Of the 250 women interviewed, seven were single women. Of these, three women in Uttar Pradesh and two in Tamil Nadu were widowed. Further, two women in Tamil Nadu were separated from their husbands and living with their parents. The median age of the respondents (mother) in Uttar Pradesh and Tamil Nadu was 25. However, almost 20 per cent of women in Uttar Pradesh were under 20 years of age whereas in Tamil Nadu there were 7.2 per cent women under 20 years of age. The median age of the fathers (husbands of the respondents) was 28 in Uttar Pradesh and 30 in Tamil Nadu.

13 WHO Anthro: Software for assessing growth and development of the world's children.

14 Agricultural Wages in India publishes data for only selected centres and districts. It is common practice to use the data of the neighbouring district for districts for which data are not available.

15 Debroy and Bhandari (2003); data from Amaresh Dubey's calculations based on NSS data for 1999–2000 and official poverty lines.

16 GoUP 2008.

17 http://www.tnstat.gov.in/nddp-constant-percapita.pdf.

18 GoUP 2008.

19 GoTN 2011.

20 GoUP 2006.

21 GoTN 2003.

22 Rajan et al. (2008) based on Census 2001.

23 In Tamil Nadu among those who said they did not own the house they lived in, many had houses on '*peramboke*' land, which officially belonged to the government (forest land) so the '*patta*' (title) was not in the name of the family although they had been living there for long. In one village (Iruvelpattu) families which had been living on the same plot of land for generations said that the land was still not in their names but belonged to the '*Reddiyar*' (the local landlord, Reddiyar is the caste name). The Reddiyar is now very old and all his heirs live in the city with no links to the village, so there was some anxiety on what will happen when he dies, at the same time some felt that he would transfer the legal rights soon as he had always been helpful to people.

24 For instance, even in the case of electric fans, this probably has to do with greater access to electricity and the government scheme of free electricity for one light, one fan and one TV per household.

25 The standard of living index is calculated by adding the following scores: *Source of drinking water:* 3 for Tap (inside home), 2 for Tap (shared), 1 for hand pump and well, and 0 for other. *Type of house:* 4 for *pakka*, 2 for semi-*pakka*, and 0 for *kachcha*. *Source of lighting:* 2 for electricity, 1 for kerosene, and 0 for other. *Fuel for cooking:* 2 for any LPG gas, 1 for any kerosene and 0 for other. *Toilet facility:* 2 for own toilet and 0 for no toilet. *Ownership of durables:* 4 each for car and tractor, 3 each for television, telephone and motorcycle/scooter, and 2 each for fan, radio/transistor, sewing machine and bicycle. The scores when totalled may vary from a lowest of 0 to a maximum of 40. On the basis of total score, households are divided into three catego-ries: (a) Low – if the total score is less than or equal to 9, (b) Medium – if the total score is greater than 9 but less than or equal to 19 and (c) High – if the total score is greater than 19.

26 Note that I have used the DLHS-2 methodology to construct the index, whereas these numbers are from DLHS-3. The SLI data could be seen as evidence of lower inequality in Tamil Nadu.

Chapter 7

Unpacking women's status in Tamil Nadu and Uttar Pradesh

The field survey was conducted in phases alternating between Tamil Nadu and Uttar Pradesh. Each time I visited one state after the other, one of the most striking aspects was how different women's lives were in each of these states. The experience of conducting the survey as a woman travelling alone was also quite different in Tamil Nadu and Uttar Pradesh. While in Tamil Nadu, mobility was much greater due to the excellent public transport system and not many restrictions on travel after dark, in Uttar Pradesh, the lack of public transport and the constant reminders by everyone that one should get back 'before dark' resulted in the survey being slower and more tedious.[1]

When looking for households in the village, in Uttar Pradesh I had to give the name of the husband and if that did not suffice, then the caste and the father's name. However, in Tamil Nadu I would start with naming the woman and then, if needed, her husband's name. Thus, although the husband's name was still important, most people in the village in Tamil Nadu knew the name of the wife as well – whereas in Uttar Pradesh the woman was not called by her name even by extended family members.

Another important difference was that in Uttar Pradesh it was almost impossible to talk to the woman alone. The mother-in-law or sister-in-law was invariably present during the interviews. In many cases, even if they were not initially present in the house they would be called for once I went in for the interview. It was quite normal for the mother-in-law to try and respond to all the questions. I had to convince them each time that I would like to hear the response from the mother of the child, even if the mother-in-law felt that she (the mother) did not know the 'correct' answers. Further, there was often a sense of suspicion in the air, so that I would feel uncomfortable in many cases in going back to the same house. After a few instances I stopped going alone and went along with a local research assistant who would help me with the weighing of children and also distract the mother-in-law or other family members during the interview.

The experience in Tamil Nadu was a complete contrast. Mostly, I was able to speak to the women alone. Even if there were other people present they would either go out after some time or once I said that I wanted only this woman to respond, they would let her do so. And even if the mother-in-law was around I rarely felt uncomfortable asking sensitive questions. It was a more open discussion, and many women understood what I was doing and why I was asking these questions. For instance, one woman in Tamil Nadu said (in Tamil), 'Oh, I understand you want to find out how empowered women[2] are.' The other difference was also the attitude of the men. Nowhere did they say, 'Why do you want to talk to the women, they don't know anything'; as was often heard in Uttar Pradesh.

As will be seen below, this does not mean that women in Tamil Nadu are completely liberated or that there was no gender bias there. Broadly, even Tamil Nadu had defined roles for men and women. While there was greater mobility among Tamil Nadu women, women did not participate as much as men in public life and in many cases also believed that men should be the prime decision makers within the household.

Kinship and relationship with natal home

As seen in the literature, there are significant differences in dominant kinship practices between the two states.[3] The symmetry in the relationship in Tamil Nadu, *vis-à-vis* the hierarchy seen in Uttar Pradesh, makes a significant difference to the lives of women in their marital homes. This does not get captured adequately in survey data.

Marriages in Uttar Pradesh are basically a transaction between two families with no role in the decision making for the girl. Primary concerns while fixing a match are caste, 'status' (the girl should not belong to a family that is of a higher 'status'; status is usually measured in terms of the wealth of the family) and ensuring that the families are not related by blood for at least seven generations. It is expected that after marriage the girl is no more a part of the natal family and will only keep minimal ties with her natal relatives.

Many of the respondents in Tamil Nadu had married their cousins or relatives. This gave them the advantage of being familiar with the family they were marrying into, resulting in fewer barriers to interaction with their in-laws, especially the father-in-law. This was not the case in Uttar Pradesh. For instance, in Uttar Pradesh, if the father-in-law walked in while the interview was on, the respondent would immediately cover her face, stand up and not talk at all. On the other hand, there were many instances in Tamil Nadu when the father-in-law was in the house or would come in and there would be very casual conversation – sometimes the daughter-in-law would even 'scold' him on some household-related issues. Unfortunately systematic data on cross-cousin or within-kin marriages were not collected. However, it was observed that many marriages were within kin – even if they were not first cousins, there were women who had married their mother's brothers/cousins, children of their parents' cousins and so on. Data from the IHDS survey (2004–5) conducted by the NCAER show that 30 per cent of women (ever-married in the age group of 15–49 years) in Tamil Nadu were married to their cousins or relatives.[4] On the other hand, only 5 per cent of women in Uttar Pradesh were married to their cousins or relatives.

Second, in Uttar Pradesh the general norm was that, when a marriage is decided upon, the girl's family must be of a lower economic status than that of the man.[5] In Tamil Nadu, on the other hand, the norm seemed to be more that they must be of a similar economic status so that there are no ego issues and that the girl can adjust easily. What was seen as more important was that the girl should come from a large family, and preferably have brothers, so that she had somebody to fall back on in times of trouble. Also the groom's family preferred this because they felt that through marriage they were also gaining greater social support and networks if there was a brother. The relationship between the brothers-in-law is one of mutual support and friendship.[6] The brother and sister relationship in Tamil Nadu is very precious. Most families have only two, or at most three, children. From the beginning there is a sense of responsibility of the brother towards the sister. Although in Uttar Pradesh too this is an important relationship with festivals like *Rakhi* being very significant, I did not see such overt show of affection as in Tamil Nadu. The brother in Tamil Nadu is expected to protect his sister all his life and is her support system. In the absence of a brother, in some cases, I even saw older sisters playing such a role.

The survey found a wide gap in the mean age at marriage between Uttar Pradesh and Tamil Nadu. The mean age at marriage among the respondents in Uttar Pradesh was 16.8 years and in Tamil Nadu it was 19.7 years.[7] Further, I met several women in Tamil Nadu who said that theirs was a 'love marriage' – and in many instances these were also cross-cousin marriages. In an environment where men and women grow up believing that these cousins are people they can get married to, they also start building such a relationship. Then it becomes a marriage of their choice and they have more space in the relationship. It is still very patriarchal and the roles are well-defined, but since there was a social relationship of the couple prior to marriage and it is seen as something that the woman also chose after being wooed by the man, she has some power.

The other instances of 'love marriage' were also mainly within the same caste and in these cases they were also from the same village. Here too, after some initial resistance both families accepted the marriage, and the woman received a lot of support from her parents' family since they were in the same village. Among the women who were included in the survey, 70 per cent in Tamil Nadu said that they had some say in deciding who they would marry; while in Uttar Pradesh this figure was only 7 per cent.[8] Even the IHDS (NCAER) survey shows a wide difference with 87 per cent in Tamil Nadu saying they had any say in marriage compared to 31 per cent in Uttar Pradesh. IHDS data also show that only 9 per cent of women in Uttar Pradesh knew their husband before marriage while 46 per cent of women in Tamil Nadu did so.

Another noticeable difference was that in many cases in Tamil Nadu, the mother or parents of the woman were present at the time I visited – they were either visiting for a long stay with the daughter or the daughter was in fact staying with the parents. This was not the case in Uttar Pradesh. In Tamil Nadu, there were cases of widowed mothers visiting, and it would be noted how she comes often to help and that she spends her time equally between her different children or that she preferred staying here than with her daughter-in-law, and so on. Such a situation was very rare among the survey households in Uttar Pradesh. In Uttar Pradesh I met two households (out of 125) where the parents were visiting, both for very specific and less usual reasons. In one case, the woman lived with her mother and brother's family, because they owned land in the village whereas there was no land in the husband's family. In the other case, the woman had delivered a baby the previous week, and since her in-laws were dead, her mother had come to help. According to the IHDS data, 27 per cent of women in Tamil Nadu were married into the same village/town, compared to 5 per cent in Uttar Pradesh and in the case of 86 per cent women in Tamil Nadu, the natal family lives nearby whereas in Uttar Pradesh this is true in the case of 55 per cent women (Desai et al. 2010). In my sample, 21 per cent of women in Tamil Nadu and 5 per cent women in Uttar Pradesh were living with their parents or in the same village as their parents.

Further, in Uttar Pradesh when people from the woman's parents' family came to visit, it was mostly the brother or father who came, whereas in Tamil Nadu it was mostly the mother as well as the rest of the family. The mothers of the respondents in Tamil Nadu were mostly independ-ent, would come and go on their own and stay at the daughter's place for a while, since they were all quite mobile. Regarding the frequency of visit to their natal homes, 81 per cent women in Tamil Nadu and 46 per cent women in Uttar Pradesh said that they visited their natal homes more than twice a year.[9] The IHDS also shows similar results with 80 per cent women in Tamil Nadu and 50 per cent women in Uttar Pradesh saying that they visited their natal homes more than twice a year.[10]

The field survey data presented in Figure 7.1 show that in both states a high percentage of women said that they get support from their natal home in case of any trouble (62 per cent in Uttar Pradesh and 89 per cent in Tamil Nadu) and that they can turn to their parents when they are in need of money (67 per cent in Uttar Pradesh and 79 per cent in Tamil Nadu). It is further interesting to see that when asked what kind of support they can get from their parents during times of difficulty (which they mostly identified with an illness), 62 per cent of women in Tamil Nadu who said they can get any support said that this would be in the form of them going and staying with their parents, while only 14 per cent women in Uttar Pradesh said that they can go and stay with their parents. In case of Uttar Pradesh, 43 per cent women who said they get support from their parents said it will be in the form of monetary support (in Tamil Nadu 22 per cent women expected to get monetary support).[11]

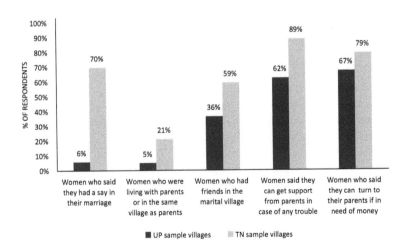

Figure 7.1 Relationship with the natal family

Source: Author's field survey

Table 7.1 Rest after delivery

Number of days after delivery women started doing household work (% respondents)	Uttar Pradesh sample villages	Tamil Nadu sample villages	Total	Number of days after delivery women started doing nonhousehold work[14]	Uttar Pradesh sample villages	Tamil Nadu sample villages	Total
Less than 15 days	32.8	11.3	22.1	Less than 30 days	12.9	1.6	7.1
15–30 days	31.2	8.9	20.1	1–2 months	37.1	1.6	19.0
30–45 days	19.2	12.9	16.1	2–3 months	14.5	1.6	7.9
more than 45 days	16.8	66.9	41.8	More than 3 months	35.5	95.3	65.9
Total N	**125**	**124**	**249**	**Total N**	**62**	**64**	**126**

Source: Author's field survey

Such a difference in regular contact and support from the natal family also directly affects women's conditions during pregnancy and delivery. Among most communities in Tamil Nadu it is seen that the traditional practice is for the woman to move to her natal home for a few months during late pregnancy and immediately after delivery. This is still followed, usually for the first two births. Of the sample children included in my survey, 60 per cent in Tamil Nadu were born in the natal home of the mother while in Uttar Pradesh 3 per cent (five cases) were born in the natal home of the mother.[12]

This has a direct relation with how much rest and time for recuperation the woman gets after delivery. While 53 per cent of women who delivered in their marital village said that they began doing household work within 30 days after delivery, only 18 per cent of those who delivered in their natal homes said so. Even in terms of nonhousehold work, 35 per cent of women who delivered in their marital homes[13] said that they start doing nonhousehold work within three months after delivery, while only 4 per cent of women who delivered in their natal homes did so. Obviously, given that it was women in Tamil Nadu who went to their natal homes for delivery, they got a longer period of rest compared to women in Uttar Pradesh.

Education

As expected there were wide differences in the education levels of the women interviewed in both states, which is clearly seen in Figure 7.2 and Table 7.2. Most women in Uttar Pradesh (78 per cent) had never

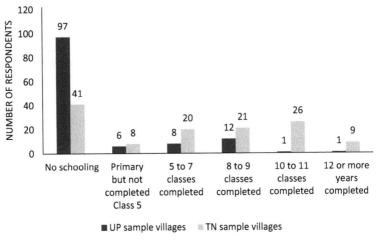

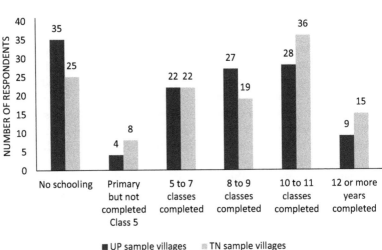

Figure 7.2 Education

Source: Author's field survey

been to school while in Tamil Nadu 67 per cent had some schooling.[15] This is reflected in the level of education as well, with 28 per cent of the respondents in Tamil Nadu having completed class 10 or more, and only 2 per cent women in Uttar Pradesh having studied up to class 10 or more.[16] During the field work as well, this difference is noticeable. In general, it was also seen that women who had some schooling (especially those who had completed elementary schooling) had greater confidence in talking to outsiders and were more 'aware'. On the other hand, it was also the case that those who were educated were less likely to be participating in employment.

According to the respondents, 28 per cent of the husbands had never been to school in Uttar Pradesh while the figure was 20 per cent in Tamil Nadu. So the gender gap is much higher in Uttar Pradesh. Among the husbands, 41 per cent had completed class 10 or more in Tamil Nadu while 30 per cent had done so in Uttar Pradesh.

In both states, there were clear caste and class differences in terms of whether women went to school or not and the level of schooling (see Table 7.3). Overall, about 65 per cent of women belonging to the SC/ST categories had no schooling, while among women of other castes 49 per cent had no schooling. However, as seen in the secondary data as well, women in the SC/ST categories in Tamil Nadu were still way ahead of women even in the other caste groups in Uttar Pradesh. For instance while 49 per cent of SC/ST women in Tamil Nadu had no schooling, 76 per cent of women in 'other' groups in Uttar Pradesh had no schooling.

Table 7.2 Education

Highest class completed	Mother's education (%)			Father's education (%)		
	Uttar Pradesh sample villages	Tamil Nadu sample villages	Total	Uttar Pradesh sample villages	Tamil Nadu sample villages	Total
No schooling	77.6	32.8	55.2	28	20	24
Primary but not completed Class 5	4.8	6.4	5.6	3.2	6.4	4.8
Class 5–7 completed	6.4	16	11.2	17.6	17.6	17.6
Class 8–9 completed	9.6	16.8	13.2	21.6	15.2	18.4
Class 10–11 completed	0.8	20.8	10.8	22.4	28.8	25.6
12 or more years completed	0.8	7.2	4	7.2	12	9.6
Total N	125	125	250	125	125	250

Source: Author's field survey

Table 7.3 Schooling amongst SC respondents and others

	SC/ST	Other
% no schooling (Uttar Pradesh)	80	76
% no schooling (Tamil Nadu)	48.9	23.1
% completed class 8 or more (Uttar Pradesh)	6	14.7
% completed class 8 or more (Tamil Nadu)	29.8	53.9

Source: Author's field survey

Note: Total N = 250, Uttar Pradesh = 125; Tamil Nadu = 125.

Similarly while almost 30 per cent women of the SC/ST category had completed class 8 or more in Tamil Nadu, in Uttar Pradesh only about 15 per cent of the women in the 'other' group had completed class 8 or more.

Employment status

Secondary data show that there is wide variation in the female workforce participation rates in Uttar Pradesh and Tamil Nadu. This is also confirmed by the field study. This is not to say that women in Uttar Pradesh do not 'work'. It was seen that many women in Uttar Pradesh were involved in work outside the home such as collecting fodder and helping out in the family fields. However, very few participated in any form of paid employment or are recognised as being engaged in work. On the other hand many women in Tamil Nadu were engaged in casual agricultural labour, NREGA works and so on.

Collecting data on women's work is difficult, especially because women do not consider many of the things they routinely do to be 'productive'. Further, since most of the work is unpaid it is not mentioned by others either. Women are responsible for almost all the household work such as cooking, cleaning, washing and caring (for children, the aged and the livestock) and this is true for both the states.[17] There was however a difference between the two states in relation to the nonhousehold outside work that women did (especially paid work).

During the field survey, women were first asked to state what their main occupation was. This question was also asked in relation to all the members of the household. In response to this, among the women interviewed, 48 per cent in Tamil Nadu and 93 per cent in Uttar Pradesh reported that their main occupation was domestic work (i.e. 52 per cent of women in Tamil Nadu reported some other occupation, while in Uttar Pradesh only about 8 per cent reported their main occupation being something other than 'domestic work').

While in Uttar Pradesh the overwhelming norm is that women should not (need not) work outside the house for paid employment, in Tamil Nadu that was not the case. This to some extent explains the women's responses when they were asked what their occupation is. When probed further and asked what else they do, more women in Uttar Pradesh said that they did work other than domestic work as well. Table 7.4 shows the respondents' occupation, including responses after probing further ('subsidiary' occupation).

Once a subsidiary occupation was included after a little probing, it was seen that about 30 per cent of women in the Uttar Pradesh sample said that they did work other than domestic work (compared with 8 per cent in the case of 'main' occupation) whereas in Tamil Nadu this difference was not so much. In the Tamil Nadu sample, 57 per cent women were 'working' when the responses for main and subsidiary occupations are included compared to 52 per cent when only main occupation is considered.

While this cannot be estimated using my field data, my observation is that in Uttar Pradesh it was only women in extremely poor families who worked for a wage, whereas in Tamil Nadu other than the few well off households, it was 'normal' for women to go out for wage work. This is also reflected in the response of women to questions relating to work and its distribution across gender. Ninety-eight per cent of women in Tamil Nadu and 65 per cent of women in Uttar Pradesh agreed with the statement 'A woman should be allowed to work for cash'. Sixty-three per cent of women in Tamil Nadu were in agreement with the

Table 7.4 Women's occupation (main + subsidiary)

Occupation	Uttar Pradesh sample villages	Tamil Nadu sample villages	Total
Casual agricultural labour	11.2	45.6	28.4
Nonagricultural labour	1.6	1.6	1.6
Cultivation	13.6	5.6	9.6
Salaried employment	1.6	0.8	1.2
Domestic work	69.6	42.4	56
Other self-employment	2.4	3.2	2.8
Nothing in particular	0	0.8	0.4
Total *N*	125	125	250

Source: Author's field survey

statement 'The husband should help with the children and household chores', while in Uttar Pradesh only 36 per cent women agreed.[18] This shows that, although in both states a large number of women agreed with the traditional gender division of labour, more women in Tamil Nadu were also open to challenging these roles. It would be interesting if such data were available for the attitudes of men and older women in the community. In many cases the husband or the mothers-in-law actually made the decision on whether women could work outside or not. Fifty-five per cent of women in Uttar Pradesh and 74 per cent of women in Tamil Nadu said that they had any say in the decision on whether they should do outside work or not.[19]

The percentage of women, who said that they had an occupation other than domestic work, was higher among the SC community than the 'others' in both the states. While in Uttar Pradesh, 40 per cent of the SC respondents said they were 'working', only 20 per cent of the non-SC respondents said so. In Tamil Nadu, 71 per cent of the SC respondents said they were 'working', only 51 per cent of the non-SC respondents said so.[20] This indicates that it is women in poorer families who have a greater tendency to be engaged in outside work in both the states.

Further in Uttar Pradesh, for women who were well educated there seemed to be an acceptance that if they got some form of salaried employment, they could take it up. For instance, in Uttar Pradesh, in most of the survey villages the para-teachers in school, the anganwadi workers and ASHAs were women from well off *thakur* households. Even though *thakurs* are the most conservative caste, with strict restrictions over mobility of women, 'respectable' jobs for educated women were acceptable. In Tamil Nadu, the range of the acceptable activities women can engage in, if they were educated, seemed to be wider, with many women saying that they would like their daughters to get jobs as sales-girls in shops or as nurses in the nearby town when they grew up.[21] In Uttar Pradesh, they typically mentioned only 'teacher'.[22]

To get further details on the work women did, the respondents were asked to list all the work they did outside the household in the last one week. The intention of this question was also to try and capture work done by women that they might not otherwise report in response to a general question on their occupation. As seen in Table 7.5, amongst all women respondents in Uttar Pradesh, 34 per cent reported doing any work out-side home in the last one week, while this figure was higher at 46 per cent in Tamil Nadu. Of these, 29 per cent in Uttar Pradesh and 68 per cent in Tamil Nadu (10 per cent in Uttar Pradesh and 31 per cent in Tamil Nadu

as percentage of all women interviewed) did any work for a wage (cash or
kind) in the last one week. Twenty-nine per cent women in Tamil Nadu
said that they did some agricultural work in the last one week,[23] while 18
per cent women in Uttar Pradesh did so. Of those who did any agricultural
work in the last one week, for 78 per cent in Tamil Nadu and 46 per cent
of the women in Uttar Pradesh it was paid work (22 per cent of all women
in Tamil Nadu and 8 per cent of all women in Uttar Pradesh).

Therefore, based on this question, the gap between women doing any
outside work in the two states is not as large as the difference in their
workforce participation as seen earlier. However, the gap between the
two states in relation to how much of this work was paid work is very
large. This again fits with what was observed in the field, with most
women in Uttar Pradesh going out either to work on their own field or
to cut grass for the cattle and in Tamil Nadu women going out for agricultural labour and/or to collect firewood.

Table 7.5 Details of women's work in the last one week

% of respondents who engaged in:	% of all respondents who did any work done in the last one week			% of those who did outside work in the last one week who were in paid work		
	Uttar Pradesh sample villages	Tamil Nadu sample villages	Total	Uttar Pradesh sample villages	Tamil Nadu sample villages	Total
Farming/ agricultural work	17.6	28.8	23.2	45.5	77.8	65.5
Tending animals/ collecting fodder	20	3.2	11.6	0	25	3.4
Nonagricultural work/ construction	0.8	0.8	0.8		100	50
Gathering food/ fuel	3.2	16	9.6			
Shop keeping	0	2.4	1.2		66.7	66.7
Service work	0.8	0.8	0.8	100	100	100
Other	1.6	8.8	5.2	50	100	92.3
Any of the above	33.6	45.6	39.6	28.6 [9.6]*	68.4 [31.2]*	
N	125	125	250	42	57	99

Source: Author's field survey
*Figures in brackets are percentage of the entire sample.

Autonomy and decision making

Increased autonomy and voice within and outside the household is considered to be one of the pathways through which women's status has an impact on child health and nutrition conditions. The field survey included many questions to assess the status of women in the two states in relation to these aspects. One of the important aspects of autonomy is how much ownership and control women have over resources. With such a wide difference in the number of women working, especially in paid work, between Tamil Nadu and Uttar Pradesh we can expect that women in Tamil Nadu would have greater control over resources since they themselves also earn money.

In response to the question on whether they have cash in hand to spend on household expenditure, roughly the same percentage of women in Uttar Pradesh and Tamil Nadu said that they do. Very few women in both the states owned any land in their own name (six in Uttar Pradesh and four in Tamil Nadu); but a higher percentage in the two states owned jewellery (43 per cent in Uttar Pradesh and 58 per cent in Tamil Nadu). Of the women who owned any land, 1 (out of 6) in Uttar Pradesh and 2 (out of 4) in Tamil Nadu said they could sell or trade this land without getting someone else's consent. With regard to jewellery, 37 per cent in Uttar Pradesh and 19 per cent in Tamil Nadu of women who personally owned jewellery or other valuables said they could use this as they wished. Therefore, in terms of ownership and control over resources not much difference is seen between the two states, with Uttar Pradesh women doing better in certain cases.

Women were asked whether they had a say in different household decisions. This too showed no clear pattern; while on certain issues women had a greater say in Tamil Nadu, for other issues this was the case in Uttar Pradesh. A greater number of women in Uttar Pradesh said they had a say in decisions such as how to spend household income and what food to cook at home. A higher proportion of women in Tamil Nadu said they had a say in decisions such as whether they could do outside work, sell or purchase jewellery, what to do when a child is sick and the kind of education to give to children. It is worth noting that the difference between the two states in most of the cases where women in Uttar Pradesh seem to have a greater say is not significant on the basis of a t-test. On the other hand, while 61 per cent of the women in Uttar Pradesh said that they were afraid to disagree with their husband, this figure was 37 per cent in Tamil Nadu and this difference is highly significant (see Table 7.6).

Table 7.6 Women's say in decision making

% women who have a say in the following decisions	Uttar Pradesh sample villages	Tamil Nadu sample villages	Total
How household's income is spent*	70.2	56.8	63.4
What food to cook	68	64	66
Sell or purchase animals	60.8	58.4	59.6
Sell or purchase jewellery	59.2	67.2	63.2
Outside work**	55.2	73.6	64.4
What to do if child is sick	79.2	83.2	81.2
How much schooling to give	72	80	76
What school to send children to	71.2	78.4	74.8
% women who said they are afraid to disagree with their husbands**	61.5	37.1	49.3

Source: Author's field survey

Note: Total N = 250, Uttar Pradesh = 125; Tamil Nadu = 125.

Based on t-tests; *p < 0.05; **p < 0.01. The difference between the two states is not significant in the other cases.

Domestic violence

On the issue of domestic violence a greater proportion of women in Uttar Pradesh said it was justified for men to beat their wives under certain circumstances such as when women were disrespectful to their parents-in-law, neglected household chores and were disobedient or did not follow orders. On the other hand, more women in Tamil Nadu felt that men were justified in beating their wives if the women beat their child frequently (this while discussing was broadly interpreted as not giving good care to the children). Most women in both these states felt that these were 'duties' they had to perform and the husband had a right to question them if they did not do it properly. Many women also said that while husbands were justified in beating the women when they did something wrong, it was also not correct to frequently beat or beat at slight provocation – they felt that he should first try talking to her and only if she didn't listen should he resort to violence.[24] The responses in Figure 7.3 do not reflect these nuances.

With regard to their personal experience with violence, while 62 per cent of women in Tamil Nadu said that they were ever beaten by their husbands since marriage, this figure was 51 per cent in Uttar Pradesh.[25] Of the women who said they were ever beaten by their husbands, 29 per cent women in Tamil Nadu and 19 per cent women in Uttar Pradesh

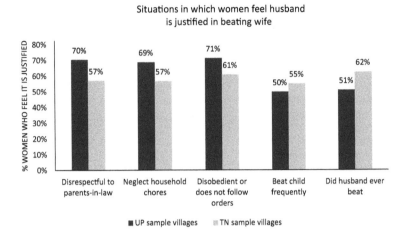

Figure 7.3 Domestic violence

Source: Author's field survey

Note: Total N = 250, Uttar Pradesh = 125; Tamil Nadu = 125.

said that they were beaten regularly.[26] As mentioned earlier this was not an easy question to ask. Further, while interpreting the findings it is important to note that this is a very subjective question. How much women report domestic violence in different places, what constitutes a violent act or is understood as violence, may vary among women across cultures. It is also very difficult to reduce women's mixed opinions on this issue into 'yes' or 'no' answers. What is reported here is the immediate response, whereas following discussions with the women were more nuanced.

Mobility

Women were asked whether they could go alone to some places and the results are presented in Figure 7.4. A higher (often much higher) percentage of women in Tamil Nadu said that they could go alone to all the places that they were asked about compared to women in Uttar Pradesh. The places where women in Uttar Pradesh could go alone to in larger numbers are to the fields, to homes of friends or relatives in the same village or to the local temple. Very few women in Uttar Pradesh had the mobility to go to any place, including their parents' house, outside the village. These figures also match well with the field experiences

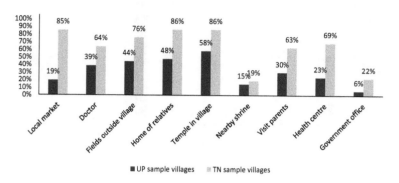

% women who can go alone to following places

Figure 7.4 Mobility

Source: Author's field survey

Note: Total N = 250, Uttar Pradesh = 125; Tamil Nadu = 125. Except in the case of 'Nearby Shrine' the difference in the percentage of women who can go alone to these different places between the two states is highly significant (p < 0.0001).

where it is very obvious that there is greater mobility among women in Tamil Nadu. The most striking difference between the two states is the number of women who can go alone to the local market. While in Tamil Nadu 85 per cent said that they could go to the local market alone, less than 20 per cent in Uttar Pradesh said they could. This also reflects on how many women can independently handle cash and make purchases.

Other than to a shrine/temple outside the village or government office outside the village, a large number of Tamil Nadu women said that they could go alone to most of the other places that they were asked about. Even within Tamil Nadu, more women could go alone to places within the village rather than those outside the village.

Most women in both states had never been to a government office outside the village (whether alone or with someone). As shown in Figure 7.5, only 5 per cent women in Uttar Pradesh and 25 per cent in Tamil Nadu had ever been to a government office outside the village.[27] Very few women had also ever participated in a public or political meeting outside the village. However, a high percentage of women in Tamil Nadu had been to a government office within the village (40 per cent). In terms of associational life, none of the women interviewed in Uttar Pradesh were members of a self-help group, while almost 45 per cent of the women in Tamil Nadu were. A greater proportion of women in Tamil Nadu had a post office or bank account,[28] had ever been to the

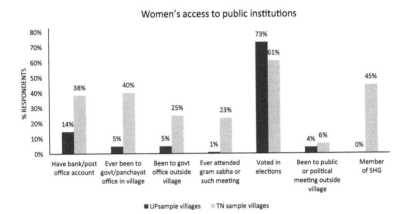

Figure 7.5 Participation in civic life

Source: Author's field survey

Note: Total *N* = 250, Uttar Pradesh = 125; Tamil Nadu = 125. Except in the case of voting in an election and attending a meeting outside the village, the difference in the between the two states is highly significant ($p < 0.0001$).

Panchayat office in the village or attended a *gram sabha*, been to a government office outside the village. On the other hand, a larger percentage of women in Uttar Pradesh reported ever having voted compared to Tamil Nadu. Seventy-three per cent of women in the Uttar Pradesh sample reported ever having voted compared to 61 per cent in the Tamil Nadu sample.[29]

Other aspects

In terms of certain other indicators as well Tamil Nadu women seemed to be freer as seen in Table 7.7. For instance, a larger number of women in Tamil Nadu said that it was safe for women to move freely in the village and that in their household the husband and wife usually eat together. However, on whether the husband would object if she visited friends alone or if he would permit higher education for the wife, a larger percentage of women in Uttar Pradesh felt that they had freedom to do these things. In Uttar Pradesh while almost all the women practised *purdah*, almost none did in Tamil Nadu.[30]

A set of statements were read out to the women and they were asked whether they agreed or disagreed (or had no opinion) with these. Table 7.8 presents the numbers of women who said they agreed with

Table 7.7 Some further aspects of women's 'autonomy'

% of respondents who:	Uttar Pradesh sample villages	Tamil Nadu sample villages	Total
Said that it was safe for women to move freely	60.8	74.4	67.6
Said that husband and wife eat meal together[31]	20	52	36
Said that husband would object to visiting friends	52.9	67.9	59.6
Said that husband would permit higher education*	43.5	34.7	39.1
Practise purdah	94.4	1.7	49.4

Note: Total N = 250, Uttar Pradesh = 125; Tamil Nadu = 125.

*The difference between the two states is not significant ($p > 0.1$). In rest of the cases, the difference is highly significant ($p < 0.01$) (for visiting friends, $p < 0.05$).

Table 7.8 Women's opinion on gender roles

% of respondents who agreed with the following statements	Uttar Pradesh sample villages	Tamil Nadu sample villages	Total
Most of the important decisions in the family should be made by the man	71	50.4	60.6
There is some work that only men should do and some work that men should not do	91.9	76.8	84.3
The husband should help with the children and household chores	36.3	63.2	49.8
A mother should not work outside the home while her children are young*	65.3	62.4	63.9
A woman should be allowed to work for cash	65.3	98.4	81.9
If a woman's opinion differs with her husband's opinion, she must accept his opinion*	58.9	46.4	52.6
Girls should be allowed to decide when and to whom they want to marry	13.7	57.6	35.7
Boys should be allowed to decide when and to whom they want to marry	34.7	68	51.4

(Continued)

Table 7.8 (Continued)

% of respondents who agreed with the following statements	Uttar Pradesh sample villages	Tamil Nadu sample villages	Total
Husbands should decide how household money is spent	53.2	26.6	39.9
Widows should be allowed to be remarried	41.6	71.2	56.4

Note: Total N = 250, Uttar Pradesh = 125; Tamil Nadu = 125.

*The difference between the two states is not significant (p > 0.1). In the rest of the cases the difference is highly significant (p < 0.01) (except for the first two statements where p < 0.1).

these statements. A higher percentage of women in Uttar Pradesh than in Tamil Nadu agreed with the statement that most of the important decisions in the family should be made by the man, that there is some work that only men should do and some that they should not. On the other hand, a higher percentage of women in Tamil Nadu agreed that husband should help in household chores, that women should be allowed to work for cash, girls and boys should be allowed to decide when and to whom they should get married and widows should be allowed to remarry. Once again, in most cases, the difference between the two states is also statistically significant.

Media exposure

More than half the women in Tamil Nadu said that they had gone to a cinema hall and watched a movie, while this was the case for less than 5 per cent of the women in Uttar Pradesh. In terms of access to media as well, almost 70 per cent of women in Uttar Pradesh said they never watched any TV and almost 95 per cent never read the newspaper. In Tamil Nadu, percentage of women who never watched TV or never read the newspaper were 8 per cent and 75 per cent, respectively. However, lesser percentage of women in Uttar Pradesh (75 per cent) compared to Tamil Nadu (81 per cent) said that they don't listen to the radio at all (see Figure 7.6).

Understanding women's status: lessons and questions from field survey

The field survey investigated the status of women in the two states of Uttar Pradesh and Tamil Nadu using different indicators as presented in

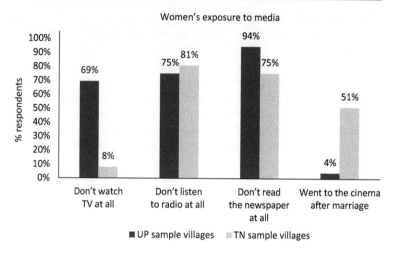

Figure 7.6 Women's access to media

Source: Author's field survey

Note: Total N = 250, Uttar Pradesh = 125; Tamil Nadu = 125.

the previous sections of this chapter. Broadly, it is seen that the status of women in Tamil Nadu is better than in Uttar Pradesh. Overall, the data from the primary survey clearly show that there is a wide difference between different aspects of women's status in both the states. Education levels are higher among women in Tamil Nadu compared to Uttar Pradesh. Even based on other indicators such as mobility and exposure to media field data shows that women in Tamil Nadu are better off compared to those in Uttar Pradesh. However, in relation to some aspects of autonomy such as having cash in hand or domestic violence, Tamil Nadu women had as poor a status as women in Uttar Pradesh.[32] Interestingly, in terms of attitudes and opinions, there is a difference in all these aspects between the women in the two states.

Further, significance tests show that while the difference in the means between the two states is significant in cases where Tamil Nadu is better, in the few instances where Uttar Pradesh seems to be better, this difference is not statistically significant. This does not, in any way, mean that there is no gender inequality in Tamil Nadu. The limited statement being made here is that women's status in Tamil Nadu is significantly better when compared to Uttar Pradesh.

Another aspect that these data bring out is the difference in the status of women in the public and private spheres. While women in Tamil Nadu are clearly better off in terms of indicators such as access to education, work, mobility, participation in associations and public life, when it comes to the private sphere of voice within the household or domestic violence there is still a long way to go. In Uttar Pradesh on the other hand, women seem to be invisible in both spheres. This difference could hold an important clue to the pathways in which women's status affects human development. In general, the literature on women's status talks about greater bargaining power, autonomy, control over resources and decision making within the household resulting in the better child health outcomes. The focus has thus been more on the intrahousehold relationships.

While this is true to some extent, what my field work shows is that it is also important to look at the 'social' role that women's status plays in improving human development outcomes. That is, better status of women affects outcomes not only through changing the household-level power dynamics but by influencing the value placed in society on issues that are generally seen to be women's 'concerns', such as education and health. When women also directly deal with public institutions more (such as ration shops, hospitals, schools and public transport) and participate to a larger extent in public life, this in turn can be seen as having an influence over what become priority issues in society. Even individual attributes can contribute to social 'status' more than to intrahousehold position. For example, education contributes not only to greater 'say' *vis-à-vis* the husband but to making the woman more confident, better informed, foresighted and so on in her dealing with the outside world as well. Therefore, women's status in the public sphere can play a very important role and this has hitherto not been given much attention.

The puzzle of women's status in certain indicators being not very different between the two states of Tamil Nadu and Uttar Pradesh can also be better understood once this distinction between the public and private spheres is made. The status of women in the public sphere between the two states is unambiguously different. Further, such a difference in the way women's status operates in the public and private spheres can also be linked to the finding in Chapter 5, where there is a difference in the 'individual' and the 'social' effects of women's work.

The field survey experience also raises doubts on how reliable some of these indicators are, especially when collected as part of large-scale surveys. Questions related to household decision making, domestic violence and so on are both sensitive and subjective. During the survey, these topics came up as part of a general conversation where the women were first made comfortable, and these subjects were broached as part of a dialogue rather than a typical investigator–respondent exercise.

Even so, many responses are also influenced by what women think is the 'right' answer rather than what they really believe or practice. This in turn is significantly influenced by the social norms in the society they live in. Since Tamil Nadu and Uttar Pradesh are so different in terms of culture and norms, it is quite possible that the responses are also influenced by their very different circumstances. Finally, while the field survey finds a sharp contrast between Tamil Nadu and Uttar Pradesh in terms of many indicators of women's autonomy and gender equality it also reiterates that this is a complex contrast and cannot be reduced to a few indicators.

To further understand the effect women's status has on health outcomes, it helps to examine the relation between women's status and the outcome-related data in a multivariate framework where confounding factors such as income/economic status are controlled for. Since the sample size is small and there are number of variables, there is a limitation to how useful such an analysis can be. The regressions based on the field survey data (details in Appendix B) reiterate what we found in the analysis using NFHS data that women's education plays a strong role in influencing child outcomes. Standard of living and the 'state' effect are also important. Other aspects of women's status are more nuanced.

The field survey data have an inherent weakness when used in regression analysis because of the small sample size and the problem of collinearity. Further, the only dependent variables available from the survey namely anthropometric indicators are not suitable for such analysis because these are primarily statistical indicators that reflect the situation for a group (or an area) better than at the individual level. Moreover, the field work and the other analysis in this study shows that it is probably the 'social' aspects that are more important (the social effect of better women's status, the availability and provisioning of public services, the representation of backward classes in government, greater accountability, etc.), which are not captured in this multivariate analysis based on the quantitative data from the field.

Notes

1 In Tamil Nadu, I stayed in a room which during the day was the office of the Tamil Nadu Science Forum. In Uttar Pradesh, I stayed with the Palanpur Village Study team in Pipli village (neighbouring Palanpur). The one instance in Uttar Pradesh where I stayed on in the village for slightly longer (up to 5.30 pm) to complete one more interview resulted in me being stranded with no transport to go back to the block headquarters from where I had to catch a train to the village where I was staying. On the other hand

in Tamil Nadu, I would usually remain in the village until much later (7.30 pm or 8 pm).

2 *Pengal nilamay (women's status).*

3 While within each state as well there are differences based on socioeconomic status, caste and religion it broadly holds true that marriages in Tamil Nadu are more among kin, close to the natal family with strong links maintained with the natal family even after marriage. On the other hand in Uttar Pradesh it is important that the bride and the groom are not related in any way and the links with the natal family are greatly weakened after the marriage.

4 This is the highest in the country. Other states with high rate of marriages to cousins or relatives are Andhra Pradesh (29 per cent), Maharashtra (26 per cent) and Karnataka (23 per cent).

5 See Drèze and Sharma (1998). Also, in the recent round of survey in Palanpur there were a couple of cases found where a Palanpur male had married someone from Bihar or West Bengal. In these cases, a dowry was not taken and in fact a small bride price was paid. One of the explanations given for this was that the family of the groom was so poor that they could not find someone even poorer and so they went further away and 'bought' women.

6 See Kolenda (2003) on this relationship in South India.

7 According to the IHDS data, mean age at marriage in Uttar Pradesh is 16.1 years and in Tamil Nadu is 18.8 years. However, the gap between the two states in terms of 'mean age at cohabiting' is not as much, with the mean age at cohabiting being 17.5 years in Uttar Pradesh and 19 years in Tamil Nadu. This is probably because of the practice of '*gauna*' in Uttar Pradesh where the bride moves to her husband's home a few years after the wedding following a ceremony called '*gauna*'. However during the field work I did not find this practice being so common anymore.

8 I did not record number of women who said it was a 'love' marriage, but asked whether they had any say in the decision on who they would marry. This therefore includes more women than those who said they had a 'love' marriage.

9 Including those who are living with their parents or in the same village as their parents.

10 In the survey I also asked about visits by natal family members and the figures were similar with 55 per cent women in Uttar Pradesh and 84 per cent women in Tamil Nadu saying that some member of their natal family visited them more than two times a year.

11 These percentages are in relation to number of women who said they can get support from their parents. Those who said that they do not get any kind of support from their parents have not been included.

12 According to the IHDS survey, 44 per cent of women in Tamil Nadu and 9 per cent of women in Uttar Pradesh had their last delivery at natal home.

13 Here, we consider only those women who have ever done any nonhousehold work, whether paid or unpaid.

14 Among those who normally do any outside work.

15 According to the respondents, 28 per cent of the husbands had never been to school in Uttar Pradesh while the figure was 20 per cent in Tamil Nadu. So the gender gap is much higher in Uttar Pradesh.

16 Among the husbands, 41 per cent had completed class 10 or more in Tamil Nadu while 30 per cent had done so in Uttar Pradesh.

17 Initially, I tried collecting information on the amount of time women spent on an average on each of these activities. However, I found that it was very difficult to get concrete responses on this. A proper time use survey was not possible given the time and resource constraints, so I decided to focus on nonhousehold work and work that is done outside the home. For the present purpose since the interest is to look at the influence of women's work on health outcomes, it was felt that focussing on outside work would be more relevant. Women's work is expected to have a positive impact on child's health because paid work increases the woman's autonomy and decision-making power, outside work exposes her to new ideas and information and also enhances mobility. On the other hand, outside work could have a negative impact because it takes away from the time women otherwise have for childcare. Since women did most of the household work in both the states, and the difference was mainly in work outside the home, I felt that it would be sufficient to focus on outside work. It must be noted, however, that women in Uttar Pradesh did a lot of work, especially livestock-related like cutting the grass and collecting the dung, which was not as common in Tamil Nadu. This was also because of fewer households having any livestock in Tamil Nadu. But women in Tamil Nadu had to collect firewood for cooking, whereas women in Uttar Pradesh used cow dung.

18 In fact in Tamil Nadu, there was usually some discussion around this statement and most women felt that the husband should help with taking care of children but not as many agreed about the rest of the household chores. So if this question had been only about husbands helping out in 'taking care of children' and did not include other 'household chores' then there may have been more women in Tamil Nadu in agreement.

19 This does not mean they were the primary decision makers but that they felt they were part of the decision making.

20 In Uttar Pradesh, there are 50 SC respondents and 75 non-SC and in Tamil Nadu 47 SC respondents and 78 non-SC.

21 However, there were no such cases among women whom I interviewed, this was more in relation to what they would like their daughters to be when they grew up.

22 The survey data show that while in Uttar Pradesh the percentage of women who are in the workforce increases as we go higher up the education scale, the reverse is true in Tamil Nadu. This is not reported here however since the sample size is small and there are very few women in the sample in Uttar Pradesh who are in the workforce and also very few women who are educated, to arrive at any conclusion. However, this matches the field observation described above. In Tamil Nadu as we move higher in the education scale, fewer women are in the workforce. Even in Tamil Nadu it was seen that as women's education increased or the economic status of the family increased women did not work outside the home. Therefore, there was also the norm in both the states that women needed to work outside the home in paid employment only if the family conditions were such that it was necessary. However, the threshold of what the level of income was beyond which women need not work seemed different between the two states.

23 Our sample being of women with children less than three years of age, there were many women who usually worked (especially in Tamil Nadu) but were currently at home because of the young children. This is why it is important to also look at the data on 'main occupation'.

24 In Tamil Nadu particularly there were discussions where women said that while it is expected of men to react (and hence justified), it is not 'fair'.

25 As mentioned earlier, especially in Uttar Pradesh, there were other people present a lot of the time when the interview was being conducted. This could have biased the response. When the mothers-in-law were present, I asked the question on domestic violence when there was a brief opportunity when the woman was alone (like when she got up to bring water) or when we were two of us (I had an assistant for help with anthropometry), one of us would distract the others and the other would quickly ask about domestic violence. I also did not probe much further into this question on personal experience with violence unless someone voluntarily wanted to talk about it, since it also raises ethical issues as a researcher who is not able to offer any help or support. Therefore, while this question does give an indication of the extent of violence, there is not much further we can say based on these data. The NFHS data presented in earlier sections show that while a smaller percentage of women in Uttar Pradesh and Tamil Nadu report any experience of spousal violence (compared to my field data), both these states are among states where the extent of spousal violence is higher than the national average and there is not much difference between the two states. The questions related to general attitude towards domestic violence and whether husbands were justified in beating their wives without reference to the woman being interviewed in particular was asked before asking her about her own experience with violence. There was more open discussion in relation to this. NFHS asks questions related to violence in much greater detail with several questions on different forms – such as physical, emotional, sexual and within each form regarding specific acts of violence such as slapping and pushing. NFHS interviewers were also provided with a list of local organisations that women could approach if they needed or asked for help.

26 While it may seem surprising that domestic violence is more prevalent in Tamil Nadu than in Uttar Pradesh, this finding is consistent with other studies and also secondary data. Studies have found that in places where more women are working and gaining autonomy in different spheres, domestic violence also is high, in reaction to the changing power balance. (Jejeebhoy 1998; IIPS 2007; Das and Kiersten 2008; Eswaran and Malhotra 2011).

27 While this is a small percentage in both states, the difference is highly significant. In Tamil Nadu many of these had to do with getting certificates or enrolling for the unemployment benefit scheme. Tamil Nadu has a scheme of giving Rs. 150 per month for those who are educated and unemployed.

28 Also to do with the fact that more number of them are SHG members.

29 Many women in Tamil Nadu said that the electoral lists were not updated and that their names were not in the voter lists in their marital village. This could also be because Uttar Pradesh had assembly elections in 2007 which was more recent than Tamil Nadu which had assembly elections in 2006.

The field work was conducted in phases during the period November 2008 to April 2010.

30 Those who did were Muslims who said they wore a *burqa* to go out, of which in the case of one it was a 'love' marriage where the girl belonged to a Hindu family and converted to Islam. They were living with her parents, and visited her in-laws once in a while. It is when she visited them or went outside the village that she wore a *burqa*.

31 In Uttar Pradesh, 64 per cent of the women said that the husband eats first and only then the wife eats, whereas in Tamil Nadu this was so for 29 per cent of the women. Rest of the women said that there is no fixed routine and it varies (14 per cent in Tamil Nadu and 3 per cent in Uttar Pradesh) or in a few cases in both the states that the wife eats first. In cases where it varies/depends, women in Tamil Nadu talked about how it depended on what work they are doing on the particular day as work timings are different for men and women.

32 For example, dowry seems to be quite a strong factor in both places. Even in cross-cousin marriages, there is dowry in Tamil Nadu.

Chapter 8

Delivering public services effectively

While doing my field work in the villages of Tamil Nadu and Uttar Pradesh, the difference in the quality and extent of public services, along with the conditions of women's lives, is something that came across as being strikingly different between the two states. Although this was expected to some extent, the way in which the difference in the role of public services in people's lives between the two states stood out during the interviews was surprising. This is also indicated by the number of persons employed in the public sector in each of these states. While there are 1,996 public sector employees per 100,000 population in Tamil Nadu, in Uttar Pradesh there are only 817 public sector employees per 100,000 population.[1] Some of the data in Chapter 4 have already shown how the coverage and quality of public services in Tamil Nadu are amongst the best in the country, whereas Uttar Pradesh ranks amongst the worst performing states. However, looking at some of the public services in details throws up some interesting insights.

Health services

It was seen earlier that per capita public expenditure on health in Tamil Nadu is higher than in Uttar Pradesh and, in fact, is one of the highest in the country. Even in terms of physical infrastructure related to health services, Tamil Nadu is ahead of most states in the country. NSS data show that more people access public health facilities in Tamil Nadu when compared to Uttar Pradesh. This also emerges from the field survey.

In the field survey I asked women where members of their household usually went for treatment when they fell sick. There was a wide variation between the two states in this (Figure 8.1). While less than 5 per cent of the respondents in Uttar Pradesh said that they go to any

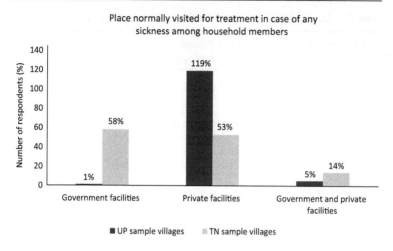

Figure 8.1 Utilisation of health services
Source: Author's field survey

government facilities[2] for treatment, in Tamil Nadu this was much higher with almost 58 per cent of women saying that they usually go to a government facility for treatment. Nineteen respondents (5 in Uttar Pradesh and 14 in Tamil Nadu) mentioned more than one place, saying that it depends on who fell sick.

Some further details were asked about visit to a health facility in the last three months and the results are presented in Table 8.1. About 81 per cent women in Tamil Nadu and 72 per cent in Uttar Pradesh visited a health facility in the last three months either for themselves or their children or with other members of the family who were ill. Of these, 63 per cent in Tamil Nadu and 11 per cent in Uttar Pradesh went to a government facility. Of those who visited a health centre in the last three months, most of them (about three-fourths) in both the states had to wait for less than one hour. Very few of them said that the health personnel were 'unfriendly'. In both states most women said that the health personnel were either 'friendly' (a slightly higher percentage in Uttar Pradesh felt so) or 'indifferent'. Similarly not many felt that the health facilities were unclean. Most felt that the health facility that they visited was 'very clean' (a higher percentage in Tamil Nadu) or 'clean'.

In Tamil Nadu, it was seen that young children are usually taken to private hospitals. It is the pregnant women and old people who mostly use the PHCs. Of those who visited any health facility in the last three

Table 8.1 Details of visit to health facility in the last three months

% of respondents who:	Uttar Pradesh sample villages	Tamil Nadu sample villages	Total
Visited health facility in the last 3 months (N = 250)	72	80.8	76.4
If visited a health facility in the last three months, type of health facility			
Government	11.1	63.4	38.7
Private	88.9	36.6	61.3
Had a waiting time of less than one hour at health facility	72.2	76.2	74.3
Attitude of nurse/doctor at the health facility			
Friendly	87.8	79.0	83.2
Indifferent	8.9	18.0	13.7
Unfriendly	3.3	3.0	3.1
Cleanliness at the health facility			
Very clean	71.0	91.2	81.5
Somewhat clean	26.9	5.9	15.9
N	90	101	191

Source: Author's field survey

months, 65 (out of 101) went for treatment of their children. Of these, about half, 33 of them, went to a government facility. Thirty-six of them went either for their own treatment or treatment of other adult members of the family. Of these, 31 (almost all) went to either the PHC or a government facility. In Uttar Pradesh, of the 10 people who needed treatment and visited a government facility in the previous three months, three were children and the rest were adults.

The respondents who said that their households generally preferred to use private facilities were further asked for reasons for not going to government facilities. The reasons for preferring private facilities over the PHCs or other government facilities seem to be manifold. As seen in Table 8.2, in Uttar Pradesh the main reasons given were not having a facility nearby (40 per cent), poor quality of care (27 per cent) and not knowing anything about government facilities (or 'we always went to private'). On the other hand, in Tamil Nadu the primary reason given was poor quality of care (the main example of this was 'they give the same white tablets for everything') and waiting time too long (14 per cent).[3]

Table 8.2 Reason for not visiting a government health facility

% of respondents who gave the following reasons	Uttar Pradesh sample villages	Tamil Nadu sample villages	Total
No nearby facility	40.0	7.8	30.1
Facility timing not convenient	5.2	5.9	5.4
Health personnel often absent	6.1	3.9	5.4
Waiting time too long	1.7	13.7	5.4
Poor quality of care	27.0	51.0	34.3
No habit/don't know about government facilities	18.3	9.8	15.7
Other	1.7	7.8	3.6
N	115	51	166
Percentage of total sample	92	40.8	66.4

Source: Author's field survey

Health seeking and childcare practices

In the field survey, women were asked about antenatal care details in relation to their last pregnancy (excluding abortions and still births). Since women who had children under three years of age were interviewed, these data basically relate to births in the last three years (Figure 8.2 and Table 8.3). Of all the women interviewed, while 63 per cent were registered with the ANM and had received a mother and child card from the ANM in Uttar Pradesh, in Tamil Nadu this was the case for 95 per cent women. Almost all women (98 per cent) in Tamil Nadu had at least one antenatal check-up during pregnancy, but this was as low as 35 per cent in Uttar Pradesh. Amongst women who had antenatal check-ups, 59 per cent went to the PHC in Tamil Nadu while none of them did in Uttar Pradesh. In Uttar Pradesh, 75 per cent of the women went to a private clinic or hospital while only 33 per cent did in Tamil Nadu (most of them also went to a government facility).

Almost all the women in Tamil Nadu were given iron and folic acid tablets and tetanus injections during their pregnancy, while in Uttar Pradesh 34.4 per cent women said they had been given IFA tables and 61.6 per cent women said that they were given at least one tetanus injection during pregnancy.

Table 8.3 Place of antenatal care

% of respondents who got their ANC (among those who received any ANC) check-up at:	Uttar Pradesh sample villages	Tamil Nadu sample villages	Total
Subcentre	6.8	5.7	6.0
PHC	0.0	59.0	43.4
Government hospital	25.0	27.0	26.5
Private clinic or hospital	75.0	32.8	44.0
N	44	122	166

Source: Author's field survey

Note: Total percentage is more than 100 because some women had an ANC check-up in more than one place.

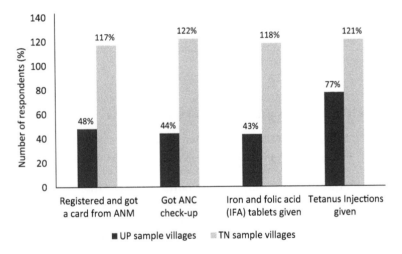

Figure 8.2 Antenatal care

Source: Author's field survey

The youngest child of 74 per cent of the women interviewed (this would be a child who is three years old or under) was born at home in Uttar Pradesh, while in Tamil Nadu 6 per cent of the women had home deliveries. Further, even amongst those who had hospital deliveries, a large percentage of these women had their deliveries in government facilities such as government hospitals or PHCs or SCs compared to private hospitals in Tamil Nadu. As shown in Figure 8.3, this was the reverse in the case of Uttar Pradesh, where most of the women had an institutional delivery in a private clinic or hospital.

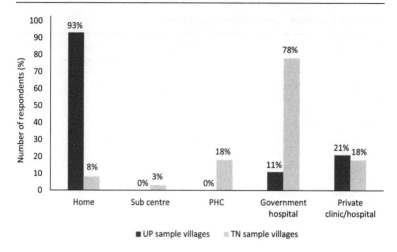

Figure 8.3 **Place of delivery**

Source: Author's field survey

Note: Figures in brackets are percentages.

More than 90 per cent of the babies (the youngest children of the mothers interviewed) were weighed at the time of birth in Tamil Nadu compared to 17 per cent in Uttar Pradesh. Further, for 62 per cent of these babies in Tamil Nadu breastfeeding was initiated immediately after birth, while this was the case for 12 per cent of the babies in Uttar Pradesh. Similar differences were also seen in the practices of feeding colostrum and prelacteals to the baby.

A higher percentage of women in Tamil Nadu said that they always wash their hands and the child's hand before feeding the child.[4] While women in Tamil Nadu, in three quarters of the cases, said that their children always eat from a separate bowl/plate, in Uttar Pradesh this was so in the case of 44 per cent of the children. The rest of the children usually shared with older children or adults, while they were eating (Table 8.4).

While a slightly higher percentage of women in Tamil Nadu felt that their children were underweight and short for their age when compared to Uttar Pradesh, the anthropometric data reveal that the percentage of children underweight or stunted is much higher in Uttar Pradesh than in Tamil Nadu. This could be interpreted to mean that women in Tamil Nadu are more aware of the health status of their children than women in Uttar Pradesh. One of the explanations for low public action on malnutrition in India, in spite of the high rates of malnutrition, is that

Table 8.4 Newborn care and childcare practices

% of cases where	Uttar Pradesh sample villages	Tamil Nadu sample villages	Total
Birthweight was recorded	17.6	91.2	54.4
Breastfeeding was initiated immediately after birth	12	62.4	37.2
Baby was given colostrum	22.4	67.2	44.8
Baby fed any prelacteals	84.8	40.8	62.8
% of mothers who said they:			
Always wash their hands before feeding the child	61.6	83.6	72.7
Always wash the child's hands before feeding	37.8	74.3	56.4
Child always eats from a separate bowl/plate	44.1	76.4	61.0
Stop feeding if the child does not eat (rest said they persuade/cajole/try giving other foods/and so on)	84	50	58
Feel their child is underweight for his/her age	27.5	36.1	31.9
Feel their child is 'short' for his/her age	14.8	21.3	18.1
Total N	125	125	250

Source: Author's field survey

there is no recognition of the problem. This is attributed to the high prevalence of chronic malnutrition leading to the situation being normalised – the average height of children is low, so a stunted child looks 'normal'. It is interesting to study further, how perceptions on what is the 'correct' height or weight are formed.

Comparing per capita public health expenditure in Tamil Nadu and Uttar Pradesh further, Figure 8.4 shows that per capita public spending on health in Tamil Nadu was more than two times that in Uttar Pradesh in the period 1975–80. Further, while Tamil Nadu showed a consistent increase in per capita public spending on health, in Uttar Pradesh while the per capita public spending on health increased between 1980 and 1995; there is a fall in spending between 1995 and 2005. There is an increase in per capita public spending on health in Uttar Pradesh relative to Tamil Nadu, in the latest period 2005–10. However, Tamil Nadu's per capita spending is still 1.5 times higher than Uttar Pradesh.

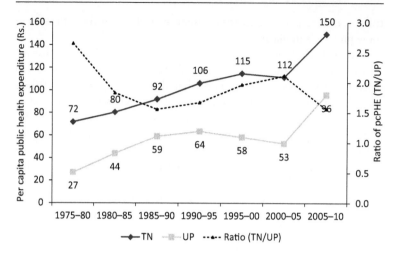

Figure 8.4 Per capita public health expenditure

Source: RBI statistics (various years)

Over this 35 year period, as seen in Figure 8.4, while there has been sustained public spending on health in Tamil Nadu (barring a slow down between 1995–2000 and 2000–5), in Uttar Pradesh there was stagnation and even slight decline in real per capita spending between the periods 1985–90 and 2000–5. In the last period under consideration here, there was a sudden increase in public spending on health in Uttar Pradesh. What is interesting here is that the per capita public spending on health in Tamil Nadu was much higher than in Uttar Pradesh even during the period when the difference between the two states in terms of per capita SDP or MPCE or poverty ratio was small, as noted in the previous section. This indicates that there was greater priority given to health spending in Tamil Nadu compared to Uttar Pradesh by the governments in power.

A remarkable difference was seen in the quality and extent of public services in Tamil Nadu, compared to Uttar Pradesh during the field work in the districts in which this study was conducted. The four PHCs that I visited in Tamil Nadu had all been painted recently in bright attractive colours (orange).[5] All of them were clean and well maintained. In each of them, there were clear protocols to be followed when patients came, especially when women in labour came in. The nurses I spoke to in these PHCs were confident of handling the cases. I asked them some questions related to what they did when there was a complication and there was a consistency in their responses indicating that there were some protocols in place.

In each PHC there was an 'EDD chart' (expected date of delivery) on the wall, with the names and details of all the women expected to deliver in the current month and what their present status is. When each ANM visits the PHC, she is expected to update this chart and in this manner every delivery in the area of a PHC is being monitored. This is on the wall and available for anyone who visits the PHC to see.

In Uttar Pradesh I did not have the opportunity to spend so much time in the PHCs. Of the four PHCs that I visited (two visits to each), there were no staff available at the time of visit in two of these. In the other two as well, there were just a handful of patients. In three of the four PHCs, there was no MBBS doctor appointed. Rather the medical officer had a BAMS[6] qualification but was expected to practise allopathy. Even during the survey in the villages, none of the women were able to tell me where the nearest PHC was. They were all aware of the bigger government hospitals in the block and district headquarters but not the PHC.

Government health services are important for this study as they are directly relevant to the human development outcomes that are under focus (infant/child mortality, malnutrition). Since this is an area in which the Tamil Nadu government has made many improvements in the recent past, it also presents a good case study on how public services in Tamil Nadu are different from the rest of the country, and from Uttar Pradesh in particular.

The District Level Health Survey (DLHS) data for 2007–8 presented in Table 8.5 show that 85 per cent of PHCs in Tamil Nadu and 80 per cent of PHCs in Uttar Pradesh have a medical officer appointed. Further, while 62 per cent of PHCs in Tamil Nadu have a lady medical officer, this was the case in only 2 per cent of PHCs in Uttar Pradesh. Ninety-four per cent PHCs in Tamil Nadu and 79 per cent in Uttar Pradesh have a pharmacist. The DLHS data show that 58 per cent villages in Tamil Nadu have SCs within the village and this is case for 31 per cent villages in Uttar Pradesh (the all India average being 41 per cent). Almost all the SCs in both the states have an ANM or female health worker in place. While almost 70 per cent of SCs in Tamil Nadu had regular electricity, only 7 per cent in Uttar Pradesh did so. Further, the DLHS classifies 98 per cent SCs in Tamil Nadu as having adequate equipment and 82 per cent having adequate essential drugs. The corresponding figures in Uttar Pradesh are 84 per cent for equipment and 35 per cent for essential drugs.[7]

Table 8.5 Facilities in PHCs and subcentres

	Tamil Nadu	Uttar Pradesh
% PHCs with a medical officer	85.3	76.9
% PHCs with a lady medical officer	62.4	2.3
% PHCs with a pharmacist	93.9	79
% villages with a subcentre within the village	58.1	31.1
% Subcentres with regular electricity	70	6.7
% PHCs with at least 60% of essential equipment	97.9	83.9
% PHCs with at least 60% of essential drugs	82.1	35.3
% Subcentres with male health workers	71.6	6.2

Source: DLHS-3 (2007–8)

According to data from the DLHS-3, 72 per cent of the SCs in Tamil Nadu had male health workers available, whereas this figure was only 6 per cent in Uttar Pradesh. At an all India level, only 40 per cent of the SCs have a male health worker available. The male health worker has an important role in many preventive activities such as health education, insecticide spraying, monitoring the availability of clean water and sanitation, while the ANM/female health worker is focussed on providing reproductive and child health services. One male multipurpose worker and one female multipurpose worker or ANM are expected to be in each SC.

Strengths of Tamil Nadu's public health services

The public health infrastructure in Tamil Nadu is above average compared to other Indian states and this also contributes to the better health outcomes in the state. Tamil Nadu is also one of the few states in the country where access to health care in the government sector continues to be universal, in the sense that there are no user fees charged for anyone, irrespective of whether they are below the poverty line or not. This is also reflected in the NSS survey on health expenditures where it is seen that Tamil Nadu is the only state where people have reported no expenditure (zero) on outpatient care in a government hospital. It is also a state where on an average people spend the least due to hospitalisation for child birth in a government hospital and lowest even in terms of the loss of household income due to hospitalisation.

In addition to investments in infrastructure, the Tamil Nadu government has taken many innovative steps in the health sector. For instance, method specific family planning targets were removed in 1992, even before this was done in the rest of the country (Visaria 2000). To enable better monitoring and management of health services, the health administration in the state is organised through 'Health Unit Districts' (HUDs). While these are usually corresponding with revenue districts, larger districts are divided into two HUDs. While there are 31 districts in Tamil Nadu, there are 42 HUDs. Each HUD is under a Deputy Director of Health Services (DDHS) who is part of the Directorate of Public Health and is in charge of all the grassroots level health staff and medical officers of the PHCs. The DDHSs have a public health qualification.

In what follows, we look at some of the features of the Tamil Nadu health system that are unique to the state and contribute to the effectiveness of the public health services.

1 **Focus on public health**: There has been a strong focus on public health activities as separate from medical services in the state. There is a separate Directorate for Public Health Services, which has been in place since 1922. The Directorate of Public Health Services has its own cadre of trained public health managers. Other than the grassroots health workers, and staff of PHCs, the Directorate of Public Health Services employs a range of technical staff such as sanitary engineers, laboratory staff, entomologists and statisticians. The public health staff are trained in nonclinical functions, given a public health perspective and are provided with opportunities for growth in their jobs. The remuneration and promotion opportunities have been designed to be better for those in the public health track than those in the medical side, to encourage doctors to take on public health jobs in the government. Those in the public health track are required to obtain a public health qualification in addition to their medical qualification.[8] All of this provides incentives for people to work in the public health field.[9]

A separate and substantial budget is dedicated for public health services. The size of the public health budget (this includes primary health care services such as PHCs and SCs) is also relatively large compared to the secondary/tertiary medical care and medical education budgets (about 35–40 per cent of the total health budget is spent on public health).[10] Although its relative share has fallen over time, the Directorate of Public Health has consistently had larger budgets than the two other Directorates in the Health Department (the Directorate for Medical Services and the Directorate for Medical Education) (Das Gupta et al. 2009).

2   **Public Health Act:** Tamil Nadu was the first state to have a Public Health Act. Tamil Nadu's Public Health Act (enacted in 1939 but substantially amended later) empowers public health functionaries to take steps to prevent health threats while also specifying the legal and administrative structures under which the public health system functions, responsibilities and powers to different levels of government and agencies, and their source of funding for discharging these duties. The main focus areas of this act are environmental health, control of communicable diseases, food hygiene and maternal and child health. A public health board under the leadership of the Minister of Public Health is set up to monitor the implementation of this act (Selvaraj n.d.). Most other states do not have such an act or have a public health act that has not been modified since the colonial period. Uttar Pradesh does not have a public health act. In Tamil Nadu this act provides the basis for planning and delivering public health services in the state, especially in relation to preventive services such as environmental health, water, sanitation and hygiene. However, the Tamil Nadu Act also needs to be amended to include new concerns related to public health such as HIV/AIDS and chikungunya. While these have been proposed they are yet to be passed by the Assembly (Kannan 2007; The Hindu 2008; Kannan 2011).

Through this system of planning and management, Tamil Nadu is able to prevent disease outbreaks and also deal with emergencies, to a large extent. It was such preparedness that helped Tamil Nadu to effectively avoid any epidemic when the tsunami hit in 2005 (WHO 2006). Das Gupta et al. (2009) also give examples of how Tamil Nadu public health teams were called in to provide support in Orissa after the cyclone in 1999 and how unprepared the governments of Maharashtra and Gujarat were when faced with a plague epidemic because they had closed down their plague surveillance units. By contrast, despite the fact that the last episode of plague in South India was in the early 1960s, in Tamil Nadu the plague surveillance unit continues to function and has been expanded to cover other vector-borne and zoonotic diseases, and gives practical training to entomologists and other public health professionals[11] (Das Gupta et al. 2009; 2010).

3   **Human resource policy:** One of the problems facing the public health system across the country is the nonavailability of doctors who are willing to work in rural and remote areas. Even when there are doctors posted in rural PHCs, the levels of absenteeism are very

high. The Tamil Nadu government provides many incentives for doctors to work in the PHCs and in remote areas, such as preference in admission to postgraduate courses, posting doctors within the zone they come from and providing accommodation at the health centres. Similar incentives are also provided to the village health nurses (or ANMs). VHNs were given free mobile phones and loans to purchase two wheelers. There are also bonuses provided for health staff working in remote areas. Further, an enabling work environment with good infrastructure, availability of drugs and opportunities for career development also encourages doctors to work in the public health sector (Datta 2009). Although many doctors are attracted towards the better paying private sector, compared to other states the incentives in the public sector have, to some extent, taken care of the problem of having enough professionals working for the government. The level of vacancy in doctors' posts in PHCs *vis-à-vis* the requirement in Tamil Nadu is nil, whereas 813 additional doctors are required in Uttar Pradesh. Doctors I met during the field visits were quite enthusiastic about their jobs. During the interviews, they spoke of the benefits, especially preferential treatment for admission into postgraduate courses and the rich experience that a rural posting provides, as incentives for working in a PHC.[12]

4   **Drug procurement policy:** A major innovative initiative in Tamil Nadu's public health system is the significant improvement in drug supply to the public health facilities. This results from centralised procurement and decentralised distribution, with the health facilities having the freedom to choose what they want and when they want it. The Tamil Nadu Medical Services Corporation Limited (TNMSC) was established in 1994 to take care of drug procurement and distribution in the entire state. The TNMSC pools budgets from all departments and procures and distributes drugs to public health facilities in the state through district-level warehouses. Also, by procuring generic drugs, rather than branded products, TNMSC has optimised purchases within the available drug budget. The TNMSC also deals with surgical instruments and other medical equipment for government medical institutions. This has been hailed as a best practice and is now being promoted as a model for the rest of the states to follow. As a result, the private expenditure on drugs for treatment in government hospitals is the least in Tamil Nadu (nil for outpatient and Rs. 637 for inpatient – refer to Table 4.7).

5   **Focus on maternal and child health and improving PHCs:** Along with general measures to run an effective public health system, special efforts have been made in Tamil Nadu, especially since the mid-1990s, to improve maternal and child health. These have a direct bearing on the outcomes studied here, such as infant and child mortality and child malnutrition. The strategies pursued by the Tamil Nadu government for safer pregnancy and newborn survival included ensuring 'prevention and termination of unwanted pregnancies; accessible, high-quality antenatal care and institutional delivery, with routine essential obstetric care and emergency obstetric first aid at the primary level; accessible, high-quality emergency obstetric care at the first referral level'.

In order to achieve this, various initiatives such as provision of safe abortion services in public health facilities; setting up 24-hour PHCs that provide emergency obstetric first-aid and attend to sick newborns and arrange for referral; improved infrastructure and environment of PHCs; improved training and protocols for emergency care, especially obstetric care; and skill upgrading of frontline health workers have been undertaken. VHNs/ANMs are provided incentives for providing antenatal care and promoting institutional deliveries. The data show acceleration in the rate of increase in the proportion of institutional deliveries. While there was a 37 percentage point increase in institutional deliveries in the two decades between 1971 (at 20 per cent) and 1991 (at 57 per cent), in the one decade between 1996 and 2005, there was a growth of nearly 30 percentage points, from 65 per cent to 94 per cent (WHO 2009).

To attract people to the PHCs, several innovative measures were introduced, such as introducing a birth companion programme, providing free meals for women who come for antenatal care, conducting 'bangle ceremonies'[13] for pregnant women, arranging for maternal picnics where pregnant women can visit the PHC and meet the staff to understand the services provided.[14]

This has resulted in more and more people utilising the public health facilities. It has been reported that there has been a tremendous rise in the number of deliveries taking place in PHCs after recent efforts towards this. A report in the Hindu newspaper states, 'The PHCs in the State have reversed the trend of migration of patients to private health care sector – as far as deliveries are concerned. There has been a 77.2 per cent increase in deliveries in the PHCs between April 2007 and January 2008 over the corresponding period in 2006–7, according to statistics available with the Public Health Department' (Kannan 2008). Figure 8.5 shows that this trend has continued with a sharp rise in the proportion of deliveries taking place in PHCs in Tamil Nadu from about 8 per cent of all deliveries in 2004–5 to over 25 per cent in 2010–11.

The data from two rounds of NSSO (52nd round in 1995–6 and 60th round in 2004) show mixed results in terms of changing preferences among people for public health facilities *vis-à-vis* private care. In the case of hospitalisation, it is seen that among the rural poor there is a slight shift to private care, whereas the urban poor and rural rich have shifted towards public facilities. However, in the case of outpatient care, there is an increase in the use of public facilities by those in the lower income quartiles. Further, in the case of maternal health care as reflected in antenatal registrations, there has been a significant increase in the role of public facilities between the last two rounds of NSSO surveys, particularly in the lowest income quartile in the rural areas (Sen et al. 2008). Many of the interventions towards improving PHCs were also carried out in the last five years, after the introduction of the National Rural Health Mission (NRHM). It would therefore be interesting to see what the next round of NSSO data would show.

Government statistics suggest that a large number of people visit the PHCs in Tamil Nadu. For instance the Tamil Nadu Human Development Report (Government of Tamil Nadu 2003) states, 'Almost 35 million

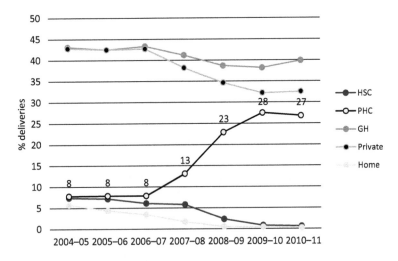

Figure 8.5 Trend in place of delivery, Tamil Nadu

Source: GoTN (2013)

outpatients are treated in PHCs annually. Allowing for repeaters, this still indicates a high degree of utilization of PHCs for minor ailments (given that the rural population of Tamil Nadu is around 45 million)'. According to the Tamil Nadu Health Department's statistics, while about 40 million outpatient cases were treated in 2000–1, this number rose to about 72 million in 2008–9. The average number of outpatients seen per PHC per day in 2008–9 was 140 (GoTN 2009).

Based on an analysis of Tamil Nadu's health system, Das Gupta et al. (2009) conclude that, 'Although it is difficult to formally prove that strong population-wide health services such as those of Tamil Nadu improve health outcomes, the connection is strongly indicated by the fact that developed countries have continued to invest public funds in these services for over 125 years, and have successfully reduced exposure to communicable diseases'. They further argue that the Tamil Nadu model is replicable in other states especially because it is based on the same administrative set up and the additional investment required to create a public health cadre is not very much.

Public health services in Uttar Pradesh

As seen in Chapter 4, there are still many gaps in Uttar Pradesh in terms of public health infrastructure. It is one of the states in the country with the lowest doctor/health workers to population ratio as well. The problem of shortage of human resources for health in Uttar Pradesh is well recognised. However, the report of the Common Review Mission comments that the Uttar Pradesh government is yet to make any considerable efforts towards resolving this problem. No innovative measures have yet been introduced to attract health professionals to the public sector, nor has any significant action been taken to train more health professionals in the state.

The PHCs that were visited during the field work were also either deserted or had very little activity. The PHC buildings were also in a state of disrepair. One of the PHCs however was recently constructed and had impressive physical infrastructure.[15] However, despite repeated visits, I could not meet the doctor who was supposed to be appointed for this PHC. The Common Review Mission (CRM) of the NRHM in its report on Uttar Pradesh observes that,

> several new PHCs constructed in the past 3–4 years were nonfunctional and kept locked because of lack of manpower, especially doctors. This phenomenon of locked new PHCs was reported to

be there across the State. The team observed that the newly constructed infrastructure in these facilities was slowly withering away due to lack of maintenance. Compound walls were found to be damaged to allow cattle and other animals to graze in. Similarly, plastering inside these premises was slowly peeling off and cracks were developing on the walls

(GoI 2011d).

The women who were in the PHCs when I visited them, or some of the women who had gone to the PHC for their delivery among the sample respondents, also complained that it was difficult to stay there because of lack of water and toilet facilities. They preferred coming back to their villages immediately after the delivery.

With regard to the equipment in the PHCs and CHCs the Common Review Mission further observes that,

during the visits, it was also observed that equipments such as radiant warmer, autoclave, generator which were in need of minor repair were lying dysfunctional for many months and even years. There seems to be both a lack of initiative on the part of the In Charge Superintendents/MO to repair these equipments and inadequate support and supervision from State Headquarters, particularly a lack of appropriate asset management systems.

(GoI 2011d)

The report of the Public Accounts Committee (PAC) of the Parliament finds that SCs are being used as warehouses and cattle sheds, many of the medicines the PAC members examined had expired, many commonly used drugs were not available and there was understaffing of trained health workers. Many of the PHCs and CHCs lacked proper water, sanitation and power supply and many of them were 'functioning' without either allopathic or AYUSH (Ayurveda, Yoga and Naturopathy, Unani, Siddha and Homoeopathy) doctors (PAC 2011). Further, the report also commented upon the huge shortfall in staff appointments in the public health centres. The data in Table 8.6 show a shortfall of as high as 76 per cent in the appointment of staff nurses.

Although there has been some recent expansion in budgets and infrastructure, the Uttar Pradesh health system has been in the news for all the wrong reasons, such as the outbreak of Japanese Encephalitis in many districts of eastern Uttar Pradesh resulting in the death of hundreds of children. This has been reported each year over the last five

Table 8.6 Availability and shortfall of human resource in Uttar Pradesh

Category	Required as per IPHS (September 2011)	Regular	NRHM contractual[16]	Total in position	Shortfall in %
Doctors	15,455	6,050	572	6,622	57
Specialist	8,599	3,226	302	3,528	59
Staff Nurses	31,187	6,435	1,127	7,562	76
MPW (male)	9,080	1,729	–	1,729	81
ANM	41,950	21,270	1,500	22,770	46
Lab technician	5,389	1,836	208	2,044	62

Source: GoI (2011d)

Note: IPHS = Indian Public Health Standards.

years, but the situation does not seem to be improving (NCPCR 2011a; Sharda 2012).[17]

Over the last two years, a major scam has been exposed in the use of the funds of the NRHM. Based on the audit by the CAG, the extent of irregularities in the use of NRHM funds between 2005 and 2011 level is about Rs. 50 billion (CAG 2011).[18] In the last two years, two chief medical officers and one deputy chief medical officer have been murdered, allegedly in connection with the fraud. An editorial in the Economic and Political Weekly (EPW 2011) says that, 'whether it is in terms of actual physical infrastructure, supply of equipment and medicines, or appointment of staff, the programme has failed to deliver except in pockets'.

Integrated Child Development Services

While health services are directly related to the outcomes being studied here, other services such as water, sanitation, Public Distribution System, education and Integrated Child Development Services (ICDS) are also expected to affect health outcomes. These are all linked to human development and the conditions in which people live. For some schemes such as the Public Distribution System and the ICDS, Tamil Nadu is well known to be one of the best performing states in the country.[19] A large household survey on the quality of public services[20] across 24 Indian states, done by the Public Affairs Committee (PAC), placed Tamil Nadu on the top based on performance of public services. In terms of overall performance, Tamil Nadu is followed by Gujarat, Karnataka, Maharashtra, Andhra Pradesh, and Kerala. In relation to public health services as well, in recent times Tamil Nadu has been recognised as one of the better performing states across the country.[21]

The ICDS scheme is the only centrally sponsored scheme providing health, nutrition and education services for children under six years of age. Along with health services, it is the other scheme that is directly relevant to the human development outcomes being studied here (child mortality and child nutrition). It is also a scheme that directly addresses the respondents of the field survey, that is, mothers of young children.

Tamil Nadu has been known for being one of the few states where the ICDS functions relatively well.[22] ICDS services, especially the food component, also constitute one of the core priorities of all the major political formations in the state. Tamil Nadu has a history of publicly funded nutrition programmes. From the 1950s onwards, there have been a variety of public feeding programmes in the state. The ICDS started in Tamil Nadu at the same time as in the rest of the country in 1975. In 1980, the Tamil Nadu Integrated Nutrition Project (TINP) was started with World Bank funding and in 1982 Tamil Nadu universalised the provision of midday meals to school children (including preschoolers).

TINP had a focus on tackling malnutrition in children under three years of age. The basic components of this programme were regular growth monitoring, targeted supplementary feeding and nutrition counselling. Nutrition counsellors were appointed in each village, who went from house to house to explain to mothers the importance of breastfeeding, introduction of complementary feeding at the right time of the right variety and so on. At the same time the weights of children were regularly taken and those identified as being malnourished were given special nutritional therapeutic food.

As seen in Table 8.7, a number of large-scale surveys also show greater coverage under ICDS in Tamil Nadu. All these surveys also show that

Table 8.7 ICDS coverage in Tamil Nadu and Uttar Pradesh

	Coverage of children (%)		Coverage of women (%)	
	Tamil Nadu	Uttar Pradesh	Tamil Nadu	Uttar Pradesh
NFHS-3 (2005–6)	43.5	22.3	50.4	9.6
PAC survey (2006)	33	19	NA	NA
FOCUS (2006)	86	57	NA	NA
IHDS (2004–5)	75	10	60	5

Note: Each of these surveys uses a different definition of coverage. This table is just to indicate that the difference in ICDS coverage between the two states is reflected by different surveys using different indicators. All these surveys report responses of households.

ICDS in Tamil Nadu is more regular and reliable, both in relation to preschool services and provision of supplementary nutrition.

This difference in the variation in coverage of nutrition and health education is also reflected in other surveys such as NFHS-3 and FOCUS (2006). The NFHS-3 report shows that more than 75 per cent of the children who are weighed are also counselled after the growth monitoring, while the national average was 49 per cent and in Uttar Pradesh it was 38 per cent. The difference in the number of children who actually benefitted from nutrition counselling is even higher because of the variation in the number of children who were weighed in the first place in each state. At the all India level, only 18 per cent of the children under five years of age were ever weighed in the previous one year; 3 per cent in Uttar Pradesh and 32 per cent in Tamil Nadu (NFHS-3).

Regarding ICDS services, the field survey results showed that amongst children over six months of age, 31 per cent had received some benefit from the ICDS in the last three months in Uttar Pradesh, while about 62 per cent of women in Tamil Nadu said that their child received some benefit.[23] In the case of services from ICDS during pregnancy, the

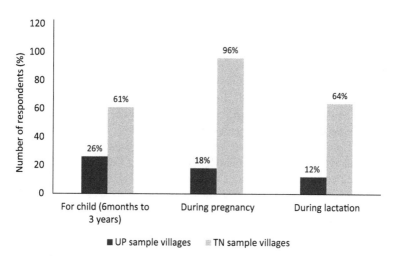

Figure 8.6 Access to ICDS services

Source: Author's field survey

Note: The question asked was in relation to: whether the child received any service from ICDS in the last three months (asked for children over six months of age); whether mother received any benefits from the ICDS while she was pregnant (during her last pregnancy) and whether mother received any benefits from the ICDS during the lactating period (for her youngest child).

Figures in brackets are percentages.

coverage in Uttar Pradesh was even lower at less than 15 per cent and in Tamil Nadu it was higher at 77 per cent. During the lactating period (up to six months after delivery), less than 10 per cent women in Uttar Pradesh said they received any services from the ICDS, while about half the women in Tamil Nadu said that they did.

In both Uttar Pradesh and Tamil Nadu, all the villages visited during the field survey had an anganwadi centre. While all of them were housed in a government building in Tamil Nadu, none of the anganwadi centres had their own buildings in Uttar Pradesh. They were mostly running out of the homes of the anganwadi worker or were given some space in the primary school. In Tamil Nadu, in six out of the eight anganwadi centres in the sample villages the anganwadi centre was functioning and the teacher and helper and on an average about 15 children were present on the day of my visit.[24] In one centre (Alangkuppam), the anganwadi worker had retired recently and a new worker had not yet been appointed. The anganwadi helper was present but there were only two children, although the helper said that more children usually come. In another village (Mamandur), the centre was closed when I visited during working hours the first time. I was told by villagers that there was a local festival and the worker did not come. However, by the end of the day the worker came and met me in the village, so she knew about my coming by the next day.

In the six centres that were functioning on the day of my visit, I also saw that the hot cooked meal for the preschool children was being prepared. It was the same in all the centres (rice, dal and some vegetables made as a *khichdi*). During my repeated visits to the village, I also saw eggs being distributed on the designated days.

In Tamil Nadu, parents are expected to bring the children under two years of age to the centre around 8 in the morning and feed the child the *urundai* made of the nutritious mix, which the anganwadi helper keeps ready every morning as soon as she opens the centre. A sample *laddu* is kept in a box each day for testing in case of any complaints of food poisoning. This was available in 6 of the 8 centres during my field visits.[25]

In all the centres visited, there were colourful posters on the walls – many made by the anganwadi workers themselves. There were beads and stones and other such local material that teachers were using to teach the children numbers and so on. The children in the anganwadi were usually able to recite poems, answer some simple questions and so on. The teachers had been trained to teach using a play-way method to develop children's motor and cognitive skills.[26] The child centres[27] in Tamil Nadu are also open for longer hours (six hours) than in Uttar Pradesh (four hours) and in the afternoon session children who stay back have a nap in the centre before their parents come to take them.

In Uttar Pradesh, of the seven centres only in three was there some activity on the day of my visit. The worker and the helper were present. There were about four to five children. All these three centres were next to the primary school. There was no cooked meal in any of the centres. Of the remaining four centres, I visited the homes of the anganwadi workers but did not see the centre functioning on any of the days of my visits to the village. All the anganwadi workers had their registers at home and were able to show me the data maintained by them.

The FOCUS study has some further data on governance aspects of ICDS, which are presented in Table 8.8. It is seen, for instance, that training of anganwadi workers seems to be taking place fairly regularly in Tamil Nadu and the workers are also paid in time, in contrast to other states.

During field visits I examined the records in the anganwadi centres in both states. Not only were the records better maintained in Tamil Nadu compared to Uttar Pradesh, the design of the registers was also such that they were more 'user-friendly'. In Tamil Nadu, the data that were recorded in some 10 different registers in Uttar Pradesh were neatly organised in one register, which had two pages each for a mother and child. These two pages had all the information from the time the mother's pregnancy was registered until the child turned 5 years old. Therefore, from this register one could see whether the mother had her

Table 8.8 ICDS in Tamil Nadu in comparison with other states

Results from FOCUS survey	Tamil Nadu	Other 'FOCUS' states
Average opening hours of the anganwadi (according to the mothers)	6½ hours a day	3½ hours a day
Average number of months that have passed since anganwadi worker attended a training programme	6	30
Proportion of anganwadi workers who have not been paid during the last three months	0	17

Source: FOCUS (2006). The FOCUS states include Chhattisgarh, Himachal Pradesh, Maharashtra, Rajasthan, Tamil Nadu and Uttar Pradesh.

antenatal check-ups, whether the delivery was normal and where it took place, date of birth of the child, whether the child was given colostrum feeding, birthweight, growth chart of the child, immunisation details and so on. This simple innovation greatly reduced the record-keeping burden of the anganwadi workers and also made more information available in a friendly format to ensure proper follow up of every mother and child.

Schools

According to the composite education development index of the NUEPA, which is an index of 27 indicators on access, infrastructure, teachers and outcome indicators, Tamil Nadu stands second only to Kerala among the major states in the country. Tamil Nadu has been a pioneer in the introduction of various schemes to enhance enrolment of children in elementary education. The most important of these schemes is the Noon Meal Scheme (NMS). The state government provides free text books and free uniforms to all children studying up to Class VIII in the government and government-aided schools. Girls in the high school are provided with free bicycles.[28]

Even before the national law on the right to education was passed, Tamil Nadu made a major legislative effort for the universalisation of education through the introduction of the Tamil Nadu Compulsory Education Act 1994. This act lays down the duty of the government to provide the necessary infrastructure for ensuring universalisation of elementary education. The state government has also put in place a policy of recruiting women for at least 50 per cent of government and panchayat union[29] school posts (Government of Tamil Nadu 2003).

During the field survey in both states, all the schools visited (six in Uttar Pradesh and eight in Tamil Nadu) were open and functioning (except for the one in Palanpur village). In all the schools in Tamil Nadu regular teachers were present. In Uttar Pradesh in all the villages, out of the six schools, in three there were regular teachers present and in the rest there were only 'para-teachers' on the day of my visit. Data show that while only 0.3 per cent of all teachers in government schools in Tamil Nadu are 'para-teachers', this figure is 38.4 per cent in Uttar Pradesh. Further, while 96 per cent of all para-teachers in Tamil Nadu have received professional training, only 33 per cent in Uttar Pradesh have done so (DISE 2011).

In the sample households in the field survey, there were 251 school-going children (165 in Uttar Pradesh and 86 in Tamil Nadu). Of these,

54 per cent in Uttar Pradesh and 64 per cent in Tamil Nadu went to government schools. In spite of the relatively good quality of the government schools in Tamil Nadu, there were many children who were being sent to private schools. However, this is to a lower extent when compared to the Uttar Pradesh sample. In Tamil Nadu, the common reasons that parents gave for sending their children to private schools was that they preferred private schools because of English medium (45 per cent) or that the quality of education in government schools was not good (36 per cent). The remaining 20 per cent said that the government school was too far. In Uttar Pradesh, 65 per cent said that they felt that the quality of education in the government school was not good, 21 per cent opted for English medium, 7 per cent said that teachers are irregular in government schools and another 7 per cent that the government school is too far (N = 76 in Uttar Pradesh and N = 31 in Tamil Nadu, for this question).

According to DISE data for 2010–11, in Tamil Nadu the percentage of children (Classes I to VIII) enrolled in government schools were 44 per cent and in private-aided schools 23 per cent (total 66.8 per cent). In one of the villages where my survey was conducted (Alangkuppam) there was only a private-aided school, which functioned just like a government school. There were no fees, midday meals and other facilities provided. In Uttar Pradesh, the percentage of children enrolled in government schools is 62 per cent and in private-aided schools is 6 per cent. Therefore, in both states a similar percentage of children went to private-unaided schools.[30] Further, according to the IHDS data, percentage of children aged 6–14 enrolled in English-medium schools is 4 per cent in Uttar Pradesh and 19 per cent in Tamil Nadu, reflecting the demand for English-medium education in Tamil Nadu.[31]

The school infrastructure in both states in the sample villages was quite similar. In fact, in Uttar Pradesh many of the buildings looked newer and in a better condition. But in Uttar Pradesh they were not used much (especially toilets, which were locked or not in use in four of the six schools). The macro-data does show some differences in infrastructure as seen in Table 8.9.

In terms of quality of education, the Annual Status of Education Report (ASER) survey shows that general learning achievement of children in the 6–14-year age group in Tamil Nadu is better than children in Uttar Pradesh. For instance, percentage of children in classes III–V who can do subtraction or more is 38 per cent in Tamil Nadu and only 29 per cent in Uttar Pradesh (ASER 2012). The skill achievement tests conducted as part of the IHDS survey (as seen in Table 8.10) also show that

Table 8.9 School-related indicators in Tamil Nadu and Uttar Pradesh

School-related indicators	Tamil Nadu	Uttar Pradesh
% schools with functional girls toilets	91.3	80.1
% schools with drinking water facility	100.0	98.2
Avg. no. of teachers per school (all schools)	6.1	3.6
Pupil–teacher ratio (PTR) (all schools)	29	44
% government primary schools with PTR > 30	20.4	63
% female teachers (all schools)	77.4	39.6
% teachers in all government schools who received in-service training during the previous year	86	17.6

Source: DISE 2010–11

Table 8.10 Quality of education

Skill achievement[34]	Tamil Nadu	Uttar Pradesh
% children aged 8–11 who can:		
Read	79	39
Subtract	71	34
Write	85	59
% children aged 8–11 enrolled in government schools who can:		
Read	78	29
Subtract	67	22
Write	82	51
% children aged 8–11 enrolled in private schools who can:		
Read	85	55
Subtract	86	52
Write	93	72

Source: IHDS (2004–5)

children in Tamil Nadu get higher scores than those in Uttar Pradesh.[32] The difference is seen in both government and private schools. The difference in achievements among children enrolled in government schools is much larger reflecting the poor state of government schools in Uttar Pradesh.[33] In fact, the skill achievement levels amongst children in government schools in Uttar Pradesh are amongst the worst in the country and much behind that in other states. This can have serious long-term consequences with a large section of Uttar Pradesh's children growing up in schools where they are not learning anything.

The midday meal scheme was running in all the schools visited in sample villages in both the states.[35] However, there was a wide variation in quality. In the field survey one of the questions asked was whether the midday meal was served in school, if there was an older school-going child present in the household. In Tamil Nadu in 83 per cent of households where older (government) school-going children were present, it was reported that midday meal was served whereas this was the case for 61 per cent of households in Uttar Pradesh. Since the survey was focussed on health services and on young children (under three years of age), further questions in relation to schools or midday meals were not asked in the survey.[36]

During my visits to the schools, in Tamil Nadu schools children gave very positive feedback about the boiled eggs being served in the school three days a week. Many children, who said that they did not like the food in school, still ate the boiled egg. While conducting the interviews I would often meet older children who came home from school during lunch bringing along their boiled egg to eat.[37] There was otherwise a complaint that the food was monotonous and so some children ate at home few days a week. Overall, there were no complaints however of disruption in the meals in any of the eight schools visited in Tamil Nadu.

On the other hand, in Uttar Pradesh, while the midday meal was being served in the villages visited, there were several complaints related to quality and regularity. In one of the villages in which the survey was conducted (Palanpur), the midday meal had not been served for more than six months, allegedly because the *pradhan* (village head) was diverting the grains supplied for the purpose of midday meal. The whole village was aware of this, but no action was taken.

Women were further asked if any other benefits/services from the government were received by them or other members of the family (see Table 8.11). In Uttar Pradesh 10.4 per cent and in Tamil Nadu 48 per

Table 8.11 Access to government schemes

% of households where	Uttar Pradesh sample villages	Tamil Nadu sample villages	Total
Midday meal given in schools if any older child in family is in government school (N = 31 in Uttar Pradesh, 34 in Tamil Nadu and 65 in total)	60.8	82.9	70.6

(Continued)

Table 8.11 (Continued)

% of households where	Uttar Pradesh sample villages	Tamil Nadu sample villages	Total
Any family member benefits/ benefited from any other government schemes	10.4	48	29.2
Which benefit?[38] (Frequency)			
Maternity benefit scheme	0	36	36
Indira Awas Yojana/house related	0	11	11
Janani Suraksha Yojana	5	6	11
Pension	7	3	10
Other	2	7	9
Total	14	63	77

Source: Author's field survey

cent did get some benefits. In Uttar Pradesh, this was mostly old-age pension or JSY. In Tamil Nadu, the benefits were mostly old-age pension, JSY or the Dr Muthulakshmi Reddy Maternity Benefit Scheme.

Public Distribution System

The Public Distribution System (PDS) is one of the important programmes run by the government towards ensuring food security. Through the PDS, subsidised foodgrains are made available to people. Households are entitled to a fixed amount of grain each month at a fixed rate. While earlier uniform entitlements were available for everyone, since 1997, a targeted PDS has been introduced across the country whereby the population below the poverty line (BPL) gets grains at a cheaper price than those who are above the poverty line (APL). The identification of who is BPL is controversial with studies showing large-scale inclusion and exclusion errors.[39]

This debate is further complicated by the fact that in practice the number of BPL persons is linked to state-wise official poverty ratios based on estimates from the NSS surveys on consumption expenditure of households spending less than the poverty line amount. It is widely claimed that the poverty lines are too low and further that they impose an arbitrary cap on the number of beneficiaries of public programmes, including the PDS. Although the details of this debate are not relevant here, what needs to be mentioned is that Tamil Nadu is the only state that refused to get into this system of a targeted PDS and continues to have a universal system where anyone who wishes to get PDS entitlements can do so.[40]

The survey done by the PAC, mentioned earlier, found that 90 per cent of households in Tamil Nadu and 86 per cent in Uttar Pradesh possessed a ration card; with 89 per cent in Tamil Nadu and 78 per cent in Uttar Pradesh using the PDS card at least once in two months. In terms of reliability, 73 per cent of households in Tamil Nadu responded that there was a regular availability of foodgrains (highest among all states), whereas only 1 per cent in Uttar Pradesh reported so (lowest among all states) (Paul et al. 2006).

According to the field survey data, a large share of respondents' households in both states, 88 per cent of the respondents in Uttar Pradesh and 92 per cent in Tamil Nadu, had a ration card. In Uttar Pradesh about 11 per cent of the respondents had BPL cards, while in Tamil Nadu there is a system of universal PDS and no differentiation made between those above and below the poverty line. Further in Tamil Nadu mostly each 'nuclear' family had a card even when they were living in joint families, which was not the case in Uttar Pradesh.

As seen in Table 8.12, there is a wide difference when we look at access to PDS. While only about 11 per cent of those who had a ration card in Uttar Pradesh said that they had bought foodgrains from the PDS in the last three months, in Tamil Nadu 97 per cent did. More than 90 per cent of the respondents in both states bought kerosene from the PDS during the previous three months. Further while only about 16 per cent of respondents in Uttar Pradesh said that the ration shop was open at least once a week, this was a higher percentage at 55 per cent in Tamil Nadu. Almost 40 per cent of respondents in Tamil Nadu said that they were not satisfied with the functioning of the PDS and about 53 per cent in Uttar Pradesh reported not being satisfied. However, the nature of dissatisfaction with the PDS was different in both the states. In Uttar Pradesh, while the people complained that the ration was very irregular and that they did not get grain most months, in Tamil Nadu the complaints were mainly in relation to other items such as the spice packet, *upma rava*, soap and tea. The people complained that these items were not available every month and in some places, the PDS dealer insisted that they buy a certain quantity of other things along with the rice, even if they did not want it.

National studies find that Tamil Nadu is one of the states with the least amount of leakages in the PDS. A study conducted by the Planning Commission in 2005 found that the leakages of foodgrains in the PDS was the least in Tamil Nadu (15.7 per cent) whereas Uttar Pradesh had a leakage of 61.3 per cent which is amongst the highest of the 16 major states included in the study (GoI 2005b). Later studies based on NSS

Table 8.12 Public Distribution System

% of respondents who:	Uttar Pradesh sample villages	Tamil Nadu sample villages	Total
Have a ration card	88.8	92	90.4
Bought foodgrains in the last three months from PDS (% of those who have a ration card)	10.8	97.3	57.8
Bought kerosene in the last three months from PDS (% of those who have a ration card)	94.1	97.3	95.8
Said ration shop is open at least once a week	16.2	54.8	35.8
Said they were not satisfied with the functioning of the PDS	52.7	38.9	45.8
Total N	125	125	250

Source: Author's field survey

data also show that Tamil Nadu has one of the most effective PDS with low leakages, high coverage and one of the highest per capita consumption of foodgrains from the PDS. These studies also rank Uttar Pradesh among the bottom states in terms of PDS performance (Himanshu and Sen 2011; Khera 2011).

Other services

Along with basic services such as health and education, Tamil Nadu also has good public infrastructure that could also contribute to better health outcomes (such as water and sanitation) and also access to health services (transport, roads). As seen in Table 8.13, there is a very large difference in availability of public infrastructure in Tamil Nadu and Uttar Pradesh. While Tamil Nadu has achieved almost universal access to electricity, in Uttar Pradesh less than 30 per cent of rural households have electricity. Similarly, while piped water is available for more than 85 per cent of rural households in Tamil Nadu, this is the case for about 2 per cent of households in Uttar Pradesh. Road density in Tamil Nadu is twice that in Uttar Pradesh. However, although slightly higher in Tamil Nadu, access to toilets is poor in both states with 19 per cent of rural households in Tamil Nadu and 15 per cent rural households in Uttar Pradesh having access to toilets. Datt and Ravallion's (1997) paper shows that as far as electricity is concerned, Tamil Nadu was much

Table 8.13 Public infrastructure services in Tamil Nadu and Uttar Pradesh

Percentage of households that:	Tamil Nadu	Uttar Pradesh
Have electricity (rural)*	91.2 (89.0)	37.9 (29.3)
Use piped drinking water (rural)*	85.9 (86.4)	7.8 (2.1)
Have access to toilet facility (rural)*	38.8 (19.5)	26.3 (15.4)
Rural road density**	71.95	36.14
(rural road length in km per 100 km² of area)		

Source: *DLHS-3, **pmgsy.nic.in

ahead of Uttar Pradesh even around 1960, with 49.7 per cent of Tamil Nadu's villages and only 2.7 per cent of Uttar Pradesh villages having electricity. The DLHS data show that 91.2 per cent of households in Tamil Nadu and 37.9 per cent in Uttar Pradesh have electricity. In terms of road density, around 1960, Tamil Nadu had 16.6 km of rural roads per 100 km² of area whereas Uttar Pradesh had a higher rural road density of 23.6 km. However, currently Tamil Nadu has a higher road density with 71.9 km of rural roads per 100 km² compared to only 36.1 km in Uttar Pradesh.

How is Tamil Nadu different?

Clearly, there is strong evidence that public services in Tamil Nadu function well, especially when compared to Uttar Pradesh and that has a big role to play in better health outcomes in the state. From the different public services reviewed, some broad features of Tamil Nadu's public services emerge that make them unique and effective.

Features of Tamil Nadu public services

1   **Universal and free services**: All the major social sector programmes in Tamil Nadu follow a universal approach even though there has been a shift in many states towards a more targeted approach where benefits are targeted towards those who are poor. The Public Distribution System is universal, the public health centres are available for all irrespective of their income status and so are government schools including provision of uniforms and books. A universal approach has the advantages of avoiding any targeting errors and also results in all people having a stake in the functioning of public services, making it more effective. It has been seen that the quality of services are better when they are also accessed by the better

off rather than when they are targeted only to the poor. As stated by Amartya Sen (1995),[41] 'Benefits meant exclusively for the poor often end up being poor benefits'.

2 **Democratised administration:** One of the reasons why the service providers in Tamil Nadu, up to the lowest level, are relatively more responsive than in other states and willing to work even in remote areas is the more democratised nature of the administration in the state. First, the history of reservations in the state for people of the backward castes[42] and also the emphasis of early social movements on education has led to a large proportion of those providing the services belonging to the communities that they are supposed to serve. Many of the doctors, teachers and so on are themselves from lower caste, poor and rural backgrounds. For example, while 38 per cent of government school teachers in Uttar Pradesh belong to the OBC groups, in Tamil Nadu this is as high as 76.4 per cent.[43] Put together with the SC teachers, slightly more than 90 per cent of the government school teachers in Tamil Nadu are from SC or OBC castes, with those from upper castes representing only 10 per cent of all government teachers. Tamil Nadu has for long had reservation in higher education for OBCs, and this in no small measure has contributed to a large number of qualified OBCs serving in the government services.

In the case of health as well, Tamil Nadu's policy of reservations in higher education over the last 40 years, has made medical education available to backward castes and classes from small towns and rural areas in the state.[44] Fifteen per cent of the seats for medicine (leading to MBBS degree) and dental courses (leading to BDS degree) are reserved for students from rural schools. These doctors are more willing to work in rural areas. Further, doctors are recruited on a zonal basis where two to three districts in the state form a zone. Doctors are recruited through the Tamil Nadu Public Service Commission to work in the zone in which their residence is located for a minimum period of 10 years. Even after five years of completion of service in the PHC, the medical officer is placed in the same zone when released to work in a hospital (Visaria 2000).[45]

3 **Human resource policies:** Along with the fact that there has been a democratisation within government service providers by greater representation of those belonging to backward castes, it is seen that Tamil Nadu also follows specific human resource policies that

encourage people to join and stay in the government and work in rural areas. As seen above, doctors are provided with many incentives such as promotions, increments and reservations for higher education if they work in rural and remote areas. Fifty per cent of the postgraduate seats in all branches of medicine are reserved for those doctors who have completed a minimum three years of service in the PHCs or district hospitals (Visaria 2000). Similarly, Tamil Nadu is a state where AWWs are paid amongst the highest across the country and receive the recognition of being workers with social security benefits and so on. Further AWWs are also provided with a channel of career progression, as the Village Health Nurse who is equivalent to female health worker is selected from amongst the list of AWWs under ICDS. Such incentives make working for the government in rural areas more attractive.

4   **Convergence**: One of the problems commonly seen in the government is that each department works in a silo, without coordination with other departments. This becomes a barrier to outcomes especially in the case of health and nutrition services, which are closely linked to other services such as water and sanitation. It is seen that there are some mechanisms in place for convergence in Tamil Nadu. For example, in the rural areas, the block health supervisors and health inspectors, along with the rest of the district public health team, provide technical and other support to the rural local bodies (panchayats) in their work. The District Collector is also mandated to hold meetings once in three months of the public health intersectoral coordination committee (Epidemic Coordination Committee), to review the measures taken to anticipate disease threats and respond to them. Other departments are called to these meetings as needed. The Deputy Director of Health Services (DDHS) must inform the Collector about issues such as mosquito nuisance, contamination of water sources and breakages of pipelines, which are recorded in the minutes for follow-up action and the departments held accountable for these actions.[46] Similarly, the monthly meetings of the anganwadi workers are held in the PHC premises. Regular joint review meetings are held at the PHC, Block and District level between health and nutrition functionaries.[47]

5   **Administrative strength**: Overall, the administration in Tamil Nadu is recognised to be efficient with proper systems in place. Although the bureaucracy belongs to the same Indian Administrative Services (IAS) cadre as in other states, the work culture in Tamil Nadu is such that there is an environment that seems to

allow things to progress and work. It is commonly accepted in policy circles,[48] that Tamil Nadu is one of the states where the bureaucracy 'works'. One example I found during the field work, is the meticulous record-maintenance that everyone seemed to be doing. They have records for all kinds of things, which are probably supposed to be available in other states as well but I could not find in Uttar Pradesh. All the panchayats I visited had well maintained registers with minutes of *gram sabha* meetings and gram panchayat meetings. The NREGA records were also well maintained.[49]

6   **Sustained public expenditure:** As seen in the earlier parts of this chapter and Chapter 4, another feature of public services in Tamil Nadu is that they have had the backing of sustained public expenditure. Even if the public expenditure on the services is not always the highest in terms of its value, what seems to be a contributing factor is that there is a continuation of support to government programmes. This is reflected on the ground in the comparatively better conditions of public infrastructure. For example, while there were few unused abandoned buildings in Tamil Nadu, in Uttar Pradesh villages I could see government buildings that were built for a purpose but were in a state of ruin because of lack of upkeep.[50] The reason behind sustained public expenditure is the political backing that public services in the state receive.

These are some of the features of public services in the state that make Tamil Nadu different. At the same time, it needs to also be mentioned that it is not the case that the public services in Tamil Nadu are perfect either in design or implementation. Public services in Tamil Nadu have been emphasised for the relatively better performance they show in comparison with the rest of the country, especially Uttar Pradesh. This is however not to argue that there are no leakages or corruption in Tamil Nadu. Or even that all the decisions of the governments in Tamil Nadu are 'pro-people' in nature. There are many gaps in the services, and there are also leakages and corruption in delivery mechanisms in the state. Tamil Nadu is also known for large-scale corruption by its leaders (however, not in relation to basic welfare services). However, in a relative sense in comparison to other Indian states there is no doubt that the basic public services in Tamil Nadu are amongst the best. The question that arises is why do such public services exist in Tamil Nadu in the first place or to put it differently what makes governments in Tamil Nadu provide (relatively) effective public services.

Notes

1 Calculated on the basis of data from the Statistical Handbooks of both the states on number of public sector employees in the state (central government employees + state government employees + local bodies employees + employees in quasi-state units) and population from Census 2011.

2 Government facilities include PHCs and government hospitals and private facilities include RMPs, private doctors/clinics and private hospitals.

3 The discussion with members of the community and mothers in the sample villages in Tamil Nadu indicated that there is still a lack of confidence among people that the quality of treatment provided in the PHCs is good. The common remarks were that children and adults are given the same medicines (no syrups for children), in one visit the dose given is not enough and requires repeated visits and that injections are not given. On the other hand, the doctor in the PHC in Iruvelpattu expressed the problem that people demand medication and injections even when they don't need these and it becomes difficult to refuse them. Therefore sometimes they run short of certain medicines because they also have to respond to the demands of the patients.

4 Although the responses to such questions cannot be verified and depend on perceptions, the difference still probably indicates something as it was asked by the same person in both places.

5 These PHCs couldn't be missed while travelling on the road in a bus or just walking by. I saw three more PHCs from the bus while travelling in Tamil Nadu.

6 Bachelor of Ayurveda, Medicine and Surgery.

7 Equipments include: Instrument sterilizer, Auto disposal syringes, Hub cutter, B.P. instrument, Stethoscope, Weighing Machine (infant/adult), hemoglobin meter, Foetoscope, SIMS speculum, IUD insertion kit, Vaccine carrier and Drugs includes, Drug kit-A/B, IFA tablets, Vitamin A solution, ORS packet (DLHS-3).

8 When young medicos with only MBBS are selected against these posts they are required to obtain Diploma in public health within four years of their appointment for regularisation as Health officers and get all the benefits like increments. They continue to get the salary during their training in public health (Datta 2009).

9 See Desikachari et al. (2010).

10 Das Gupta et al. 2009 and Budget Documents, GoTN (2011).

11 When the plague outbreak took place in western India in 1994, a team was sent from this unit to help control the outbreak, along with their plague labourers experienced in finding rats and isolating their fleas.

12 There are blog sites of PHCs and PHC doctors, where doctors share information and experiences related to their work. This is just another example of the vibrancy of the sector (Kannan 2011). The Tamil Nadu CM also opposed a recent move by the Government of India to have common entrance tests for postgraduate medical courses stating that this would distort the incentive system that Tamil Nadu government has carefully developed (*Times of India* 2012).

13 A 'bangle ceremony' is traditionally performed in Tamil Nadu (as well as in some other South Indian states) when a woman is in the last stages of

pregnancy to invoke blessings for a safe delivery and a healthy child. In this ceremony, the custom is for women (usually older relatives) to place bangles on the pregnant women's hands along with gifting her other items like '*kum-kum*' and saree.

14 WHO (2009), GoTN (2009), Padmanaban et al. (2009).

15 PHC in Village Akrauli, Moradabad District, Uttar Pradesh.

16 The Tamil Nadu CRM report states that 'there is minimal contractual appointments in the state'. On the other hand, the Uttar Pradesh CRM report observes that 'there was a substantial lack of motivation amongst the contractual staff. It was apparent that this was due to poor service conditions; reluctance on the part of State to depute contractual staff for longer skill-based training, outdated contract renewal policies and a clear demarcation between the regular and contractual employees'.

17 'Casual approach and red-tapism are the reasons behind encephalitis deaths in Uttar Pradesh', concluded the National Commission for Protection of Child Rights (NCPCR) after examining the measures taken by Uttar Pradesh government to save children from Japanese Encephalitis (JE) and Acute Encephalitis Syndrome (AES) in eastern districts of the state (*Times of India* 2012). The National Commission for Protection of Child Rights' letter to the Government of Uttar Pradesh on this issue states, 'The visiting team was highly disappointed over the unpreparedness of the Health Department to stop the deaths because the villages that the Commission visited are sample villages selected by the administration and the situation in those villages was pathetic and an eye-opener' (NCPCR 2011b).

18 Performance Audit Report of the National Rural Health Mission for the year ended 31 March 2011, CAG.

19 Srinivasan (2014), Drèze and Khera (2012), Himanshu and Sen (2011), Drèze (2006), Paul et al. (2006).

20 The public services included in this study are drinking water, health care, road transport, public distribution system, primary schools and childcare system.

21 Shiva Kumar et al. (2011) and Das Gupta et al. (2009, 2010).

22 FOCUS (2006), Drèze (2006), Rajivan (2006), Sinha and Bhatia (2009), Viswanathan (2003).

23 This does not say anything about regularity, quality and so on. It only says that some service (food, counselling, growth monitoring, preschool) was received at least once in the last three months.

24 What is reported here is the situation on the first day I visited the village when I made an unannounced visit. During follow-up visits, I usually also spent some time in the anganwadi, but by then the anganwadi worker was also expecting me.

25 During the field work, many women in the Tamil Nadu villages mentioned that they were counselled by the ANM or the anganwadi worker about breastfeeding and also about what to give children as complementary feeding. Many women narrated that once the child completes six months old they should be given 'mashed rice, dal, beetroots and carrots', in a manner where it seemed that the source of information for all was the same. Although this might not be practiced in many households due to time and resource constraints, I found that most women had the knowledge on what

is to be fed and they even reported that they were informed by the ANM or the anganwadi worker.

26 I heard from the teachers and the parents that many were now sending their children to private schools because they had English medium there.

27 The anganwadi centres in Tamil Nadu are also known as child centres.

28 While travelling during the field survey, seeing girls on bicycles going to school in the morning was a common sight.

29 Panchayat Union in Tamil Nadu is the group of village panchayats that serve as the link between the villages and the district administration (coterminous with the Block level in other states). Tamil Nadu has 385 panchayat unions. Panchayat union council consists of elected ward members from the villages.

30 The IHDS survey (2004–5) finds that 43 per cent of children in the age group of 6–14 in Uttar Pradesh and 23 per cent in Tamil Nadu are in private schools. According to the ASER report (2012); 48.5 per cent of children in the age group of 6–14 in Uttar Pradesh and 29 per cent in Tamil Nadu are in private schools.

31 In Tamil Nadu, when speaking with parents on why many of them sent their children to the private school when there was a government school in the village, the common response was that they wanted their children to go to English medium schools. Sometimes, they even said that they sent their children to private schools as they had kindergarten classes and started at an earlier age, whereas the government school was for those who had completed five years of age. On the other hand, in Uttar Pradesh parents said that they sent their children to private schools because the government schools are not of good quality, teachers are absent or do not teach.

32 Among the schools visited by me, the environment in the schools in Tamil Nadu was very different compared to Uttar Pradesh. In Tamil Nadu the teachers were very welcoming and willing to share information. One teacher in Mamandur, when we asked why they took the trouble to come to the school every day and stay all day, especially because this village was not very well-connected, responded saying, 'this is our duty – we have no choice'.

33 Based on the school visits during the field survey, it was seen that in Tamil Nadu innovations in teaching methods to improve quality of teaching were being tried out. In all the primary schools that I visited, the teachers talked about the 'Activity-Based Learning' system that the Tamil Nadu government had recently introduced. The environment in the schools and among the teachers was also more vibrant in Tamil Nadu. I would also meet teachers (including many female teachers) in the bus each morning while going to the villages for the survey, who would quite often be discussing the happenings in their respective schools, exam schedules and so on. For example, on Republic Day they were all in the bus dressed in their best attire for the celebrations in school, exchanging notes on what the children would be performing. On the other hand, this kind of enthusiasm about their work was largely missing among teachers in Uttar Pradesh. It is also possible that other than in the school, I did not get to meet the teachers and see how they interacted with each other because of the absence of a public transport system in the district.

34 Reading ability is defined as being able to read at least a simple paragraph with three sentences. Two-digit subtraction is considered to be a basic numerical skill that all 8–11 year olds should have, so being able to do this is defined as having arithmetic skill. Writing ability is defined as being able to write a simple sentence with two or fewer mistakes.
35 Again, with an exception of Palanpur in Uttar Pradesh.
36 The India Human Development Survey (IHDS) (2004–5) finds that around 85 per cent of government primary school students have access to midday meals in both states. The Public Affairs Committee (PAC) survey finds that in Tamil Nadu 95 per cent of households are aware of midday meals and of those aware 100 per cent utilise the scheme. In Uttar Pradesh, 67 per cent are aware and among those aware 57 per cent utilise midday meals.
37 Since the change in government in 2011, eggs are being given five days a week in the MDMS in Tamil Nadu. Further, the eggs are also being cooked in a variety of ways and not just boiled.
38 Four respondents reported more than one benefit (one in Uttar Pradesh and three in Tamil Nadu).
39 Ram et al. (2009), Hirway (2003), Saxena Committee Report (2009).
40 The idea of targeting was briefly considered and then given up following protests (Vivek 2010; based on an interview with an IAS officer).
41 See Sen (1995) for a discussion on targeting.
42 Up to 69 per cent of seats in Tamil Nadu are reserved for backward castes and SCs/STs.
43 DISE 2010–11.
44 Ravichandran (2005).
45 From Government of Tamil Nadu (1998).
46 Das Gupta et al. (2010).
47 Tamil Nadu FORCES (2008).
48 Based on discussions with a number of bureaucrats from different cadres.
49 Numerous examples of such record-keeping were experienced during the field work. The time keeper at the bus stop had a recording system in which he had a book where there was one row printed for each bus route, with their correct timings, and he had to keep filling the arrival and departure times of each of these buses. This allows him/her to provide information on timings and expected bus arrivals and departures. There is one such notebook for each day. Then the conductor has a sheet where he has to enter the number of tickets of each category he has sold and this has to be verified and signed by the time keeper. The person doing the antimosquito spray had a register in which he recorded details of the villages where it had been sprayed, the date and so on. In the internet cafe, the Village Health Nurse would be seen completing her data entry every evening. There are many such examples that I came across during my field visits in Tamil Nadu.
50 The seed store in Palanpur for instance – a beautiful big building, in ruins now. This was also the case with internal village roads. As mentioned earlier this is also one of the comments of CRM on the state of PHCs and CHCs in Uttar Pradesh.

Chapter 9

Public action for public services

What are the conditions in Tamil Nadu that make provision of effective public services related to education and health a priority for governments? Conversely, why is it that Uttar Pradesh has not yet seen a similar kind of push in government towards basic public services for the people of the state? Multiple factors related to the sociopolitical and cultural history of the states play a role. I look at the explanations for this in broadly three categories – the nature of the state governments and ruling parties; the history of social movements and backward caste/class mobilisation; and role of women/gender in politics.[1]

Nature of governments: stability, identity and subnationalism

Some basic features of the governments in the states of Uttar Pradesh and Tamil Nadu show that Tamil Nadu has had more stable governments since the 1950s onwards. During this period Uttar Pradesh has had 16 legislative assembly elections, and in Tamil Nadu there have been 14. However, within each term of government, there were frequent changes in leadership in Uttar Pradesh. This is reflected in the fact that Uttar Pradesh has seen the Chief Minister change 31 times during the 60 years period since 1952, whereas in Tamil Nadu the change has occurred only 16 times. Therefore, in Tamil Nadu a CM was changed only twice in the middle of the terms of a government. Once this was because of the death of the serving CM, M.G. Ramachandran and in the second instance, Dr Jayalalitha had to step down for a year because of a court case against her. In Uttar Pradesh on the other hand, on an average, in every term of government there were two different CMs. In fact, of all the CMs only Mayawati has completed a full term (2002–7). The state never had any other CM work continuously for five years (The Hindu 2012).

Not only has there been frequent change in leadership in Uttar Pradesh, they were also different leaders each time. During this entire period, Tamil Nadu has seen nine persons who have held CM posts, but in Uttar Pradesh there have been 20 persons who have held the post of CM. Therefore, there was greater stability in the leadership in the state of Tamil Nadu. Stability in state governments and the leadership in Tamil Nadu contributed to ensuring continuity in policy priorities and also enough time for a CM to implement policies and see the impact. On the other hand, the frequent changes in leadership in Uttar Pradesh did not allow for this kind of stability and continuity.

One of the factors, which contributed to the instability in Uttar Pradesh, also explains to an extent the lack of priority on basic social services in the state. This is the fact that Uttar Pradesh's leaders were more preoccupied with national politics and also largely controlled by national leadership. Uttar Pradesh has contributed to 8 out of the 13 Prime Ministers India has had, and still continues to be one of the most backward states in the country. For most of the time since Independence the party in power in Uttar Pradesh was a national party (Indian National Congress for 33 years and BJP for 6 years). Chief Ministers were chosen by the national leadership with national priorities in mind. The state leaders also saw state politics as a stepping stone to positions in the central government. This is also reflected in the fact that a number of CMs of Uttar Pradesh have also been Cabinet Ministers (11 out of 20) at the Centre, whereas this is not the case with Tamil Nadu. It is in fact also stated that the National Congress deliberately appointed 'weak' leaders in the state, so that they do not become a threat to the national leadership based on the sheer size of Uttar Pradesh (Ramesh 1999; Hasan 2001; Singh 2012).

Table 9.1 Stability in government[2]

Since 1952	Uttar Pradesh	Tamil Nadu
No. of persons who held Chief Minister position in the state	20	9
No. of times Chief Minister's terms have changed	31	16
No. of times President's Rule has been imposed in state	9	4
No. of years under national party rule (Congress or BJP)	39	17
No. of assembly elections	16	14

Source: Compiled from Election Commission of India website

The dominance of national parties resulted in the state government following national priorities rather than any stated objectives for the betterment of the people of Uttar Pradesh (Zenini-Bortel 1998; Kudaisiya 2007). Elections were largely fought on national issues and data from election surveys shows the lack of interest amongst the people of Uttar Pradesh in state politics compared to those in other states, including Tamil Nadu.[3] While the large size of Uttar Pradesh and its population has made it a very influential state in national politics (the 'heartland'; the largest number of MPs in the Parliament are from Uttar Pradesh), Singh (2012) argues that this preoccupation with national politics is one of the factors that led to the relative neglect of the welfare of the people in the state. Uttar Pradesh has therefore experienced a neglect of social services reflected in low investments and poor monitoring (as seen in the earlier chapters) by the state government. Further, many have noted the lack of 'public action' in Uttar Pradesh in response to the poor state of affairs to be a significant factor in explaining the poor performance in the state (Drèze and Gazdar 1997). The politics in the state has shaped people's expectations in a manner where they are more concerned with national issues and issues of identity than with obligations of the government towards social and human development.[4]

However, it must be noted that politics in Uttar Pradesh has also seen a change in the last two decades with the emergence of regional parties such as the Samajwadi Party (SP) and the Bahujan Samajwadi Party (BSP). These parties represent backward castes and Muslims and *dalits*, respectively. On the other hand, with the onset of coalition governments at the Centre the regional parties of Tamil Nadu have been playing a critical role in the national government. Members of these regional parties have been holding key Cabinet portfolios in the national government. How these recent changes affect state politics needs to be observed for a few more years.

Singh (2012) theorises that it is the subnational identity in a state that results in stronger state governments and better social development outcomes. Using detailed historical case studies of the states of Tamil Nadu and Kerala on one hand and Uttar Pradesh and Rajasthan on the other, Singh (2012) shows how a cohesive subnational identity contributes to progressive social policy;[5] and the spread of subnationalism through social and political movements spur greater people's engagement in society, which combined together result in better social development in the state. Tamil Nadu governments were elected on the basis of a 'Tamil' identity and to do good for the Tamilians. This contributed to the nature of the Tamil Nadu government with its focus on welfare services.

Many have characterised the Tamil Nadu governments as being 'populist'. Subramanian (1999) makes a distinction in the types of populism and talks about affirmative populism of the DMK and paternalistic populism of the AIADMK where one is more empowering than the other. However, in both cases the state sees a major role for itself in providing services and welfare to people. Public services, especially those related to food and nutrition therefore became a part of the agenda of the political parties to the extent that people now expect them do more and better on this front. Tamil Nadu was one of the first states where the price at which PDS rice would be sold became an election issue. Even now, issues such as PDS prices and number of eggs to be served in the school midday meals make it to the election manifestos of the political parties, widely publicised and seen to be affecting voting patterns.

Rajivan (2008)[6] summarises that the reason for better public services in Tamil Nadu is a combination of pressure from above (e.g. top-down budgetary allocations for public services, political will) and pressure from below (bottom-up demand for services, which is influenced by women's status, voice and political participation). She argues that these two are synergistic – that is, each feeds upon and strengthens the other, resulting in sustainable change. The bottom-up is important as it helps retain political will overtime making it worthwhile in an electoral democracy to respond to people's expectations.[7] Top-down political will, on the other hand, can trigger off expectations from below; and once bottom-up pressure is generated it helps in retaining political will even through changes in the ruling political party or coalitions.

Backward caste/class mobilisation

Tamil Nadu has a history of progressive social reform movements. The Self-Respect Movement (SRM) which began in the 1920s under the leadership of *Periyar* (E. V. Ramaswamy Naicker) is generally considered to have had a significant impact on Tamil Nadu society and politics in the twentieth century.[8] This movement mobilised backward castes to create an equal society – where people of all castes are equal, there is economic equality and equality between men and women. It was a movement against the dominance by Brahmins in economic and social fields. The movement sought to instil a sense of pride amongst people of their Dravidian and Tamilian identities. The movement also campaigned against superstitions and sought to spread rational thinking.

At the beginning of the twentieth century Brahmins constituted only 3 per cent of population of Madras Presidency, but exercised disproportionate control over the political, economic and social life of the province. For example, in 1912, Brahmins held 55 per cent of the Deputy Collectors' posts, 83.3 per cent of subjudges and 72.6 per cent of District munsifs (Arooran 1980). The non-Brahmin elites began to organise themselves around a 'Tamil' identity against the 'foreign' Brahmins. Although the leadership of these movements were the elites amongst the backward castes, the mobilisation was around bringing together everyone who was not Brahmin and therefore their politics spoke of the welfare of the vast majority of the people of the region/ state. With the emphasis on the betterment of 'Tamil' people, more than 90 per cent of the state's population were included in the movement (Arooran 1980).

This movement first took shape in the form of the Justice Party launched in 1916 with a 'non-Brahmin' manifesto. The movement made specific gains such as introducing reservation for backward castes in the legislative assembly in 1923. The SRM became a part of the Justice Party that later transformed itself into the Dravidar Kazhagam (DK). Later, Annadurai split the DK and formed the Dravidar Munnetra Kazhagam (DMK). While this split occurred because of the differences of opinion on the relationship the state should have with the Indian union and also personal differences with *Periyar*, the DMK otherwise chose to follow the ideals of the SRM.

Although the Congress won the first election post-Independence, when there was a wave across the country in its support following the role it played in the national movement, in Tamil Nadu (then 'Madras' state) Congress failed to get an absolute majority. However, it managed to form the government with the support of smaller parties. Even the Congress government in the state, which was in power until 1967, had to focus on the development of the state and take on issues related to the welfare of backward castes (BCs) due to the strong impact of the SRM on the people of the state.

The first CM, C. Rajagopalachari (a 'brahmin') was forced to resign from Government because of his proposal to introduce the New Scheme of Elementary Education (critics called it the 'Hereditary Education Scheme'; *Kula Kalvi Thittam*) where students were to spend time learning the occupations of their parents. This was seen as a casteist scheme aimed at perpetrating caste hierarchies. While the opposition to the scheme was led by the DMK, there was also a lot of opposition from within the Congress Party itself and Rajaji was made to resign.

K. Kamaraj who followed him as the Congress CM in the state, in 1954, dropped this scheme. He also formulated policies in the state, which were focussed on welfare of backward castes and classes, which were in tune with the mood in the state. As seen above, Kamraj during his tenure as CM focussed immensely on education. Kamraj was also greatly respected by *Periyar*. Kamraj moved on to serve the Congress party in the Centre after nine years of being CM of Tamil Nadu (in 1963). Bakthavatsalam, the CM from Congress who followed Kamraj, was not as charismatic and was also faced with the anti-Hindi agitations led by the DMK by the end of his tenure.

With the widespread support gained during the anti-Hindi struggle, the DMK came into power in 1967, under the leadership of C. Anna-durai (succeeded by Dr M. Karunanidhi from 1969 onwards). In the 1970s, there was a split in the DMK and the ADMK (later called the AIADMK) was formed. This was led by M. G. Ramachandran (MGR), another charismatic leader from the tradition of Dravidian politics. Since the late 1960s onwards, all state governments in Tamil Nadu have been formed by one of the Dravidian parties. Since the political parties that came to power in Tamil Nadu belonged to this lineage, although they took on a different form once they became a political party and ran governments, they had similar political positions. Because of their lineage, these Dravidian parties contributed to the spread of education among the backward castes; provision of health, education, nutrition and housing services to the poor and so on.

This history of social movements and rise of regional political parties representing the backward castes/classes in the state contributed to the rise of the backward classes and their role in administration and service provision and also the need for the government to be seen as working for the 'people'. These movements addressed themselves to a majority of the population and worked for the welfare of the population as a whole. Therefore, the backward caste mobilisation in Tamil Nadu influenced the politics of the state in two ways – one, by making 'welfare' an agenda for state intervention and two, by increasing representation of people from the backward castes in the state administration, thereby democra-tising the administration in the state.

Similar social and economic change among the lower castes was not witnessed in Uttar Pradesh in the colonial period or postcolonial period (Pai et al. 2005). Until recently, there was no major movement in the state that mobilised people from the backward castes and/or *dalits*. Fol-lowing the credibility gained during the freedom struggle, the Congress party was seen to represent the interests of the marginalised such as Mus-lims, *dalits* and backward castes. However, the Congress leadership was predominantly upper caste, with little space being given to *dalits*. For example, in 1968, there was not even one representative from the lower castes and only one SC member among the presidents of its branches at district or town level (Jafferlot 2003).

While Congress continued to dominate Uttar Pradesh politics until the 1980s (with small periods of dissent in the 1970s with Chaudhury Charan Singh's farmers' mobilisation); the backward and lower castes' parties challenged this hegemony by the late 1980s. This was also a period of heightened communal tensions in the state, resulting in a deep polarisation and rise of the BJP.[9] The Congress in the state declined not only because of the upsurge of new forces but also its own failures in the form of neglect of the backward castes and lack of performance in relation to the social development and welfare of the state (Kohli 1987; Drèze and Gazdar 1997; Singh 2010).

The rise of the Bahujan Samaj Party (representing the *dalits*) and the Samajwadi party (representing the backward castes) effectively countered the dominance of the Congress in the state. However, these parties, and the massive mobilisation of backward castes and *dalits* by them, did not result in making universal welfare services a priority for the governments they formed as it did in Tamil Nadu. One of the reasons for this is that these movements were very sectarian in nature representing narrow sections of society (*dalits* are 20 per cent of the population and upper castes 15 per cent of the population in Uttar Pradesh, whereas in Tamil Nadu more than 90 per cent of the population that was non-Brahmin was included in the agenda of the SRM). Although Kanshi Ram, the leader who started the BSP, sought to mobilise 85 per cent of the population (which included the Muslims, backward castes and *dalits*) against the 15 per cent upper castes, this movement soon reduced into one being just for the *dalits*. An attempt at a coalition between the SP and BSP failed, with the two competing with each other for political supremacy (Mishra 1995).

While the BSP's main agenda was to form a government in the state, it did not spell out any development agenda even for the *dalits* (Pai 2004). In fact, even now the BSP does not have an election manifesto. One of the main programmes taken up by the BSP during both its terms in the state government has been the setting up of statues of dalit leaders and parks. While such symbolism could be important,[10] what has been missing in the state's politics is a strong emphasis on the welfare of the people of the state.

In her earlier tenure as Chief Minister, one of Mayawati's focus programmes was the Ambedkar Village Programme (AVP), where funds were targeted at villages that had a majority dalit population for an improvement in their social and physical infrastructure. However, many argued that such targeted interventions were not useful in a state where the entire state had such low levels of economic and social development.[11] Singh (2010) reports that,

> there is a feeling among the middle level BSP leaders that lack of interest in the party in rural developmental programmes has shifted the focus of government from the very important social sectors like health and education. Earlier party functionaries used to receive information about the government's prominent social welfare programmes but now they are not receiving any message from the high command regarding health and education or other welfare programmes.

The Samajwadi party on the other hand, is also not known for any development initiatives. The SP governments of the past were notorious for tacitly supporting those indulging in criminal activities such as kidnapping and black marketing. The SP has come back to power in 2012; this time on a plank of improving the social and economic development in the state and it is yet to be seen if this will bear any fruit.

Ramesh (1999) summarises the failure of the backward caste movements in Uttar Pradesh to transform into a positive development agenda for the state in the following manner:

> the elite in Uttar Pradesh, unlike in Tamil Nadu and Maharashtra, have themselves not been great champions of education and social reforms. . . . Uttar Pradesh has almost 18 per cent of India's poor but gets just around 8 per cent of cereal allocations from the PDS. Never has this been made an issue by Uttar Pradesh politicians. Of course, Uttar Pradesh does not lift all that is allocated to it – less than 50 per cent of the wheat allocated to Uttar Pradesh under the PDS actually gets taken by Uttar Pradesh. Kerala MPs, for example, will do anything to keep their share in the PDS going. . . . Uttar Pradesh has been most unconcerned about the low level of PDS coverage. There was a time when Uttar Pradesh's development administration was the envy of the rest of the country
>
> (Ramesh 1999).

Therefore, while empowerment in Tamil Nadu for the backward castes translated itself into the seeking of education and social reforms (along with political power, but at a later stage); in Uttar Pradesh the focus has solely been on political power. The leadership in Uttar Pradesh has not yet made social reforms in the form of welfare of the people they represent through better education and health opportunities their main agenda. Therefore, although there is an effective backward caste and dalit mobilisation and significant symbolic victories have been gained it is yet to be seen how much this translates into social development of the people.

Role of women/gender

The role of women's status in public and private spaces has been discussed extensively in previous chapters. Better status of women, especially in the public sphere in Tamil Nadu has influenced the politics in the state to focus towards the social and human development of the people. Along with stable governments focussed on the development of the state, a strong mobilisation of the backward castes and classes and their representation in government, the presence of women and their concerns in government (the percentage of women amongst public sector employees in Tamil Nadu is 30 per cent, whereas it is around 11 per cent in Uttar Pradesh) and social movements is a significant factor that makes the government work in Tamil Nadu.

The way the Dravidian movement took shape, it gave a lot of importance to education and even women's empowerment. For example, the movement propagated the use of contraception and reproductive choice among women to rid women of the burden of frequent child-bearing (Hodges 2005). Choice-based and intercaste marriages were encouraged. The movement organised women's conferences, self-respect marriages and involved women in mass agitations. The conferences of the SRM demanded for equal property rights for men and women and for women to be recruited in the army and police. These Conferences were also opportunities for women activists to speak and for public discussion on issues related to women's emancipation (Bharadwaj 1991; Pandian et al. 1991; Thiruchandran 1997).

In the later periods as well, women were addressed as a constituency. M G Ramachandran one of the most popular Chief Ministers of the state, was a film star and through his movies and speeches sought to appeal to women as a separate vote bank. The noon meal scheme was introduced by MGR in 1982 across the state and this was one of the schemes through which he was trying to reach out to women voters. The following excerpt from MGR's speech on the eve of start of this scheme is an indication of how he tried to address women specifically.

> This scheme is an outcome of my experience of extreme starvation at an age when I only knew to cry when I was hungry. But for the munificence of a woman next door who extended a bowl of rice gruel to us and saved us from the cruel hand of death, we would have departed this world long ago. *Such merciful women folk, having great faith in me, elected me as Chief Minister of Tamil Nadu.* To wipe the tears of these women I have taken up this project. . . . to picture lakhs and lakhs of poor children who gather to partake of nutritious meals in the thousands of hamlets and villages all over Tamil Nadu, and blessing us in their childish prattle, will be a glorious event' [emphasis added]
>
> (as quoted in Harriss-White 1991)

The paternalistic politics of MGR and his party the ADMK resonated with women and *dalits*, with women continuing to vote for his party in large numbers even after his death. Even in the 1991 elections where ADMK was led by Jayalalitha, post the death of MGR, one of the main issues of campaign against the DMK government was that women were unsafe under the DMK rule. The safety of women was linked to the DMK's scheme of setting up government licensed cheap liquor shops (Suresh 1992).

In this manner, in each round of elections the political parties try to raise issues to address women voters. However, the manner in which women's issues were addressed by MGR and his party was qualitatively different and retrogressive from the SRM's focus on women, which was more radical in its vision for gender equality. MGR on the other hand, had a more 'protective' attitude. Women were portrayed as 'mothers' or 'sisters' who symbolised the Tamil pride. This fell into the typical patriarchal imagery of women whose chastity had to be protected (Pandian 1989; Rajadurai and Geetha 1991; Hancock 2008). While this is an interesting and pertinent debate, what is relevant here is that in spite of the changes in the Dravidian movement and the splits in the political parties, women and their issues continued to be one of the central themes for politics and governance.

My field work also showed that in Tamil Nadu many more women (than in Uttar Pradesh) access public institutions and public services. Most of the people in the queues outside the ration shops under the Public Distribution System were women. It was women who were meeting school teachers regarding concerns related to their children and women who were accompanying the elderly and children to health facilities. Women were using public transport to go for work, accessing banks as members of self-help groups or recipients of government benefits (maternity entitlements, unemployment allowance) and visiting gram panchayat and other government offices for accessing various public services. Therefore, although not many women are still part of political leadership or public life in Tamil Nadu, compared to Uttar Pradesh they are much more present in public spaces, especially in terms of accessing and providing public services. This has an impact on how public services are designed and implemented.

On the other hand in Uttar Pradesh, women's empowerment has not yet been spoken about in any serious or effective manner by any of the mainstream political parties or social movements in the state. Rather the history of the state has been one where women have only become even more marginalised.

While studies looking at the influence of women on politics have mostly focussed on direct participation of women in politics as activists or leaders, there is a need for further research on how women can shape political agenda through just being independent participants in social life.

Notes

1 For a detailed study on factors contributing to effective public services in Tamil Nadu, see Vivek (2010); Singh (2012).
2 Data in this section have been compiled from websites of the Election Commission of India and state governments of Uttar Pradesh and Tamil Nadu.
3 Figures from National Election Survey (NES) conducted by CSDS presented in Singh (2012) show percentage of respondents with 'Somewhat' or 'Great deal of Interest' in Election Campaign was 57.7 per cent in Tamil Nadu and 34.2 per cent in Uttar Pradesh. Similarly respondents with 'Somewhat' or 'Great deal of Interest' in Politics & Public Affairs is 53 per cent in Tamil Nadu and 37 per cent in Uttar Pradesh. In the same survey, less than 14 per cent of the residents of Uttar Pradesh could correctly name their state Chief Minister and 51 per cent in Tamil Nadu (Singh 2012).
4 There are reports especially during and after the recent Assembly elections in the state that this is changing with people being more concerned with the development record of the governments while deciding to vote.
5 The national policy agenda set by the Congress in New Delhi emphasised industrialisation rather than social development. The policies of most state Congress governments, such as Uttar Pradesh, reflected these central priorities. While the Congress regime in Tamil Nadu did not completely neglect

industrialisation, its adoption of a significant social programme set it apart from Congress governments in New Delhi, and the rest of India. Only a few weeks into the first session of the democratically elected legislature in independent India, education and health were the subjects of very lengthy and lively debates, involving many participants and covering issues such as the challenges of providing basic education, school infrastructure, teachers' salaries and the education of marginalised groups such as the former 'untouchables', Muslims and girls as well as primary health infrastructure; the number of doctors, nurses; their salaries; the means of tackling diseases such as TB and cancer; and the establishment of medical colleges to produce trained personnel (Tamil Nadu State Assembly 1952) (Singh 2012).

6 This was discussed by her in personal communication. Also see box by Rajivan in Focus (2006).

7 Although there was no recent instance of any 'public action' in the villages that I visited in Tamil Nadu, in conversations with people they repeatedly mentioned how they would take it up with higher authorities if they did not get their services. For example, the doctors and pharmacists in the four PHCs that I visited mentioned that if medicines were not available, then people would question them and even go to higher authorities. The patients in the PHC and even villagers I spoke to mentioned that they would complain to higher officials if the ANM was irregular or treatment was not available in the PHC. People were aware of the relevant phone numbers to call and make complaints. Vivek (2010) presents an interesting account of collective action, especially by the dalits that led to them getting each of the public services in the village for one village in Tamil Nadu.

8 More information on the Self-Respect Movement's influence, backward caste mobilisation and also on the developments in Tamil Nadu has been described in Bharadwaj (1991), Goyal (2006), Harriss (2001), Subramanian (1999), Lakshman (2011), Vivek (2010), Singh (2012) and the references cited there.

9 The Mandal Commission report recommending reservations for backward castes also contributed to caste-based polarisation.

10 While they began with statues of Ambedkar, during the second term huge parks were built with statues of other dalit leaders including Kanshiram and Mayawati who are leaders of BSP. In Tamil Nadu also there was such symbolic politics – the propagation of the 'Tamil' language, anti-Hindi stance, people started to give their children very classic Tamilian names, the use of the image of Tamilttay (Mother Tamil) and so on; but along with the rhetoric of welfare of Tamil people through education, health and so on.

11 In contrast, in Tamil Nadu the focus was on upliftment of all Tamil people.

Chapter 10

Summing up and way forward

This study set out to explain the variations in human development across Indian states, with special focus on Tamil Nadu and Uttar Pradesh. There are multiple factors that affect human development outcomes and it is not necessary that change occurs in the same manner across all states. Nevertheless, this study brings out and reconfirms certain important features. First, it is found that economic growth only has a limited role to play in ensuring improved health and human development outcomes. In fact, improved human development can also contribute to economic growth, while economic growth can provide opportunities for greater investments in human development. Tamil Nadu started off as a state that was slightly above the all India average in terms of human development and below the all India average in terms of economic conditions. It has now progressed to be one of the best states with regard to health outcomes and among the better-off in terms of economic conditions. Uttar Pradesh, on the other hand, has remained a poor state both in terms of economic conditions as well as human development outcomes.

Second, the role of women's status is extremely important. Women matter, not just through their role within the household but also as a collective voice in society. It therefore becomes important to understand why women's status is so different across regions. The role of kinship structures, sustained public investments in education and health, whether women participate in the labour force or not, how social movements have shaped around women's issues are all relevant explanations.

There are multiple pathways through which women's status affects health and human development outcomes. Female education is a crucial factor through which women's status and human development can be improved. Educated and economically independent women have a greater say in household decision making and better bargaining power within the household. It is seen that this has a positive influence on decisions related to health and education in the family. However, in quantitative analysis even when direct autonomy related indicators are not significantly associated with health outcomes, it is seen that women's education continues to be important. Female education it appears has its own independent effect. The ways in which education contributes to better outcomes can be studied further.

Further, it could be argued that better women's status also has a 'social' role. Therefore, areas where more women are engaged in employment outside the household are places where health outcomes are relatively better even though at the household level mother's employment could have a negative association with child health outcomes. In spite of increasing education among women and other changes in the economy such as out migration by men, shift of men into nonagricultural activities, there seems to be rigidity in women's employment in some areas such as Uttar Pradesh, especially western Uttar Pradesh where I conducted my field work. Considering the enormous potential for social change that women's employment has the factors that contribute to women's participation in the workforce also need to be studied further.

Women's status, especially in the public sphere, also influences the way public services function and what the demands of public action are. In Tamil Nadu, women are seen as a 'vote bank' and politicians try to appeal for their votes. It is because women are more visible in public spaces and participate in public activities that they can be seen as a separate constituency. In Uttar Pradesh, women are largely 'hidden' from public agenda. This link between women's status and how that affects political priorities is made here tentatively but needs further investigation. As mentioned earlier, it is neither being claimed that there is no gender inequality in Tamil Nadu nor that there is no progress in Uttar Pradesh, just that there is a contrast between the two states and this is being highlighted.

Third, this comparison of Tamil Nadu and Uttar Pradesh shows that public services can be effective and that they can make a difference. It is possible for governments to provide universal and free basic services in a manner where they have an impact on human development outcomes. The quality of public services is also related to the level of accountability to people. It was found that Tamil Nadu had in-built transparency and accountability mechanisms as part of many of its public programmes. For example, panchayat secretaries and mates were required to send an SMS to the block official with the number of workers attending the NREGA worksite on any given day. The block official would then do a random check of a few worksites each day and do a headcount to verify if the number of workers recorded was indeed the same as the number of workers working. Similarly, PHCs displayed prominently numbers of infant and child deaths, institutional deliveries and immunisation details for the area. Further, it was found that people were aware of their entitlements and also had an idea of who to complain to and what they should do in case of denial. Phone numbers of officials were easily available at the school, PDS shop, health centre and so on. It is probably having these systems in place that made the service providers in Tamil Nadu also more professional in their approach than their counterparts in Uttar Pradesh.

The question that then arises is why is it that public services became a priority in Tamil Nadu in the first place. The history of backward class mobilisation in the state, emergence of regional parties, possibility of unifying the people of the state along cultural and language lines, availability of progressive political alternatives right from the beginning of Independence are all factors in Tamil Nadu that have contributed to shaping the politics of the state. Along with this, greater democratisation of society and governance by improved status of backward castes and classes as well as of women contributed to the politics of the state. The combination of state action (provision of services) and public action (including demanding for services, accountability) is what probably makes a difference. Therefore, even while studying provision of public services, it is important to understand the social context that allows these services to be effective.

This study focussed primarily on why Tamil Nadu is better than most other states in relation to its health outcomes and therefore the positive aspects in the state have been highlighted. Early surge in literacy led by the state governments' priority to expansion of schooling, followed by a comprehensive set of social policies related to food, social security and health, sustained public expenditures and the universal approach to welfare programmes in Tamil Nadu have substantially contributed to the state's progress in improving the health status of its people. Some related issues such as the nature of economic growth in the two states, role of high degree of urbanisation in Tamil Nadu, regional and caste differences, overall revenue and expenditure of the states have not been included but need to be studied.

Further, it also remains a puzzle that Tamil Nadu has been able to achieve all of this while at the same time its politicians are notorious for being involved in large-scale scams (the 2G case, for example). Corruption at the state and central level is one of the big issues during every election, with the major political parties and their leaders in the state having been accused of being involved in corrupt practices. There are also reports from Tamil Nadu about people being evicted from slums forcefully, people in rural areas being displaced and continuing atrocities against *dalits* and so on. The field experience also showed that the segregation in living between *dalits* and the others continues in Tamil Nadu, with the SC colonies having relatively poorer infrastructure and a higher proportion of landless wage workers. What is interesting is that despite all this public services function reasonably well, and there are major improvements in human development outcomes across the board.

In Uttar Pradesh too, although there has been very little progress there are some signs of change in the recent past. There has been a significant rise in literacy rates, even among girls and women. The last three decades have seen major mobilisation of backward castes and *dalits* with the two major political parties in the state claiming to represent these groups. The previous government in the state was led by the BSP a party that primarily represents *dalits*, with a clear majority. The current government in the state is of the SP, which represents the OBCs. The SP also won (in 2012) with a clear majority with media reports claiming that the reason they won is that they took up 'development' issues rather than only narrow caste-based ones. While the BSP did take up some development work, it was focussed largely only on transferring direct benefits to *dalits* and was quite limited (like the Ambedkar Gram Yojana). The last one year of the SP government does not show any major change in the nature of politics in the state in spite of the changed rhetoric seen during elections. How these developments will shape the future agenda of the state is hence yet to be seen.

As of now, what has been witnessed in Uttar Pradesh in the last two or three decades is very different from the nature of Tamil Nadu's backward class mobilisation in the early 1920s or the immediate post-Independence era. The SRM under the leadership of E. V. Ramaswamy ('*Periyar*') mobilised the Tamil people on the basis of their Dravidian and Tamil identity against Brahmin domination. Brahmins in the state formed a mere 3 per cent of the state's population but had cornered a majority share of political and administrative space. The regional parties, DMK and AIADMK that have been forming governments in the state from the 1960s onwards are both offsprings of this movement. Moreover, the SRM contributed to the deepening of Tamil solidarity and offered a plank for bringing together the vast majority of Tamilians. Although within the non-Brahmins as well there are caste-based hierarchies with the *dalits* facing discrimination by the others there was at least a rhetoric of universal progress for all Tamilians in Tamil Nadu.

This history contributed to the principle of universalism gaining importance in the state.

In Tamil Nadu, this mobilisation was able to link itself to public services such as education and health and second, garner near universal support by creating universal agendas. In Uttar Pradesh on the other hand, a larger proportion of the state's population belong to the upper castes (than in Tamil Nadu), making it difficult to forge broad-based alliances. The nature of mobilisation of backward castes and *dalits* by political parties has also further fragmented people's interests. In terms of women's mobilisation as well, the experience of the two states has been very different. In Tamil Nadu, women's issues were central in the early social movements in the region contributing to there being a focus on human development issues. Uttar Pradesh is yet to see any major mainstream movement taking up women's issues as effectively.

This history of social movements in Tamil Nadu also led to greater democratisation of public services in the state where a large number of those providing the services belong to rural areas and are themselves from disadvantaged classes and castes. This has also helped in making public services effective. As a result of the backward caste and anti-Brahmin mobilisation, Tamil Nadu is one of the states that had the highest level of reservations in higher education even before the OBC reservations were introduced nationwide. Human resource policies in the health sector are also such that they encouraged students from rural and backward communities to join the public health cadres. For example, while 38 per cent of government school teachers in Uttar Pradesh belong to the OBC groups, in Tamil Nadu this is as high as 76 per cent. The presence of a large number of service providers who belong to similar backgrounds as the people they serve also adds to the quality of services. Fifteen per cent of the seats for medicine (leading to MBBS degree) and dental courses (leading to BDS degree) are reserved for students from rural schools. Similarly, women are also better represented among public servants, among other things as doctors and teachers, in Tamil Nadu than in Uttar Pradesh making health and education services more accessible for girls and women. While 62 per cent of PHCs in Tamil Nadu have a lady medical officer, this was the case in only 2 per cent of PHCs in Uttar Pradesh.

Education, especially female education, is well recognised in the literature as one of the prime movers behind human development. In this study, I include female education as one of the main aspects of women's status and it is indeed found that this is one of the most important factors explaining interstate differences in health outcomes. Similarly, while looking at public services, schooling and education services are also included. Beyond this, special attention to education has not been given in this study because the role of education in human development is relatively well understood. This does not in any way deny the role that education plays in the Tamil Nadu-Uttar Pradesh contrast.

Another related factor, which is important but has not been studied in detail, is the role of social inequities, other than those based on gender. Even though there are serious intercaste differences in Tamil Nadu, compared to Uttar Pradesh, those belonging to the backward castes and classes have been able to assert their rights to a considerable extent through long struggle and participation in public action. While *dalits* continue to be discriminated against in Tamil Nadu and segregated living is widely practised in rural areas, in a relative sense they are better off in terms of access to public services and a representation in public action. What is witnessed is that there is the principle of universalism in public discourse, some consensus against discrimination in public life and some empowerment of *dalits*/OBCs. Tamil Nadu, Kerala and Himachal Pradesh have dealt with social divisions based on caste and gender through different means, including mass education and this contributes to the overall higher levels of human development in these states. In the northern states on the other hand, representatives of these oppressed groups continue to be almost absent in public life. This aspect of greater democratisation of society needs in-depth analysis. This issue has not been dealt with in this book in detail, but mentioned only so far as it is linked with women's status and nature of public action.

What this analysis of human development in Tamil Nadu and Uttar Pradesh also brings out is that no single factor can explain the difference in the development experiences of these two states. While some very useful insights have been gained especially in relation to women's status, public services and public action, it cannot be claimed that this is the 'full picture'. In the sections above, I have tried to list out some of the grey areas in relation to what has been studied in detail in the previous chapters. Further, each of the factors studied interact with each other mutually reinforcing their combined strength. Therefore, in Tamil Nadu massive public investment in education contributes to improvement in women's status, which in turn has an effect on better delivery of public services. At the same time, the history of social movements and the backward class mobilisation also contribute to challenging age-old social hierarchies, which in turn have a role in improving the reach of public services. Although in Tamil Nadu, many problems related to caste oppression and gender inequality remain, relatively it is a story of success because of this combination of factors.

On the other hand, what we see in Uttar Pradesh is a failure in each of these aspects, which result in a vicious cycle of low female educa- tion, poor public services and deep-rooted caste inequities. As a way out of this vicious cycle, this study calls for active involvement of the state in provision of public services with higher investments and greater accountability with a special emphasis on female education. Public action can significantly contribute to effective public services being put in place. In the present context, where the role of public services is being questioned I hope that this study also contributes to a better understanding on how and when they can be useful.

Appendix A

Details of state-level analysis

Variables used

Table A1 State-level variables used in the analysis

Variable	Name and definition	Source
ln_U5MR	Under-five mortality rate: the probability of dying (per 1,000) before completing the fifth birthday	SRS for 2009
ln_IMR	Infant mortality rate: the probability of dying (per 1,000) before completing the first birthday.	SRS for 2009
ln_femlit	Female literacy rate: % of females above six years of age who are literate	Census (2011)
ln_nfhslit	Female literacy rate: % of women in reproductive age who are literate	NFHS-3 (2005–6)
ln_gendergap	Gender gap in literacy rate: male literacy rate – female literacy rate	Census (2011)
ln_hcr_rural	Head count ratio: % of population below the poverty line in rural areas	NSS, 61st round (2009–10)
ln_MPCE	Average monthly per capita consumption expenditure	NSS, 61st round (2009–10)
ln_pucca_house	Percentage of households residing in *pakka* house	NFHS-3 (2005–6)
ln_nfhs_employed	Female employment: % of women who reported that they had done any work in the 12 months prior to the survey	NFHS-3 (2005–6)

Variable	Name and definition	Source
ln_wprf	Workforce participation rate of females in rural areas: % of workers in total female population in rural areas	NSS, 61st round (2009–10)
ln_mobility	% of women allowed to go to three specified places alone (market, health facility, and to places outside the village/ community)	NFHS-3 (2005–6)
ln_decisionmaking	% of women who participate in decisions related to own health care, making major household purchases, making purchases for daily household needs and visits to her family or relatives.	NFHS-3 (2005–6)
ln_PHC	PHC coverage: Average population covered by a primary health centre in the state	Rural Health Bulletin (2009)

Note: All the variables are entered as log in the regressions.

Results

Table A2 Factors affecting child mortality rates at the state level (OLS regression)

Variables	(1)	(2)	(3)	(4)	(5)	(6)
	ln_U5MR	ln_U5MR	ln_U5MR	ln_U5MR	ln_U5MR	ln_U5MR
ln_femlit		−2.603*** (0.596)	−2.655*** (0.673)	−2.697*** (0.625)		
ln_nfhslit						−1.306*** (0.429)
ln_gendergap	0.914*** (0.148)				0.871*** (0.202)	
ln_hcr_rural	0.388** (0.131)					0.344 (0.220)
ln_MPCE		−0.650* (0.352)	−0.634 (0.374)	−0.774* (0.404)	−0.164 (0.345)	
ln_wprf					−0.287 (0.172)	
ln_nfhs_ employed	−0.630*** (0.177)	−0.523* (0.244)	−0.509* (0.263)	−0.568** (0.257)		−0.489* (0.265)

(Continued)

Table A2 (Continued)

Variables	(1)	(2)	(3)	(4)	(5)	(6)
	ln_U5MR	ln_U5MR	ln_U5MR	ln_U5MR	ln_U5MR	ln_U5MR
ln_PHC	−0.242*	−0.324*	−0.321*	−0.330*	−0.295	−0.479**
	(0.132)	(0.166)	(0.173)	(0.170)	(0.196)	(0.210)
ln_mobility				0.162		
				(0.241)		
ln_decision-making			0.0582			
			(0.298)			
Constant	5.054***	23.96***	23.80***	24.73***	6.753*	14.86***
	(1.406)	(3.916)	(4.154)	(4.161)	(3.413)	(3.783)
Observations	18	18	18	18	18	18
R-squared	0.861	0.762	0.763	0.771	0.760	0.679

Source: Author's own estimates. The details of variables used are presented in Table A1

Note: Standard errors are in parentheses. *$p < 0.1$, **$p < 0.05$, ***$p < 0.01$.

Table A3 Factors affecting IMR at the state level (OLS regression)

Variables	(1)	(2)	(3)	(4)	(5)
	ln_IMR	ln_IMR	ln_IMR	ln_IMR	ln_IMR
ln_gendergap	0.899***	0.860***			
	(0.139)	(0.145)			
ln_hcr_rural	0.259*				
	(0.123)				
ln_nfhs_employed	−0.530***	−0.381**	−0.408	−0.404	−0.456*
	(0.167)	(0.166)	(0.231)	(0.251)	(0.243)
ln_PHC	−0.239*		−0.349**	−0.349*	−0.356**
	(0.124)		(0.158)	(0.165)	(0.161)
ln_pucca_house		−0.215*			
		(0.110)			
ln_femlit			−2.470***	−2.483***	−2.573***
			(0.566)	(0.640)	(0.590)
ln_MPCE			−0.466	−0.462	−0.601
			(0.334)	(0.356)	(0.381)
ln_mobility					0.177
					(0.228)
ln_decisionmaking				0.0146	
				(0.284)	
Constant	4.911***	3.653***	21.95***	21.91***	22.79***
	(1.322)	(0.723)	(3.722)	(3.954)	(3.931)

	(1)	(2)	(3)	(4)	(5)
Variables	ln_IMR	ln_IMR	ln_IMR	ln_IMR	ln_IMR
Observations	18	18	18	18	18
R-squared	0.851	0.832	0.740	0.740	0.753

Source: Author's own estimates. The details of variables used are presented in Table A1

Note: Standard errors are in parentheses. $*p < 0.1$, $**p < 0.05$, $***p < 0.01$.

Details of district-level analysis

Variables used

Table A4 District-level variables used in the analysis

Variable	Name and definition	Source
Cmr	The probability of dying (per 1,000) before completing the fifth birthday (under-five mortality rate) (rural)	Derived from Census (2001)
Imr	The probability of dying (per 1,000) before completing the first birthday (rural)	Census (2001)
nss_hcr	Head Count Ratio: Percentage of population below the poverty line in rural areas	Derived from NSS, 55th round (1999–2000)
dlhs_sli	Percentage of households with low standard of living	DLHS-2 (2002–4)
f_literacy_rate	Female Literacy Rate: % of females above 6 years of age who are literate (rural)	Census (2001)
main_wpr_f	Percentage of female main workers among entire female population in the age group of 15–59 years (rural)	Census (2001)

(Continued)

Table A4 (Continued)

Variable	Name and definition	Source
st_pop	Percentage of ST population to total population (rural)	Census (2001)
sc_pop	Percentage of SC population to total population (rural)	Census (2001)
Phc	Percentage of villages that have a PHC	Census (2001)
health_facility	Percentage of villages that have any medical facility	Census (2001)
Pavedroad	Percentage of villages that can have an access by paved road	Census (2001)
Tapwater	Percentage of villages that have access to tap water	Census (2001)
Puswpr	Principal Status Workforce Participation Rate (Female)	NSS (1983–4)
main_nonalworkers_ male	Proportion of main nonagricultural workers (male) to main workers (male)	Census (2001)

Poverty rates (measured by the head count index at the district level based on NSS data) have been used as an indicator of economic conditions. The data closest to Census 2001 are from the 55th round of the NSS survey that was conducted in 1999–2000.[1] The district-level estimates of poverty ratios from this round of NSS data are from Amaresh Dubey's calculations in the 'District-level deprivation in the New Millennium' report by Debroy and Bhandari (2003). Due to problems of sample size, it is not possible to disaggregate poverty ratios at the district level into rural and urban, and therefore the district poverty ratio is used in this analysis, even when considering rural mortality rates. This is the closest proxy available as there are no other data available for poverty ratios at the district level. Instead of the NSS poverty ratio I also tried using the percentage of population having a low standard of living index (SLI) based on DLHS data (DLHS-2 conducted in 2002–4). The correlation between the percentage of population in a district based on low SLI of DLHS-2 and the district poverty ratios based on consumption expenditure data of NSS is 0.62. The regression results do not differ much when we use the DLHS SLI instead of poverty ratios from NSS.

As before, the two main variables indicating women's status in a district used in this analysis are the female literacy rate and the female workforce participation rate. The female literacy rate is defined as the proportion of females aged seven years and above who are literate. The female workforce participation rate in the present context is defined as the number of female workers (main) as a proportion of the total female population in a district in the age group of 15–59 years.[2] Both these datasets are available from Census 2001. The data related to only rural areas have been considered in the regressions where rural mortality rates are the dependent variables.

The data related to village amenities from Census 2001 have been used for the indicators in relation to availability of services. In the regression equations, I have included percentage of villages in a district where any medical facility is available. The Census data show what kind of medical facility is available, but do not classify into government or private facilities. Replacing availability of medical facility with the percentage of villages with a PHC (as an indicator of public health facility) did not make any difference to the results.

To capture the variation in availability of public infrastructure, the proportion of villages that have a paved access road is used. Other indicators that were tried are the percentage of villages where tap water is the source of drinking water and percentage of villages that have bus services available.

All the data used for this district-level analysis are from the Census 2001, except for poverty ratios based on NSS and ratio of low SLI population from DLHS. Five hundred and seventy-three districts have been included in the present analysis. These represent districts of all states (except Union Territories and districts that do not have any rural population).

Results

Table A5 Factors affecting child mortality rates at the district level (OLS) – I

Variables	(1)	(2)	(3)	(4)
	Cmr	Cmr	Cmr	Cmr
nss_hcr	0.378*** (0.0562)			0.252*** (0.0596)

(Continued)

Table A5 (Continued)

Variables	(1)	(2)	(3)	(4)
	Cmr	Cmr	Cmr	Cmr
dlhs_sli		0.360***	0.286***	
		(0.0538)	(0.0573)	
f_literacy_rate	-0.572***	-0.496***	-0.575***	-0.600***
	(0.0680)	(0.0728)	(0.0692)	(0.0646)
main_wpr_f_15	-0.0578	-0.0846†	-0.0258	-0.00240
	(0.0580)	(0.0576)	(0.0584)	(0.0580)
st_pop	0.0691**	0.00842	-0.00743	-0.0110
	(0.0352)	(0.0370)	(0.0374)	(0.0383)
Phc	-0.526***	-0.498***		
	(0.0938)	(0.0941)		
health_facility			-0.209***	-0.112**
			(0.0426)	(0.0519)
Pavedroad				-0.191***
				(0.0539)
Tapwater				
Constant	93.91***	84.49***	95.21***	110.1***
	(4.150)	(5.204)	(5.488)	(4.663)
Observations	573	573	573	573
R-squared	0.386	0.386	0.382	0.397

Source: Author's own estimates. The details of variables used are presented in Table A4

Note: Standard errors are in parentheses. *$p < 0.1$, **$p < 0.05$, ***$p < 0.01$, †$p < 0.15$.

Table A6 Factors affecting child mortality rates at the district level (OLS) – 2

Variables	(1)	(2)	(3)	(4)
	Cmr	Cmr	Cmr	Cmr
nss_hcr	0.378***			0.252***
	(0.0562)			(0.0596)
dlhs_sli		0.360***	0.286***	
		(0.0538)	(0.0573)	
f_literacy_rate	-0.572***	-0.496***	-0.575***	-0.600***
	(0.0680)	(0.0728)	(0.0692)	(0.0646)
main_wpr_f_15	-0.0578	-0.0846†	-0.0258	-0.00240
	(0.0580)	(0.0576)	(0.0584)	(0.0580)
st_pop	0.0691**	0.00842	-0.00743	-0.0110
	(0.0352)	(0.0370)	(0.0374)	(0.0383)
Phc	-0.526***	-0.498***		
	(0.0938)	(0.0941)		

Variables	(1)	(2)	(3)	(4)
	Cmr	Cmr	Cmr	Cmr
health_facility			-0.209***	-0.112**
			(0.0426)	(0.0519)
Pavedroad				-0.191***
				(0.0539)
Tapwater				
Constant	93.91***	84.49***	95.21***	110.1***
	(4.150)	(5.204)	(5.488)	(4.663)
Observations	573	573	573	573
R-squared	0.386	0.386	0.382	0.397

Source: Author's own estimates. The details of variables used are presented in Table A4

Note: Standard errors are in parentheses. *p < 0.1, **p < 0.05, ***p < 0.01, †p < 0.15

Table A7 Factors affecting infant mortality rates at the district level (OLS) – I

Variables	(1)	(2)	(3)	(4)
	Imr	Imr	Imr	Imr
nss_hcr	0.358***			0.250***
	(0.0493)			(0.0524)
main_wpr_f	-0.102**	-0.127**	-0.0752†	-0.0523
	(0.0509)	(0.0506)	(0.0514)	(0.0510)
f_literacy_rate	-0.507***	-0.437***	-0.510***	-0.537***
	(0.0597)	(0.0640)	(0.0609)	(0.0568)
Phc	-0.475***	-0.449***		
	(0.0824)	(0.0826)		
st_pop	0.0913***	0.0344	0.0206	0.0230
	(0.0309)	(0.0325)	(0.0329)	(0.0337)
dlhs_sli		0.339***	0.274***	
		(0.0473)	(0.0504)	
health_facility			-0.183***	-0.103**
			(0.0375)	(0.0456)
Pavedroad				-0.160***
				(0.0474)
Constant	84.29***	75.57***	85.03***	98.31***
	(3.643)	(4.572)	(4.828)	(4.103)
Observations	573	573	573	573
R-squared	0.411	0.410	0.404	0.419

Source: Author's own estimates. The details of variables used are presented in Table A4

Note: Standard errors are in parentheses. *p < 0.1, **p < 0.05, ***p < 0.01, †p < 0.15.

Table A8 Factors affecting infant mortality rates at the district level (OLS) – 2

Variables	(5) Imr	(6) Imr	(7) Imr	(8) Imr
nss_hcr		0.275***		0.195***
		(0.0519)		(0.0545)
main_wpr_f	−0.0743†	−0.0809†	−0.106**	
	(0.0511)	(0.0503)	(0.0504)	
f_literacy_rate	−0.508***	−0.467***	−0.437***	−0.542***
	(0.0606)	(0.0594)	(0.0633)	(0.0559)
Phc		−0.360***	−0.358***	
		(0.0850)	(0.0857)	
st_pop	−0.00425	0.0293	−0.00139	0.0346
	(0.0340)	(0.0333)	(0.0337)	(0.0279)
dlhs_sli	0.215***		0.239***	
	(0.0548)		(0.0545)	
health_facility	−0.112**			−0.127***
	(0.0458)			(0.0387)
Pavedroad	−0.134***	−0.175***	−0.153***	
	(0.0507)	(0.0390)	(0.0428)	
Tapwater				−0.142***
				(0.0295)
Constant	93.08***	94.22***	88.43***	95.90***
	(5.682)	(4.209)	(5.779)	(3.621)
Observations	573	573	573	573
R-squared	0.412	0.432	0.423	0.430

Source: Author's own estimates. The details of variables used are presented in Table A4

Note: Standard errors are in parentheses. $*p < 0.1$, $**p < 0.05$, $***p < 0.01$, $†p < 0.15$.

Individual level

For ease of interpretation, the values given in the tables that follow are of the odds ratios rather than of the coefficients. In the case of a categorical independent variable, the odds ratio of any one category of the variable is calculated by dividing the odds of the independent variable being equal to 1 for that particular category by the odds of the independent variable being equal to 1 for the category chosen as the reference category (Kishor and Parasuraman 1998). The odds ratio for the reference category is 1 by definition. Almost all the independent variables used in the equations are also categorical and therefore odds ratios are easy to interpret.

Table A9 Factors affecting infant deaths at the household level

Infant death	(1)	(2)	(3)	(4)
Variables	Odds ratio	Odds ratio	Odds ratio	Odds ratio
Mother's education (ref: no education)				
Incomplete primary	1.16*	1.17*	1.17*	0.89**
Complete primary	0.95	0.92	0.95	0.82***
Incomplete secondary	0.83***	0.83***	0.82***	0.71***
Complete secondary	0.72**	0.71**	0.71**	0.54***
Higher	0.49***	0.48***	0.49***	0.37***
Social group (ref: SC)				
ST	0.87*	0.91	0.91	0.94
BC	0.88**	0.88**	0.88**	1.01
OC	0.88*	0.90*	0.89*	0.94
Wealth index (ref: poorest)				
Poor	1.05	1.08	1.06	0.94
Middle	0.89*	0.94	0.90	0.78***
Rich	0.81**	0.85*	0.81**	0.71***
Richest	0.72***	0.75***	0.72***	0.58***
Mobility (ref: cannot go alone to any of three places: market, health facility, outside village/community)				
Can go alone to some places	1.13	1.12	1.15	1.06
Media exposure (ref: no media exposure)				
Have some media exposure	1.12**	1.11*	1.13**	1.04
Decision making (ref: have no role in any of four decisions)[3]				
Have some decision making	0.95	0.94	0.95	0.96
Have role in all decisions	0.93	0.94	0.94	0.93*
Employment (ref: mother unemployed)				
Mother employed (has worked in last 12 months)	1.06	1.06	1.06	1.05

(Continued)

Table A9 (Continued)

Infant death	(1)	(2)	(3)	(4)
Variables	Odds ratio	Odds ratio	Odds ratio	Odds ratio
Mother's BMI (ref: low BMI, i.e. < 18.5)				
Normal BMI	0.96	0.97	0.97	1.00
Mother's anaemia status (ref: not anaemic)				
Mother anaemic	1.18***	1.18***	1.17***	1.17***
Sex of the child (ref: male)				
Female child	0.95	0.95	0.95	0.90***
Area of residence (ref: urban)				
Rural	0.94	0.95	0.96	1.02
Education (social effect) (continuous variable)				
% women educated at the PSU level	0.994*** (Coeff = −0.006)	0.995*** (Coeff = −0.004)	0.994*** (Coeff = −0.005)	
Employment (social effect) (continuous variable)				
% women employed at the PSU level	0.999 (Coeff = −0.0003)	0.999 (Coeff = −0.0001)	0.999 (Coeff = −0.0002)	
Access to government services (ref: state with less than average access to government health services)				
More than average access			0.87***	
Region (ref: East)				
North		0.93		
West		0.87		
Central		1.22***		
Northeast		0.89		
South		0.75***		
Constant	0.08***	0.07***	0.08***	0.08***
Observations	43,560	43,560	43,560	91,865

Source: Author's own estimates. All the variables included are from NFHS-3

Note: *$p < 0.1$, **$p < 0.05$, ***$p < 0.01$ (odds ratios presented in table).

However, in the case of a continuous variable it is better to look at the coefficient because the odds ratios do not have the same meaning. The odds ratio is interpreted as the proportionate change in the odds of the event occurring for a unit change in the value of the independent variable. In the case of continuous independent variables the odds ratios tend to be close to one, because a one unit change in the variable usually do not make a big difference to the odds of the dependent variable being one or the other. This does not mean that the variable does not have a significant effect. In such a case, it makes more sense to look at the coefficient and level of significance. This is done in the case of continuous independent variables, in the results presented below. In the Table A9, the reference category is mentioned in brackets and the variables are labelled in such a manner that their definition is understood. Those variables that have been computed and are not obvious are explained.

Notes

1 Although the NSS consumption expenditure data of 1999–2000 were criticised for using different reference periods for collection of consumption data, this may be more important and a limitation for intertemporal exercise. However, since the regression exercise here is primarily cross-sectional, the 1999–2000 poverty estimates are used to understand the impact of poverty. The implicit assumption here is that the bias, if any, is systematic across districts and states.
2 The other studies mentioned here such as Murthi et al. (1997), Kapoor (2010) also use the proportion of main workers in the definition of female workforce participation.
3 The four decisions include decisions related to own health care; making major household purchases; making purchases for daily household needs and visits to her family or relatives.

Appendix B

Determinants of stunting among children: results from the field survey

A multivariate analysis is done with the data from the primary survey. The field survey has the limitation of having a very small sample size and also being restricted to data from a single block in each of the two states. While not claiming to be representative of the state, the field survey was still very useful in understanding the nuances of how each of the factors being studied here work towards influencing health outcomes. In a way, the field survey improved the understanding of the data that are available from secondary sources. In the same spirit, the purpose of the data analysis in this section is more to validate what is found on the basis of the analysis in the previous chapters based on large data sets such as the Census and NFHS. The results are therefore only indicative. The results of the regression analysis must not be looked at in isolation, but as adding further insights to the larger study.

The data show that there was a large difference between the two states in terms of indicators of women's status, children's malnutrition, access to health care (health seeking behaviour and health care practices) and so on, with Tamil Nadu doing much better on all of these indicators. This also fits well with the secondary data and the experience of the field work.

In this section a multivariate analysis based on this data is conducted to understand what the factors are that affect health outcomes. The only health 'outcome' indicator in this survey is related to children's heights and weights. Nutrition status is more complex than 'mortality' indicators. There is also a difference between factors affecting different indicators of malnutrition such as stunting, wasting and underweight. In the present analysis, I look at stunting as it is a more long-term indicator, representing chronic undernutrition.

Second, the difference between Tamil Nadu and Uttar Pradesh is large in terms of almost all the indicators looked at (dependent and explanatory) and the different factors are also highly correlated within each state. Moreover, while the field survey yielded a lot of data on indictors related to women's status, the indicators related to public services from the survey cannot be included in the regression analysis related to explaining variation in health outcomes at the individual level as public services have more of a social effect. This is because it is not the case that only those who access public services (PHC rather than private clinic, anganwadi rather than private nursery) are getting any services. At an individual level it might not make a difference to the health outcome whether the health care is being provided by a public or private provider, but at the population level whether public services are available and of what quality influence not just health outcomes but quality and availability of private health facilities as well. Therefore, what matters is whether there are public services available or not in the area, rather than which service an individual is utilising. On the other hand, women's status has both a household effect and a social effect and therefore can be included.

Based on the field survey data, I have included indices related to different aspects of women's status in the regression. The field survey further reinforces that women's status is complex and cannot be reduced to a single indicator. Therefore, multiple indicators related to decision making, exposure to media, mobility, participation in civic life and opinions on gender relations have been used. Each of these indicators however is a composite index of the responses to a number of questions asked in relation to them.[1]

While keeping in mind the fact that reducing women's status into few multiple indicators is complicated, for the purposes of the present analysis I develop five indicators of women's status. The steps followed to arrive at these five indicators are described below. These five indicators are in addition to indicators related to women's education and employment, which are also included in the final analysis.

Step 1: Sum all related indicators based on 0–1 responses. The responses to the following indicators have been added:

- Eight questions related to decision making (Table 7.6) – indicating number of aspects in which the woman has a 'say' in decision making within the household.
- Four in relation to exposure to media (Figure 7.6) – indicating the number of media the respondent has access to.

- Nine in relation to mobility (Figure 7.4) – indicating the number of places the respondent can go alone to.
- Six in relation to participation in civic life (Figure 7.5) – indicating the number of activities related to civic life the respondent has participated in.
- Nine in relation opinion on gender roles (Table 7.8) – indicating the number of statements in response to which the woman agreed with an opinion that is favourable to gender equality.

Step 2: Normalising the indicator using the formula

$$Y_i = (X_i - X_{min}) / (X_{max} - X_{min})$$

where Y_i is the normalised indicator for respondent i, X_i is the corresponding prenormalisation figure, and X_{max} and X_{min} are the maximum and minimum values, respectively, of the same indicator across all respondents. The normalised indicator varies between 0 and 1 for all respondents, with 0 being the worst and 1 being the best.

Step 3: Since it is convenient to have categorical variables for a logistic regression these normalised indicators are further converted into a categorical variable by dividing the values into three categories (0, 1 and 2 with the higher number indicating a better status) in the following manner:

$$0 - Y_i \leq 1SD$$
$$1 - Y_i \geq 1SD \ \& \ Y_i \leq 1SD$$
$$2 - Y_i > 1SD$$

where Y_i is the normalised indicator for respondent i and SD is standard deviation

Based on these three steps I arrive at one categorical variable to represent each of the following indicators of women's status.

(1) Decision making
(2) Mobility
(3) Exposure to media
(4) Participation to civic life
(5) Opinions on gender roles

Each of these variables takes the value of either 0, 1 or 2. These variables are then included in the regression equations (Table B2).

The regression also includes the status of childcare practices among the sample women. While there are many indicators of childcare practices that were included in the survey, all of them cannot be included because most are relevant only to children who have completed six months (e.g. complementary feeding practices) or one year (e.g. full immunisation). This would further reduce the sample size. Therefore, I construct a childcare practice index that has elements that are relevant to all children under the age of three years. The index of childcare practices is arrived at in the same manner as the women's status indices. The components are presented in Table B1.

The index of childcare related knowledge[3] is an index of scores based on indicators related to what the women felt should be the first feed of

Table B1 Components of index of childcare practices (N = 304)[2]

Indicator	Definition	Scores*	Percentage
(1) First feed	Woman thinks baby's first feed should be breast milk or colostrum = 1; otherwise = 0	0 1	42.8 57.2
(2) Exclusive breastfeeding	Woman says that a baby should be exclusively breastfed for six months = 1; otherwise = 0	0 1	73.4 26.6
(3) Initiation of complementary feeding	Woman says that complementary feeding must be initiated at six, seven or eight months = 1; otherwise = 0	0 1	54.3 45.7
(4) Continued breastfeeding	Woman says breastfeeding must be continued for one year or beyond = 1; otherwise = 0	0 1	48.7 52.3
(5) Response to diarrhoea	If the woman said that response to diarrhoea must be giving more liquids or giving ORS or taking to doctor = 1; otherwise = 0	0 1	14.8 85.2
Index of childcare knowledge		0 1 2	21.4 51.6 30

Note: *For all these questions if the response was 'Don't know', the score given is 0.

Source: Author's field survey

a baby, how long exclusive breastfeeding and continued breastfeeding must be practised, what the timing of complementary feeding should be and what must be done in case a child has diarrhoea. The scores of the different components of the childcare knowledge are first summed up and then this is normalised based on the maximum and minimum scores. Further, the normalised indicator is given three values of 0, 1 and 2 based on whether it is ≤1SD, ≥1SD or between the two.

The results of the logistic regression including these indices and other factors are discussed below.

Dependent variable

As the dependent variable, I have included Stunting. Children who have height-for-age z-scores ≤2SD have been coded as being stunted, '0' and the rest (with complete information) as being not stunted, '1'. Data related to 272 children have been included in the regression exercise.[4]

Explanatory variables

Table B2 gives details of the independent variables used in the different logistic regression models presented later. Indicators related to the main factors being studied such as economic conditions and women's status have been included. As mentioned earlier, the impact of access to public services cannot be assessed with such a small sample. Public services can be expected to have a 'social' effect.[5] Further, the field survey has a small sample size and therefore, it is not conducive to including too many explanatory variables in the regression equation. The main variables being studied are included.

With being stunted as the dependent variable ('0' stunted; '1' not stunted) I tried different models of logistic regression with the explanatory variables given above. Table B3 presents the odds ratios of not being stunted based on some of these models.

Children from a higher SLI show significantly higher odds of being not stunted. This is true even when controlled for state, mother's education and other indicators of women's autonomy. The SLI group 'High' is probably not significant because of the small sample size. There are only three women[6] who have been ranked as being high SLI and all three are from Uttar Pradesh. The analysis based on NFHS data also showed that the wealth quintile children belong to is a significant factor in determining odds of being stunted.

Table B2 Independent variables

Variable	Definition	Value	Percentage
Standard of living index	A standard of living index was based on scores used in DLHS-2; with some minor changes based on data available. Three groups – '0' – Low SLI; '1' – Medium SLI and '2' – High SLI	0 1 2	38.9 60.1 1.0
Mother's education	Women have been divided into three categories – '0' – Less than class 4; '1' – Class 5 to Class 8 and '2' More than Class 8	0 1 2	60.7 19.8 19.5
Mother's education (2)	Women have been divided into three categories based on their level of education, which has been normalised taking into account the minimum and maximum level of education among the sample. (Level is equal to the class completed in school Graduation and above considered to be 15)	0 1 2	0 70.7 29.3
Women's employment	Indicator of whether woman does any outside work. '0' – No outside work; '1' – Any outside work (paid or unpaid)	0 1	62.5 37.5
Paid employment	Indicator of whether woman is involved in paid work. '0' – No paid employment; '1' Any paid employment	0 1	84.2 15.8
Index of childcare knowledge	Based on a sum of five indicators related to breastfeeding, complementary feeding and diarrhoea '0' – Poor Practices; '1' – Better Practices	0 1 2	21.4 51.6 30
Decision-making index	Index of mother's say in decision making. '0' – Lowest; '2' – Highest	0 1 2	17.8 82.2 0
Mobility index	Index of mother's ability to go alone to different places. '0' – Lowest; '2' – Highest	0 1 2	24.3 52.3 23.4
Exposure to media index	Index of mother's exposure to different media. '0' – Lowest; '2' – Highest	0 1 2	29.6 54.9 15.5
Participation in civic life index	Index of mother's participation in civic activities. '0' – Lowest; '2' – Highest	0 1 2	81.6 0 18.4
Opinions (on gender roles) index	Index of mother's response to statements on gender roles. '0' – Lowest; '2' – Highest	0 1 2	17.1 68.4 14.5

Source: Author's field survey

Table B3 Results of logistic regression

Variables	(1) Odds ratio	(2) Odds ratio	(3) Odds ratio	(4) Odds ratio	(5) Odds ratio	(6) Odds ratio	(7) Odds ratio
SLI (ref: low)							
SLI_group: Medium	2.01**	2.07***	2.06**	2.08***	2.13***	2.10***	2.30***
	(0.556)	(0.582)	(0.581)	(0.587)	(0.598)	(0.601)	(0.669)
SLI_group: High	2.70	2.66	2.60	2.85	3.94	3.58	3.97
	(3.979)	(3.894)	(3.822)	(4.194)	(5.795)	(5.261)	(5.912)
Mother's education (ref: mother's education 2 = 0)							
Mother's education 2 = 2	2.66***	2.45***	2.48***	2.41***	2.17**		2.40***
	(0.815)	(0.763)	(0.779)	(0.755)	(0.709)		(0.797)
Mother's education (ref: less than class 4)							
Class 5--8						0.94	
						(0.327)	
More than 8						2.96**	
						(1.284)	
State (ref: Uttar Pradesh)							
Tamil Nadu					1.86*	1.71	1.91*
					(0.593)	(0.568)	(0.663)
Childcare knowledge (ref: childcare index = 0)							
Childcare index = 1	2.30**	1.97*	1.98*	2.06**	1.90*	1.87*	1.77
	(0.798)	(0.696)	(0.701)	(0.737)	(0.704)	(0.693)	(0.658)
Childcare index = 2	2.44**	2.05*	2.10*	2.12*	1.76	1.81	1.55
	(0.976)	(0.838)	(0.872)	(0.871)	(0.788)	(0.825)	(0.696)
Opinion on gender roles (ref: opinion index = 0)							
Opinion index = 1		1.56	1.57	1.66			
		(0.569)	(0.573)	(0.614)			

	(1)	(2)	(3)	(4)	(5)	(6)	(7)
Opinion index = 2	3.45** (1.736)						
Decision making (ref: decision making index = 0)							
Decision making index = 1		3.63** (1.900)	3.68** (1.879)				
Mobility (ref: mobility index = 0)							
Mobility index = 1				0.66 (0.248)	0.69 (0.260)	0.72 (0.265)	
Mobility index = 2						1.58 (0.574)	0.86 (0.403)
Woman's work (ref: no outside work)							
Does any outside work					1.10 (0.314)		
Woman's paid work (ref: no paid work)							
Has done any paid work						1.15 (0.440)	1.20 (0.459)
Participation in civic life (ref: civic life index = 0)							
Civic life index = 1			0.88 (0.325)				
Constant	0.24*** (0.080)	0.17*** (0.075)	0.17*** (0.075)	0.22*** (0.110)	0.28*** (0.123)	0.30*** (0.131)	0.16*** (0.068)
Observations	272	272	272	272	272	272	272

Source: Author's estimates based on field survey data

Note: Dependent variable: stunted = 0, not stunted = 1 (odds ratios in the table are odds of not being stunted); standard error in parentheses; *p < 0.1, **p < 0.05, ***p < 0.01.

While being educated up to class 8 does not make a significant difference to odds of being not stunted, the mother being educated more than class 8 significantly increases the odds of being not stunted. This is true controlled for most of the other variables as well. Further, even when the alternate index for level of mother's education (based on normalisation) is used it turns out to be significant. What is important is that female education still emerges a significant factor.

Of the different indicators of women's status, the mother's having a more equitable view on gender roles and having some mobility significantly increases the odds of the children not being stunted. The decision-making indicator and participation in civic life index have no significant impact.

From the survey data, children of women who work, have higher odds of not being stunted compared to women who do not work. However, this is not a significant effect in the case of either any outside work or paid work.

The 'state' dummy is significant and shows that children in Tamil Nadu have a greater chance of not being stunted compared to children in Uttar Pradesh even when other complicating factors are controlled for. This 'state' effect could be because of the public (health and other) services and public action, which – based on the experience of the field work – stood out as important factors. Having a better knowledge of childcare improves the odds of not being stunted, but the coefficient is sometimes not significant.

Women's views on gender roles and mobility matter to whether their children are stunted or not. On the other hand women's employment status, decision-making index and participation in civic life are not significant. This raises questions on the commonly understood pathways through which women's status affects child health outcomes. Assuming that women's opinions are more influenced by the general status of women in the society, this could be seen as an indicator of the social status of women rather than intrahousehold decision making.

Notes

1 As seen in the previous sections there were multiple questions asked in relation to each aspect of women's status in order to understand how women's lives differ in the two states. For the purpose of the regression analysis it is necessary to reduce these indicators into fewer indices. While I attempted developing a single 'women's status' indicator, these results are not presented here because of two reasons. One is that given the complexity of measuring women's status, the fewer indicators one tries to reduce it to the

more problems arise. It needs to be kept in mind that women's status is multidimensional and difficult to reduce into a single indicator. Second, such a single indicator was also not yielding any meaningful results in the regression analysis. Whereas using separate indicators for each aspect of women's status provides some useful insights.

2 Includes all children under three in the sample. Since there was more than one child in the eligible age group in some households, this figure is more than 250. Among the 250 respondents there were 304 children under three years of age for whom data were collected.

3 I choose to use childcare knowledge and not practices because of sample size issues. Since many of the relevant childcare practices can be measured only after the child is six months (complementary feeding) to one year (full immunisation) old, to include this variable in the regression, the sample size would have to be further reduced to include only those children who have completed one year of age.

4 Among the 250 children in the sample, there are 304 children under the age of three years. After excluding children for whom there is no complete information on heights and date of birth and those whose height for age z-scores and $\leq 6SD$ or $>6SD$, I am left with 272 cases.

5 In the present sample, of the five villages within each state there is not much variation and so it is not possible to come up with a dummy to represent public services at the village level. A state dummy has been included.

6 There are four children in these three households. Therefore, four cases are included here with each child being one 'case'.

References

Acharya, Meena and Lynn Bennett. 1981. 'Rural Women of Nepal. An Aggregate Analysis and Summary of 8 Village Studies', *The Status of Women in Nepal*, Volume II, Part 9. Field Studies, Centre for Economic Development and Administration Kathmandu, Tribhuvan University.

Adabar, Kshamanidhi. 2004. 'Convergence of Standards of Living across Indian States', Working Paper No. 153, Bangalore: Institute for Social and Economic Change (ISEC).

Agarwal, Bina. 1986. 'Women, Poverty and Agricultural Growth in India', *Journal of Peasant Studies*, 13(4): 165–220.

Agarwal, Bina. 1994. 'Gender and Command over Property', *World Development*, 22(10): 1455–1478.

Agarwal, Bina. 1997. '"Bargaining" and Gender Relations. Within and Beyond the Household', *Feminist Economics*, 3(1): 1–51.

Agarwala, S. N. 1957. 'The Age of Marriage in India', *Population Index*, 23(2): 96–107.

Agnihotri, Satish. 1997. 'Workforce Participation, Kinship and Sex Ratio Variations in India', *Gender Technology and Development*, 1(75): 77–112.

Agrawal, Ankush. 2010. 'Infant Mortality in India. 1972–2007: An Exploratory Analysis', *Journal of Social and Economic Development*, 12(2): 1–37.

Ahluwalia, Montek S. 2000. 'Economic Performance of States in Post-Reform Period', *Economic and Political Weekly*, 35(19): 1637–1643.

Akerlof, George A. 1970. 'The Market for Lemons: Quality Uncertainty and the Market Mechanism', *Quarterly Journal of Economics*, 84(3): 488–500.

Anand, Sudhir. 1994. 'Population, Well-being, and Freedom', in Gita Sen, Adrienne Germain and Lincoln C. Chen (eds), *Population Policies Reconsidered. Health, Empowerment and Rights*. Harvard Series on Population and International Health, Cambridge: Harvard Centre for Population and Development Studies, pp. 75–85.

Anand, Sudhir and Martin Ravallion. 1993. 'Human Development in Poor Countries: On the Role of Private Incomes and Public Services', *Journal of Economic Perspectives*, 7: 133–150.

Arokiaswamy, P., Kirsty McNay and Robert H. Cassen. 2004. 'Female Education and Fertility Decline. Recent Developments in the Relationship', *Economic and Political Weekly*, 41(39): 4491–4495.

Arooran, Nambi K. 1980. *Tamil Renaissance and Dravidian Nationalism, 1905–1944*. Chennai: Koodal Publishers.

Arrow, Kenneth J. 1963. 'Uncertainty and the Welfare Economics of Medical Care', *The American Economic Review*, 53(5): 941–973.

ASER Centre. 2012. *Annual Status of Education Report Rural, 2012*. New Delhi: Pratham Resource Centre.

Aturupane, H., P. Glewwe and P. Isenman. 1994. 'Poverty, Human Development, and Growth. An Emerging Consensus?', *The American Economic Review*, 84(2): 243–249.

Baldacci, Emanuele, Benedict Clements, Sanjeev Gupta and Qiang Cui. 2004. 'Social Spending, Human Capital, and Growth in Developing Countries. Implications for Achieving the MDGs', IMF Working Paper, WP/04/217, Washington: IMF.

Baldacci, Emanuele, Maria Teresa Guin-Sui and Luiz de Mello. 2003. 'More on the Effectiveness of Public Spending on Health Care and Education: A Covariance Structure Model', *Journal of International Development*, 15: 709–725.

Banerjee, Abhijit V. and Esther Duflo. 2011. *Poor Economics*. Noida: Random House India.

Barro, Robert J. 1991. 'Economic Growth in a Cross-Section of Countries', *Quarterly Journal of Economics*, 1062: 407–443.

Basu, Alaka M. and K. Basu. 1991. 'Women's Economic Role and Child Survival. The Case of India', *Health Transition Review*, 1(1): 83–103.

Batliwala, Srilata. 1994. 'The Meaning of Women's Empowerment. New Concepts from Action', in Gita Sen, Adrienne Germain and Lincoln C. Chen (eds), *Population Policies Reconsider(ed) Health, Empowerment and Rights*. Harvard Series on Population and International Health Harvard, Cambridge: Harvard Centre for Population and Development Studies, pp. 127–138.

Benhabib, Jess and Mark M. Spiegel. 1994. 'The Role of Human Capital in Economic Development. Evidence from Aggregate Cross-Country Data', *Journal of Monetary Economics*, 342: 143–174.

Berman, Peter and Rajeev Ahuja. 2008. 'Government Health Spending in India', *Economic and Political Weekly*, 43(26–27): 209–216.

Bhalla, S., S. Saigal and N. Basu. 2003. 'Girls' Education Is It – Nothing Else Matters Much', Background Paper for World Development Report 2003/04, New Delhi: Oxus Research & Investments.

Bhalotra, Sonia. 2007. 'Spending to Save? State Health Expenditure and Infant Mortality in India', IZA DP No. 2914, Bonn: IZA.

Bharadwaj, Anandhi S. 1991. 'Women's Question in the Dravidian Movement c. 1925–1948', *Social Scientist*, 19(5/6): 24–41.

Bhat, Ramesh and Nishant Jain. 2006. 'Analysis of Public and Private Healthcare Expenditures', *Economic and Political Weekly*, 41(1): 57–68.

Bhatia, Rajesh. 2002. 'Measuring Gender Disparity using Time Use Statistics', *Economic and Political Weekly*, 37(33): 3464–3469.

Bhattacharya, B. B. and S. Sakthivel. 2004. 'Regional Growth and Disparity in India. Comparison of Pre and Post Reform Decades', *Economic and Political Weekly*, 39(10): 1071–1077.

Binder, Michael and Georgios Georgiadis. 2010. 'Determinants of Human Development. Insights from State-Dependent Panel Models', *Human Development Research Paper*. 2010/24, United Nations Development Programme.

Bloom, David E. and David Canning. 2005. 'Health and Economic Growth: Reconciling the Micro and Macro Evidence', CDDRL Working Paper No. 42, Stanford: Centre on Democracy, Development and the Rule of Law, Stanford University.

Bokhari, Farasat A. S., Yunwei Gai and Pablo Gottret. 2006. 'Government Health Expenditures and Health Outcomes', *Health Economics*, 16: 257–273.

Bose, Ashish. 2000. 'North-South Divide in India's Demographic Scene', *Economic and Political Weekly*, 35(20): 1698–1700.

Bose, Ashish. 2007. 'Beyond Population Projections. Growing North-South Disparity', *Economic and Political Weekly*, 42(15): 1327–1329.

Bourguignon, François, Agnès Bénassy-Quéré, Stefan Dercon, Antonio Estache, Jan Willem Gunning, Ravi Kanbur, Stephan Klasen, Simon Maxwell, Jean-Philippe Platteau and Amedeo Spadaro. 2008. 'Millennium Development Goals at Midpoint: Where Do We Stand and Where Do We Need to Go?', *European Report on Development*, Brussels: European Commission.

CAG. 2011. *Audit Report on National Rural Health Mission NRHM, Uttar Pradesh For the Year 2010–11*. Comptroller and Auditor General of India.

Caldwell, J. 1979. 'Education as a Factor in Mortality Decline', *Population Studies*, 33(3): 395–413.

Caldwell, J. C. 1986. 'Routes to Low Mortality in Poor Countries', *Population and Development Review*, 12: 171–220.

Caldwell, J. C., P. H. Reddy and P. Caldwell. 1982. 'The Causes of Demographic Change in Rural South India: A Micro Approach', *Population and Development Review*, 8(4): 689–727.

Central Statistical Organisation CSO. 1999. *Time Use Survey July. 1998–June. 1999. Brief Details and Important Findings of the Survey*. Ministry of Statistics and Programme Implementation, Government of India, New Delhi, http://mospi.nic.in/stat_act_t5_2.htm (accessed on 10 May 2013).

Chakraborty, Achin. 2011. 'Human Development. How Not to Interpret Change?', *Economic and Political Weekly*, 46(51): 16–19.

Chakraborty, Tanika and Sukkoo Kim. 2010. 'Kinship Institutions and Sex Ratios in India', *Demography*, 47(4): 989–1012.

Chaurasia, Alok Ranjan. 2005. 'Inter-state Inequality in Infant Mortality in India: 1981–2000', *Journal of Health and Population in Developing Countries*, http://www.longwoods.com/content/17649 (accessed on 1 February 2016).

Cleland, J. and C. Wilson. 1987. 'Demand Theories of the Fertility Transition. An Iconoclastic View', *Population Studies*, 411: 5–30.

Commission on Macroeconomics and Health. 2001. *Macroeconomics and Health. Investing in Health for Economic Development.* Geneva: World Health Organization.

Conley, D. and K. W. Springer. 2001. 'Welfare State and Infant Mortality', *The American Journal of Sociology*, 107(3): 768–807.

CSDH. 2008. *Closing the Gap in a Generation. Health Equity through Action on the Social Determinants of Health.* Final Report of the Commission on Social Determinants of Health.

Cutler, David, Angus Deaton and Adriana Lleras-Muney. 2006. 'Determinants of Mortality', *The Journal of Economic Perspectives*, 20(3): 97–112.

Das Gupta, M. 1987. 'Selective Discrimination against Female Children in Rural Punjab, India', *Population and Development Review*, 13: 77–100.

Das Gupta, Monica, B. R. Desikaraju, Rajendra Shukla, T. V. Somanathan, P. Padmanaban and K. K. Datta. 2010. 'How Might India's Public Health System Be Strengthened? Lessons from Tamil Nadu', *Economic and Political Weekly*, 65(10): 46–60.

Das Gupta, Monica, B. R. Desikaraju, T. V. Somanathan and P. Padmanaban. 2009. 'How to Improve Public Health Systems? Lessons from Tamil Nadu', Policy Research Working Paper 5073, The World Bank.

Das, Maitreyi Bordia and Kiersten Johnson. 2008. 'Spousal Violence in Bangladesh as Reported by Men. Prevalence and Risk Factors', *Journal of Interpersonal Violence*, 24(6): 977–995.

Dasgupta, Partha. 1993. *An Inquiry into Well-Being and Destitution.* Oxford: Clarendon Press.

Datt, Gaurav and Martin Ravallion. 1997. 'Why Have Some Indian States Performed Better Than Others at Reducing Rural Poverty?', FCND Discussion Paper No. 26, Food Consumption and Nutrition Division, International Food Policy Research Institute IFPRI, Washington, DC.

Datta, K. K. 2009. *Public Health Workforce in India: Career Pathways for Public Health Personnel*, Background Paper for the National Consultation on Public Health Workforce in India, Organized by the Ministry of Health and Family Welfare, Govt. of India in Collaboration with the WHO Country Office for India on 24–25, June. 2009 at New Delhi.

Deaton, Angus. 2003. 'Health, Inequality and Economic Development', *Journal of Economic Literature*, 41(1): 113–158.

Deaton, Angus. 2004. *Health in an Age of Globalisation*, Report Prepared for the Brookings Trade Forum, Brookings Institution, Washington, DC, http://www.princeton.edu/rpds/papers/pdfs/deaton_healthglobalage.pdf (accessed on 15 May 2011).

Debroy, Bibek and Laveesh Bhandari. 2003. *District-Level Deprivation in the New Millennium.* New Delhi: Konark.

Deolalikar, Anil B. 2005. 'Infant and Under-Five Mortality in India. Levels, Patterns, and Correlates', http://www.esocialsciences.com/data/articles/Document 12682005348.054751E-02.pdf (accessed on 15 May 2011).

Desai, Sonalde. 1994. 'Women's Burdens. Easing the Structural Constraints', in Gita Sen, Adrienne Germain and Lincoln C. Chen (eds), *Population Policies Reconsidered: Health, Empowerment and Rights.* Harvard Series on Population and International Health, Cambridge: Harvard Centre for Population and Development Studies, pp. 139–150.

Desai, Sonalde and Devaki Jain. 1994. 'Maternal Employment and Changes in Family Dynamics. The Social Context of Women's Work in Rural South India', *Population and Development Review*, 20(1): 115–136.

Desai, Sonalde B., Amaresh Dubey, Brijlal Joshi, Mitali Sen, Abusale Shariff and Reeve D. Vanneman. 2010. *Human Development in India: Challenges for a Society in Transition*. New Delhi: Oxford University Press.

Desikachari, B. R., K. K. Datta, Monica Das Gupta, P. Padmanaban, Rajendra Shukla and T. V. Somanathan. 2010. 'How Might India's Public Health Systems Be Strengthened? Lessons from Tamil Nadu', *Economic and Political Weekly*, 55(10): 46–60.

Dev, Mahendra S. and C. Ravi. 2007. 'Poverty and Inequality. All-India and States, 1983–2005', *Economic and Political Weekly*, 42(6): 509–521.

Dholakia, Archana R. and Ravindra H. Dholakia. 2004. 'Expenditure Allocation and Welfare Returns to Government, a Suggested Model', *Economic and Political Weekly*, 39(24): 853–856.

Dholakia, Ravindra H. 2003. 'Regional Disparity in Economic and Human Development in India', *Economic and Political Weekly*, 38(39): 4166–4172.

DISE. 2011. *Elementary Education in India. Progress Towards UEE*, Flash Statistics. 2010–11, National University of Education Planning and Administration, New Delhi.

Dommaraju, Premchand and Victor Agadjanian. 2009. 'India's North-South Divide and Theories of Fertility Change', *Journal of Population Research*, 263: 249–272.

Drèze, Jean. 2006. 'Universalisation with Quality. ICDS in a Rights Perspective', *Economic and Political Weekly*, 41(34): 3706–3715.

Drèze, Jean and Amartya K. Sen. 1989. *Hunger and Public Action*. New Delhi: Oxford University Press.

Drèze, Jean and Amartya Sen (eds). 2002. *India: Development and Participation*. New Delhi: Oxford University Press.

Drèze, Jean and Amartya Sen. 2013. *An Uncertain Glory: India and its Contradictions*. New Delhi: Penguin India.

Drèze, Jean and Haris Gazdar. 1997. 'Uttar Pradesh: The Burden of Inertia', in Jean Drèze and Amartya Sen (eds), *Indian Development: Selected Regional Perspectives*. New Delhi: Oxford University Press, pp. 33–128.

Drèze, Jean and Mamatha Murthi. 2001. 'Fertility, Education and Development Evidence from India', *Population and Development Review*, 27: 33–64.

Drèze, Jean and Naresh Sharma. 1998. 'Palanpur. Population, Society Economy', in Peter Lanjouw and Nicholas Stern (eds), *Economic Development in Palanpur over Five Decades*. Oxford: Clarendon Press, pp. 3–113.

Drèze, Jean and Reetika Khera. 2012. 'Regional Patterns of Human and Child Deprivation in India', *Economic and Political Weekly*, 47(39): 42–49.

Duflo, Esther. 2011. 'Women's Empowerment and Economic Development', NBER Working Paper No. 17702, Cambridge, MA, National Bureau of Economic Research.

Durrant, Valerie L. and Zeba A. Sathar. 2000. 'Greater Investments in Children through Women's Empowerment. A Key to Demographic Change in Pakistan?', Policy Research Division Working Paper No. 137, Population Council, http://www.popcouncil.org/pdfs/wp/137.pdf (accessed on 10 May 2013).

Dyson, T. and M. Moore. 1983. 'On Kinship Structure, Female Autonomy and Demographic Behaviour', *Population and Development Review*, 1(3): 5–60.

Easterly, W. 1999. 'Life during Growth', *Journal of Economic Growth*, 43: 239–276.

Economic and Political Weekly EPW. 2011. 'A Costly Lesson from Uttar Pradesh', *Economic and Political Weekly*, 46(32): 9.

Eswaran, Mukesh and Nisha Malhotra. 2011. 'Domestic Violence and Women's Autonomy. Evidence from India', *Canadian Journal of Economics*, 44(4): 1222–1263.

Fay, Marianne, Danny Leipziger, Quentin Wodon and Tito Yepes. 2005. 'Achieving Child Health Related Millennium Development Goals – The Role of Infrastructure', *World Development*, 33(8): 1267–1284.

Filmer, Deon and Lant Pritchett. 1999. 'Child Mortality and Public Spending on Health. How Much Does Money Matter?' World Bank Policy Research Working Paper No. 1864.

FOCUS. 2006. *Focus on Children under Six Report*. New Delhi: Citizen's Initiative for the Rights of Children Under Six.

Georgiadis, Georgios, José Pineda and Francisco Rodríguez. 2010. 'Has the Preston Curve Broken Down? Human Development Research'.

Ghosh, Jayati. 2009. *Never Done and Poorly Paid: Women's Work in Globalising India*. New Delhi: Women Unlimited.

Government of India. 2001. *Sample Registration System Bulletin*, 35(2), October 2001. New Delhi: Office of the Registrar General.

Government of India. 2005a. *Report of the National Commission on Macroeconomics and Health*, New Delhi: Ministry of Health and Family Welfare.

Government of India. 2005b. *Performance Evaluation of Targeted Public Distribution System (TPDS)*, Report No.189, New Delhi, 2005 Programme Evaluation Organisation, Planning Commission, Government of India.

Government of India. 2011a. *Provisional Population Totals. India, Paper 1 of 2011, Series 1 India*, Census of India, New Delhi: Office of the Registrar General.

Government of India. 2011b. *Sample Registration System Bulletin*, 46(1), December 2011. New Delhi: Office of the Registrar General.

Government of India. 2011c. *Level and Pattern of Consumer Expenditure 2009–10*. Report No. 538. New Delhi: National Statistical Survey Organisation.

Government of India. 2011d. *5th Common Review Mission Report. Uttar Pradesh*, National Rural Health Mission, Ministry of Health and Family Welfare.

Government of India. 2011e. *Selected Socio-Economic Statistics. India, 2011*, Ministry of Statistics and Programme Implementation, Central Statistics Office, New Delhi.

Government of India. 2012. *Press Note on Poverty Estimates 2009–10*. New Delhi: Planning Commission.

Government of India. 2014a. *Sample Registration System Bulletin*, 49(1), September 2014. New Delhi: Office of the Registrar General.

Government of India. 2014b. *Maternal Mortality Ration Bulletin 2013*. New Delhi: Office of the Registrar General.

Government of India. 2015. *Economic Survey 2014–15*. New Delhi: Ministry of Finance.

Government of Tamil Nadu. 1998. *Notes on Family Welfare and MCH Activities in Tamil Nadu (prepared for the visit of high level delegates from the People's Republic of China, March 24–25)*. Chennai: Health and Family Welfare Department.

Government of Tamil Nadu. 2003. *Tamil Nadu Human Development Report*. New Delhi: Social Science Press.

Government of Tamil Nadu. 2009. *Annual Public Health Administration Report, 2008–09*, Government of Tamil Nadu, http://www.tn.gov.in/departments/health/APHAR_2008_09/index.htm (accessed on 10 May 2013).

Government of Tamil Nadu. 2011. *Statistical Handbook, 2011*, Department of Economics and Statistics, Government of Tamil Nadu.

Government of Tamil Nadu. 2013. *Programme Implementation Plan, 2012–13*, State Health Society, NRHM.

Government of Uttar Pradesh. 2006. *Uttar Pradesh Human Development Report*, Government of Uttar Pradesh.

Government of Uttar Pradesh. 2008. *District Statistical Handbook, 2008*, Department of Economics and Statistics, Government of Uttar Pradesh.

Goyal, Sangeeta. 2006. 'Human Development in Tamil Nadu and Karnataka. A Comparison', in Vikram Chand (ed), *Reinventing Public Service Delivery in India*. New Delhi: Sage Publications, pp. 294–332.

Guilmoto, C. Z. and S. Irudaya Rajan. 1998. 'Regional Heterogeneity and Fertility Behaviour in India', Working Paper No. 290, Centre for Development Studies Thiruvananthapuram, CDS.

Gupta, Sanjeev, Marijn Verhoeven and Erwin Tiongson. 2002. 'The Effectiveness of Government Spending on Education and Health Care in Developing and Transition Economies', *European Journal of Political Economy*, 18(4): 717–737.

Gupta, Sanjeev, Marijn Verhoeven and Erwin R. Tiongson. 2003. 'Public Spending on Health Care and the Poor', *Health Economics*, 12: 685–696.

Haddad, Lawrence. 1999. 'Women's Status. Levels, Determinants, Consequences for Malnutrition, Interventions and Policy', *Asian Development Review*, 17(1–2): 96–131.

Hancock, Mary E. 2008. *The Politics of Heritage from Madras to Chennai*. Bloomington, IN: Indiana University Press.

Harriss, John. 2001. 'Populism, Tamil Style. Is It Really a Success?', DESTIN Working Paper Series, Nos. 1–15, London School of Economics.

Harriss-White, Barbara. 1991. *Child Nutrition and Poverty in South India: Noon Meals in Tamil Nadu*. New Delhi: Concept Publishing Company.

Hasan, Zoya. 2001. 'Transfer of Power? Politics of Mass Mobilisation in Uttar Pradesh', *Economic and Political Weekly*, 36(46–47): 4401–4409.

Himanshu and Abhijit Sen. 2011. 'Why Not a Universal Food Security Legislation?', *Economic and Political Weekly*, 66(12): 38–47.

Hirway, Indira. 2000. 'Tabulation and Analysis of the Indian Time Use Survey Data for Improving Measurement of Paid and Unpaid Work', ESA/STATA/AC.79/20, Expert Group Meeting on Methods for Conducting Times Use Surveys, 23–27 October 2000, Statistics Division, United Nations Secretariat, New York.

Hirway, Indira. 2002. 'Indian Experience of Time Use Survey', Proceedings of the National Seminar on Applications of Time Use Statistics, Organized by Central Statistical Organisation and UNIFEM held at New Delhi during 8–9 October 2002.

Hirway, Indira. 2003. 'Identification of BPL Households for Poverty Alleviation Programme', *Economic and Political Weekly*, 38(45): 4803–4808.

Hirway, Indira. 2005. 'Measurements Based on Time Use Statistics. Some Issues', Paper Prepared for the Conference on 'Unpaid Work and Economy. Gender, Poverty and Millennium Development Goals' to be organized at Levy Economics Institute, New York, on 1–3 October 2005.

Hirway, Indira. 2012. 'Missing Labour Force. An Explanation', *Economic and Political Weekly*, 67(37): 68–72.

Hobcraft, J. 1993. 'Women's Education, Child Welfare, and Child Survival: A Review of the Evidence', *Health Transition Review*, 3: 159–175.

Hobcraft, John. 2000. 'The Consequences of Female Empowerment for Child Well-being. A Review of Concepts, Issues and Evidence in a Post-Cairo Context', in Harriet Presser and Gita Sen (eds), *Women's Empowerment and Demographic Processes*. Oxford: Clarendon Press, pp. 159–185.

Hodges, Sarah. 2005. 'Revolutionary Family Life and the Self Respect Movement in Tamil South India, 1926–49', *Contributions to Indian Sociology*, 39(2): 251–277.

Huffman, Wallace and Peter Orazem. 2007. 'Agriculture and Human Capital in Economic Growth: Farmers, Schooling and Nutrition', in R. Evenson and P. Pingali (eds), *Handbook of Agricultural Economics*, Volume 3. Amsterdam: Elseiver B.V., pp. 2281–2341.

Institute of Applied Manpower Research. 2011. *India Human Development Report 2011, Towards Social Inclusion*. New Delhi: Government of India.

International Institute for Population Sciences. 2007. *National Family Health Survey NFHS 3. 2005–06*. Mumbai: IIPS.

Jafferlot, Christophe. 2003. *India's Silent Revolution: The Rise of the Lower Castes in North India*. New York, Hurst, London: Columbia University Press and New Delhi: Permanent Black.

Jain, A. K. 1985. 'Determinants of Regional Variations in Infant Mortality in Rural India', *Population Studies*, 39(3): 407–424.

Jatrana, S. 1999. 'Determinants and Differentials of Infant Mortality in Mewat Region of Haryana State, India', Unpublished PhD Thesis, Demography Program, Research School of Social Sciences, Canberra, The Australian National University.

Jayachandran, Usha. 2008. *Socioeconomic Analysis of Elementary Education in India*, PhD Thesis, Delhi School of Economics, University of Delhi.

Jayaraman, Rajshri and Peter Lanjouw. 1999. 'The Evolution of Poverty and Inequality in Indian Villages', *World Bank Research Observer*, 14(1): 1–30.

Jeffery, R. and A. Basu. 1996. *Girls' Schooling, Women's Autonomy and Fertility Change in South Asia*. New Delhi: Sage Publications.

Jejeebhoy, Shireen J. 1991. 'Women's Status and Fertility: Successive Cross-Sectional Evidence from Tamil Nadu, India', *Studies in Family Planning*, 22: 217–230.

Jejeebhoy, Shireen J. 1995.*Women's Education, Autonomy and Reproductive Behaviour. Experience from Developing Countries*. Oxford: Clarendon Press.

Jejeebhoy, Shireen J. 1998. 'Wife-Beating in Rural India: A Husband's Right? Evidence from Survey Data', *Economic and Political Weekly*, 33(15): 855–862.

Jejeebhoy, Shireen J. 2000. 'Women's Autonomy in Rural India: Its Dimensions, Determinants and Influence of Context', in Harriet Presser and Gita Sen (eds), *Female Empowerment and Demographic Processes*. Oxford: Clarendon Press, pp. 204–238.

Jejeebhoy, Shireen J. and Shiva S. Halli. 2006. 'Marriage Patterns in Rural India: Influence of Sociocultural Context', in Cynthia B. Lloyd, Jere R. Behrman, Nelly P. Stromquist and Barney Cohen (eds), *The Changing Transitions to Adulthood in Developing Countries: Selected Studies*. Washington, DC: National Academies Press, pp. 172–199.

Jejeebhoy, Shireen J. and Zeba A. Sathar. 2001. 'Women's Autonomy in India and Pakistan. The Influence of Religion and Region', *Population and Development Review*, 27(4): 687–712.

Joshi, Seema. 2006. 'Impact of Economic Reforms on Social Sector Expenditure in India', *Economic and Political Weekly*, 61(4): 358–365.

Kabeer, Naila. 2001. 'Reflections on the Measurement of Women's Empowerment', in *Discussing Women's Empowerment-Theory and Practice*, Sida Studies No. 3, Stockholm: NovumGrafiska AB.

Kak, Shakti. 1994. 'Rural Women and Labour Force Participation', *Social Scientist*, 22(3–4): 35–59.

Kannan, Ramya. 2007. 'PHCs Deliver Better Performance', *The Hindu*, Newspaper Article, 8 November 2007.

Kannan, Ramya. 2008. 'More Women Choose PHCs for Deliveries', *The Hindu*, Newspaper Article, 27 February 2008.

Kannan, Ramya. 2011. 'PHCs Take the Blog Route to Reach Out', *The Hindu*, Newspaper Article, 10 November 2011.

Kapoor, Shruti. 2010. 'Infant Mortality Rates in India. District Level Variations and Correlations', Paper Presented at 6th Annual Conference on Growth and Development, 16–18 December 2010, Indian Statistical Institute, New Delhi.

Kar, Sabyasachi and S. Sakthivel. 2007. 'Reforms and Regional Inequality in India', *Economic and Political Weekly*, 42(47): 69–77.

Karve, Irawati. 1965. *Kinship Organisation in India*. Mumbai: Asia Publishing House.

Kenny, Charles. 2005. 'Why Are We Worried About Income? Nearly Everything that Matters is Converging', *World Development*, 33(1): 1–19.

Kenny, Charles. 2009. 'There's More to Life Than Money. Exploring the Levels/ Growth Paradox in Income and Health', *Journal of International Development*, 21: 24–41.

Khera, Reetika. 2011. 'Revival of the Public Distribution System. Evidence and Explanations', *Economic and Political Weekly*, 46(44, 45): 36–50.

Khilnani, Sunil. 2011. 'The Glaring North-South Gap', *The Mint*, Newspaper Article, 14 April 2011.

Kingdon, Geeta Gandhi and Jeemol Unni. 2001. 'Education and Women's Labour Market Outcomes in India', *Education Economics*, 9(2): 174–196.

Kishor, Sunita. 1995. 'Autonomy and Egyptian Women. Findings from the 1988 Egypt Demographic and Health Survey', Occasional Papers 2, Calverton, MD: Macro International Inc.

Kishor, Sunita. 2000. 'Women's Contraceptive Use in Egypt. What Do Direct Measures of Empowerment Tell Us?', Paper Prepared for Presentation at the Annual Meeting of the Population Association of America, 23–25 March 2000, Los Angeles, CA.

Kishor, Sunita and Parasuram Sulabha. 1998. 'Mother's Employment and Infant and Child Mortality in India', NFHS Subject Reports No. 8, International Institute for Population Sciences and Marco International Inc.

Kohli, Atul. 1987. *The State and Poverty in India, Politics of Reform*. New York: Cambridge University Press.

Kolenda, Pauline. 1987. *Regional Differences in Family Structures in India*. Jaipur: Rawat Publications.

Kolenda, Pauline. 2003. *Caste, Marriage and Inequality: Essays on North and South India*. Jaipur: Rawat Publications.

Kravdal, O. 2003. 'Child Mortality in India. Exploring the Community-level Effect of Education', Health Economics Research Programme, University of Oslo, Working Paper No. 4.

Krishnaji, N. 1983. 'Poverty and Fertility. A Review of Theory and Evidence', *Economic and Political Weekly*, 18: 19–21.

Kudaisiya, G. 2007. 'Region, Nation, "Heartland"', in Sudha Pai (ed.), *Political Process in Uttar Pradesh. Identity, Economic Reforms, and Governance*. New Delhi: Pearson Longman, pp. 1–31.

Kumaradoss, Vincent Y. 2004. 'Kamaraj Remembered', *Economic and Political Weekly*, 39(17): 1655–1657.

Kurian, Oommen C. 2006. *Economic Evaluation in Health Care. The Foundations, Methods and the Context in a Historical Perspective*, MPhil Dissertation, Centre for Social Medicine and Community Health, Jawaharlal Nehru University.

Lakshman, Narayan. 2011. *Patrons of the Poor: Caste Politics and Policymaking in India*. New Delhi: Oxford University Press.

Mahal, Ajay, Abdo S. Yazbeck, David H. Peters, G. N. V. Ramana. 2001. 'The Poor and Health Service Use in India', Health Nutrition and Population Discussion Paper, Washington: World Bank.

Mahmud, Simeen and Anne M. Johnston. 1994. 'Women's Status, Empowerment, and Reproductive Outcomes', in Gita Sen, Adrienne Germain and Lincoln C. Chen (eds), *Population Policies Reconsider(ed). Health, Empowerment and Rights*, Harvard Series on Population and International Health, Harvard Centre for Population and Development Studies, pp. 151–160.

Malhotra, Anju and Mark Mather. 1997. 'Do Schooling and Work Empower Women in Developing Countries? Gender and Domestic Decisions in Sri Lanka', *Sociological Forum*, 124: 599–630.

Malhotra, Anju, Reeve Vanneman and Sunita Kishor. 1995. 'Fertility, Dimensions of Patriarchy, and Development in India', *Population and Development Review*, 21(2): 281–305.

Malhotra, Anju, Sidney Ruth Schuler and Carol Boender. 2002. Measuring Women's Empowerment as a Variable in International Development, Background Paper Prepared for the World Bank Workshop on Poverty and Gender. New Perspectives.

Martin, Teresa Castro. 1995. 'Women's Education and Fertility. Results from 26 Demographic and Health Surveys', *Studies in Family Planning*, 26(4): 187–202.

Martorell, R., U. Ramakrishnan, D. G. Schroeder, P. Melgar and L. Neufeld. 1998. 'Intrauterine Growth Retardation, Body Size, Body Com position and Physical Performance in Adolescence', *European Journal of Clinical Nutrition*, 51(S1): S43–S53.

Mason, Karen Oppenheim. 1986. 'The Status of Women. Conceptual and Methodological Issues in Demographic Studies', *Sociological Forum*, 1(2): 284–300.

Mazumdar, Indrani and N. Neetha. 2011. 'Gender Dimensions. Employment Trends in India, 1993–94 to 2009–10', Occasional Paper No. 56, Centre for Women's Development Studies, New Delhi.

McGuire, J. 2001. 'Social Policy and Mortality Decline in East Asia and Latin America', *World Development*, 2910: 1673–1697.

Mehrotra, S. 2006. 'Well-being and Caste in Uttar Pradesh – Why Uttar Pradesh is not like Tamil Nadu', *Economic and Political Weekly*, 41(40): 4261–4271.

Mehta, Pradeep S. and Bipul Chatterjee. 2011. *Growth and Poverty: The Great Debate*. Jaipur: CUTS International.

Mencher, J. P. 1980. 'The Lessons and Non-Lessons of Kerala – Agricultural Labourers and Poverty', *Economic and Political Weekly*, 15(41–43): 1781–1802.

Miller, Barbara. 1981. *The Endangered Sex-Neglect of Female Children in Rural North India*. Ithaca: Cornell University Press.

Miller, Jane E. and Yana V. Rodgers. 2009. 'Mother's Education and Children's Nutritional Status. New Evidence from Cambodia', *Asian Development Review*, 26(1): 131–165.

Mishra, Amaresh. 1995. 'Uttar Pradesh Opportunity for the Left', *Economic and Political Weekly*, 30(46): 2910–2911.

Mishra, Vinod K. and Robert D. Retherford. 2000. 'Women's Education Can Improve Child's Nutrition in India', *NFHS Bulletin*, Number 15, International Institute for Population Sciences Mumbai and East West Center Research Program Population and Health Honolulu.

Moestue, H. and S. Huttly. 2008. 'Adult Education and Child Nutrition the Role of Family and Community', *Journal of Epidemiology and Community Health*, 62: 153–159.

Mooij, Jos and Mahendra S. Dev. 2002. 'Social Sector Expenditures in the. 1990s. Analysis of Central and State Budgets', *Economic and Political Weekly*, 37(9): 853–856.

Moursund, A. and O. Kravdal. 2003. 'Individual and Community Effects of Women's Education and Autonomy on Contraceptive Use in India', *Population Studies*, 57(3): 285–301.

Murthi, Mamta, Anne-Catherine Guio and Jean Drèze. 1997. 'Mortality, Fertility and Gender Bias in India. A District-Level Analysis', in Jean Drèze and Amartya Sen (eds), *Indian Development: Selected Regional Perspectives*. New Delhi: Oxford University Press, pp. 357–406.

Musgrove, P. 1996. 'Public and Private Roles in Health. Theory and Financing Patterns', World Bank Discussion Paper No. 339, Washington, DC.

Nag, M. 1989. 'Political Awareness as a Factor in Accessibility of Health Services: A Case Study of Rural Kerala and West Bengal', *Economic and Political Weekly*, 24(8): 417–426.

Nakkeeran, N. 2003. 'Women's Work, Status and Fertility: Land, Caste and Gender in a South Indian Village', *Economic and Political Weekly*, 38(37): 3931–3939.

Nayyar, Gaurav. 2008. 'Economic Growth and Regional Inequality in India', *Economic and Political Weekly*, 43(6): 58–67.

NCPCR National Commission for Protection of Child Rights. 2011a. Letter to Government of Uttar Pradesh, Letter No. Uttar Pradesh/Comp/2011/20536.

NCPCR National Commission for Protection of Child Rights. 2011b. *NCPCR Visit to Gorakhpur Division. A Report*, Assessment of Large-scale Deaths of Children due to Japanese Encephalitis/Acute Encephalitis Syndrome, Government of India.

Neetha, N. 2006. 'Invisibility Continues? Social Security and Unpaid Women Workers', *Economic and Political Weekly*, 41(32): 3497–3499.

Nurul Alam. 2006. 'Women's Position in the Household and Community and the Care of Sick Children in Rural Bangladesh', Paper Presented at Population Association of America. 2006 Annual Meeting Program, Los Angeles, California, 20 March–1 April 2006, http://paa2006.princeton.edu/abstractViewer.aspx?submissionId=60239 (accessed on 14 June 2013).

Osmani, S. R. 1997. 'Poverty and Nutrition in South Asia', in Nutrition and Poverty. Papers from the ACC/SCN 24th Session Symposium, Kathmandu.

Padmanaban, P., Parvathy Sankara Raman and Dileep V. Mavalankar. 2009. 'Innovations and Challenges in Reducing Maternal Mortality in Tamil Nadu, India', *Journal of Health Population and Nutrition*, 27(2): 202–219.

Pai, Sudha. 2004. 'Dalit Question and Political Response', *Economic and Political Weekly*, 34(11): 1141–1150.

Pai, Sudha, Pradeep Sharma, Pralay Kanungo and Rahul Mukherji. 2005. 'Uttar Pradesh in the 1990s. Critical Perspectives on Society, Polity and Economy', *Economic and Political Weekly*, 40(21): 2144–2147.

Pal, Parthapratim and Jayati Ghosh. 2007. 'Inequality in India. A Survey of Recent Trends', DESA Working Paper No. 45, United Nations Department of Economic and Social Affairs.

Pandian, M. S. S. 1989. 'Culture and Subaltern Consciousness: An Aspect of MGR Phenomenon', *Economic and Political Weekly*, 24(30): PE62–PE68.

Pandian, M. S. S., S. Anandhi and A. R. Venkatachalapathy. 1991. 'Of Maltova Mothers and Other Stories', *Economic and Political Weekly*, 26(16): 1059–1064.

Panikar, P. G. K. 1985. 'Health Care System in Kerala and Its Impact on Infant Mortality', in S. B. Halstead, J. Walsh and K. Warren (eds), *Good Health at Low Cost*. New York: Rockefeller Foundation, pp. 47–55.

Parashar, Sangeeta. 2005. 'Moving Beyond the Mother-Child Dyad. Women's Education, Child Immunization, and the Importance of Context in Rural India', *Social Science & Medicine*, 61: 989–1000.

Paul, Samuel, Suresh Balakrishnan, Gopakumar K. Thampi, SitaShekhar and M. Vivekananda. 2006. *Who Benefits from India's Public Services*. New Delhi: Academic Foundation (in collaboration with Public Affairs Centre, Bangalore).

Peabody, W. J. 1999. *Policy and Health: Implications for Development in Asia*. USA: Cambridge University Press.

Pelletier, D. L., E. A. Frongillo Jr., D. G. Schroeder and J. P. Habicht. 1995. 'The Effects Of Malnutrition on Child Mortality in Developing Countries', *Bulletin of the World Health Organization*, 734: 443–448.

Phillips, D. R. and Y. Verhasselt. 1994. *Health and Development*. London: Routledge.

Prabhu, Seeta. 2001. *Economic Reform and Social Sector Development*. New Delhi: Sage Publications.

Prabhu, Seeta K. and V. Selvaraju. 2006. 'Public Financing for Health Security in India. Issues and Trends', in Sujata Prasad and C. Sathyamala (eds), *Securing Health for All. Dimensions and Challenges*. New Delhi: Institute for Human Development, pp. 401–413.

Preston, Samuel. 1975. 'The Changing Relation between Mortality and Level of Economic Development', *Population Studies*, 29(2): 231–248.

Preston, S. 1980. 'Mortality Declines in Less Developed Countries', in R. Easterlin (ed.), *Population and Economic Change in Developing Countries*. New York: National Bureau of Economic Research, pp. 289–360.

Pritchett, L. and L. H. Summers. 1993. 'Wealthier is Healthier', Policy Research Working Paper Series, WPS 1150, World Bank.

Pritchett, Lant and Martina Viarengo. 2010. 'Explaining the Cross-National Time Series Variation in Life Expectancy. Income, Women's Education, Shifts, and What Else?', Human Development Research Paper. 2010/31, United Nations Development Programme.

Public Accounts Committee (PAC). 2011. *Report on National Rural Health Mission*, Report No. 32, Lok Sabha.

Purfield, Catriona. 2006. 'Mind the Gap – Is Economic Growth in India Leaving Some States Behind?', IMF Working Paper, WP/06/103, Asia and Pacific Department, International Monetary Fund.

Rajadurai, S. V. and V. Geetha. 1991. 'Dravidian Politics End of An Era', *Economic and Political Weekly*, 26(26): 1591–1592.

Rajan, S. Irudaya, P. Mohanachandran Nair, K. L. Sheela, Lalitendu Jagatdeb and Nihar Ranjan Mishra. 2008. *Infant and Child Mortality in India: District Level Estimates*. New Delhi: Population Foundation of India.

Rajivan, Anuradha K. 2006. 'Tamil Nadu. ICDS with a Difference', *Economic and Political Weekly*, 41(34): 3685–3688.

Rajivan, Anuradha K. 2008. 'Targeted Interventions Against Hunger. A Case for Preschool and School Feeding', Hunger Briefing Paper Series No. 1, UNDP Regional Centre in Colombo.

Ram, F., S. K. Mohanty and U. Ram. 2009. 'Understanding the Distribution of BPL Cards: All India and Selected States', *Economic & Political Weekly*, 44(7) 14 February.

Ramachandran, V. K. 1997. 'On Kerala's Development Achievements', in Jean Drèze and Amartya Sen (eds), *Indian Development: Selected Regional Perspectives*. New Delhi: Oxford University Press, pp. 205–356.

Ramakrishnan, U., R. Manjrekar, J. Rivera, R. Gonzales-Cossio and R. Martorell. 1999. 'Micronutrients and Pregnancy Outcomes: A Review of the Literature', *Nutrition Research*, 19(1): 103–159.

Ramalingaswami, V., U. Jonsson and J. Rohde. 1996. 'The Asian Enigma', in *Progress of Nations*. New York: United Nations Children's Fund, pp. 11–17.

Ramaswamy, K. V. 2007. 'Regional Diegnancy Outcomes: A Review of the Literature', *Nutrition Research*, 19(1): 103–159 dimension of Growth and Employment', *Economic and Political Weekly*, 42(49): 47–56.

Ramesh, Jairam. 1999. 'Future of Uttar Pradesh. Need for a New Political Mindset', *Economic and Political Weekly*, 34(31): 2127–2131.

Ranis, Gustav and Frances Stewart. 2000. 'Strategies for Success in Human Development', *Journal of Human Development and Capabilities*, 1(1): 49–69.

Ranis, Gustav and Frances Stewart. 2010. 'Success and Failure in Human Development. 1970–2007', Human Development Research Paper. 2010/10, United Nations Development Programme.

Ranis, Gustav, Frances Stewart and Alejandro Ramirez. 2000. 'Economic Growth and Human Development', *World Development*, 28(2): 197–219.

Ravallion, Martin. 1997. 'Good and Bad Growth. The Human Development Reports', *World Development*, 25(5): 631–638.

Ravichandran S. 2005. *Historical and Political Economy Perspectives of Fertility Transition in the states of Tamil Nadu and Uttar Pradesh*, PhD Thesis, International Institute for Population Sciences deemed university, Mumbai.

Registrar General of India. 2008. Vital Rates of India. 1971 to 2007 based on the Sample Registration System SRS.

Reidpath, D. D. and P. Allotey. 2003. 'Infant Mortality Rate as an Indicator of Population Health', *Journal of Epidemiology & Community Health*, 57: 344–346.

Reserve Bank of India. 2011. *State Finances. A Study of Budgets, 2010–11*, Government of India: RBI.

Rice, T. 2013. 'The Behavioral Economics of Health and Health Care', *Annual Review of Public Health*, 34: 431–447.

Rosenzweig, Mark R. 1995. 'Why Are There Returns to Schooling?', *The American Economic Review*, 85(2), Papers and Proceedings of the Hundred and Seventh Annual Meeting of the American Economic Association Washington, DC, 6–8 January 1995: 153–158.

Saxena Committee Report. 2009. 'Identification of BPL Households in Rural India', *Planning Commission*, Government of India.

Selvaraj, n.d. Scope of the Public Health Act in Protecting the Health of the Community. Presentation, www.pitt.edu/~super7/30011–31001/30491.ppt (accessed on 10 January 2012).

Sen, Amartya K. 1981. 'Public Action and the Quality of Life in Developing Countries', *Oxford Bulletin of Economics and Statistics*, 43: 287–319.

Sen, Amartya K. 1995. 'The Political Economy of Targeting', in D. van de Walle and K. Nead (eds), *Public Spending and the Poor: Theory and Evidence*. Baltimore, MD: Johns Hopkins University Press, pp. 11–22.

Sen, Amartya K. 1999. *Development as Freedom*. New Delhi: Oxford University Press.

Sen, Amartya K. 2011. 'Quality of Life. India vs. China', *The New York Review of Books*, 12 May 2011, http://www.nybooks.com/articles/archives/2011/may/12/quality-life-india-vs-china/?pagination=false (accessed on 5 September 2012).

Sen, Gita. 1992. 'Social Needs and Public Accountability: The Case of Kerala', in Marc Wuyts, Maureen Mackintosh and Tom Heuilt (eds), *Development Policy and Public Action*. Oxford: Oxford University Press, pp. 253–277.

Sen, Gita. 1993. 'Women's Empowerment and Human Rights. The Challenge to Policy', Paper Presented at the Population Summit of the World's Scientific Academies.

Sen, Gita, Aditi Iyer and Asha George. 2008. 'Structural Reforms and Health Equity: A Comparison of NSS Surveys, 1986–87 and 1995–96', *Economic and Political Weekly*, 37(14): 1345–1352.

Sharda, Shailvee. 2012. 'Uttar Pradesh's "Casual Approach" Behind High Encephalitis Deaths. NCPCR', *The Times of India*, Newspaper Report, 5 October 2012.

Shiva Kumar, A. K., Lincoln C. Chen, Mita Choudhury, Shiban Ganju, Vijay Mahajan, Amarjeet Sinha and Abhijit Sen. 2011. 'Financing Health Care for All. Challenges and Opportunities', India. Towards Universal Health Coverage, *The Lancet*, January: 92–102.

Singh, Prerna. 2012. *'We'-ness and Welfare. Subnationalism and Social Development across Indian States*. Book Manuscript in Progress.

Singh, Shyam. 2010. 'Dalit Movement and Emergence of the Bahujan Samaj Party in Uttar Pradesh. Politics and Priorities', Working Paper No. 242, The Institute for Social and Economic Change, Bangalore.

Sinha, Dipa and Vandana Bhatia. 2009. *Learning from Models of ECCD Provision in India*. Hyderabad: Kusuma Foundation.

Sivakami, M. 1997. 'Female Work Participation and Child Health. An Investigation in Rural Tamil Nadu, India', *Health Transition Review*, 7: 21–32.

Smith, Lisa C. and Lawrence Haddad. 2000. 'Explaining Child Malnutrition in Developing Countries. A Cross Country Analysis', Research Report 111, International Food Policy Research Institute, Washington, DC: IFPRI.

Smith, Lisa C., Usha Ramakrishnan, Aida Ndiaye, Lawrence Haddad and Reynaldo Martorell. 2003. 'The Importance of Women's Status for Child Nutrition in Developing Countries', Research Report 131, International Food Policy Research Institute, Washington, DC: IFPRI.

Soares, Rodrigo R. 2007. 'On the Determinants of Mortality Reductions in the Developing World', *Population and Development Review*, 33(2): 247–287.

Srinivasan, Vivek. 2014. *Delivering Public Services Effectively: Tamil Nadu and Beyond*. New Delhi: Oxford University Press India.

Subramanian, N. 1999. *Ethnicity and Populist Mobilization: Political Parties, Citizens and Democracy in South India*. Delhi: Oxford University Press.

Subramanian, S. V., Ichiro Kawachi and George Davey Smith. 2007. 'Income Inequality and the Double Burden of Under- and Overnutrition in India', *Journal of Epidemiology and Community Health*, 61: 802–809.

Subramanyam, M. A., I. Kawachi, L. F. Berkman and S. V. Subramanian. 2011. 'Is Economic Growth Associated with Reduction in Child Undernutrition in India?', *PLoS Med*, 83: e1000424. doi: 10.1371/journal.pmed.1000424.

Sundararaman, T. and Vandana Prasad. 2006. 'Accelerating Child Survival', Book 3, *Public Health Resource Network*, New Delhi.

Suresh, V. 1992. 'The DMK Debacle. Causes and Portents', *Economic and Political Weekly*, 27(42): 2313–2322.

Suri, Tavneet, Michael Boozer, Gustav Ranis and Frances Stewart. 2011. 'Paths to Success. The Relationship between Human Development and Economic Growth', *World Development*, 39(4): 506–522.

Suryanarayana, M. H., Ankush Agrawal and K. Seeta Prabhu. 2011. *Inequality Adjusted Human Development Index for India's States 2011*. New Delhi: UNDP.

Swaminathan, P. 1997. 'Work and Reproductive Health. A Hobson's Choice for Indian Women?', Working Paper No. 147, Madras Institute of Development Studies, Madras.

Szretzer, S. 1997. 'Economic Growth, Disruption, Deprivation, Disease and Death. On the Importance of the Politics of Public Health for Development', *Population and Development Review*, 23(4): 693–728.

Tamil Nadu FORCES. 2008. *Status of Young Children in Tamil Nadu*. Chennai: Tamil Nadu-FORCES.

The Hindu. 2008. 'Self-reliant PHCs Increase Institutional Deliveries', *The Hindu*, Newspaper Report, 24 April 2008.

The Hindu. 2012. 'Mayawati the First CM to Complete Five Years in Uttar Pradesh', *PTI*, Newspaper Report, 7 March 2012.

The Times of India. 2012. 'Jayalalithaa Opposes Common Medical Entrance Test', 2 October 2012.

Thiruchandran, Selvi. 1997. *Ideology, Caste, Class and Gender*. UBS Publishers.

Thorbecke, Erik and Chutatong Charumilind. 2002. 'Economic Inequality and Its Socioeconomic Impact', *World Development*, 30(9): 1477–1495.

UNDP. 1990. *Human Development Report 1990*. New York: UNDP.

UNDP. 2010. *Human Development Report 2010*. New York: UNDP.

UNDP. 2014. *Human Development Report 2014*. New York: UNDP.

UNICEF. 1998. *The State of the World's Children, Focus on Nutrition*. New York: UNICEF.

Venkatesan P. and N. Sivakumar. 2012. 'Glimpses of Kamaraj's Rule 1954–63 AD', *Review of Research*, 1(12): 1–4.

Visaria, Leela. 2000. 'Innovations in Tamil Nadu', *Seminar*, Issue No. 489. New Delhi.

Visaria, P. M. 1969. 'The Sex Ratio of the Population of India', Monograph No. 10, Census of India 1961. New Delhi: Office of the Registrar General.

Viswanathan, Brinda. 2003. *Household Food Security and Integrated Child Development Services in India*, A Report Prepared as Part of Collaborative Study by Centre for Economic and Social Studies CESS, Hyderabad and International Food Policy Research Institute IFPRI, Washington on Food Security at Household Level in India, www.righttofoodindia.org (accessed on May 2013).

Vivek, S. 2010. *Understanding Public Services in Tamil Nadu. An Institutional Perspective*, Doctoral Dissertation, Syracuse University, Syracuse, NY.

Wang, L. 2003. 'Determinants of Child Mortality in LDCs: Empirical Findings from Demographic and Health Surveys', *Health Policy*, 65(3): 277–299.

Ware, Helen. 1984. 'Effects of Maternal Education, Women's Roles, and Child Care on Child Mortality', *Population and Development Review*, 10(Suppl.): 191–214.

Whalley, John and Xiliang Zhao. 2010. 'The Contribution of Human Capital to China's Economic Growth', Working Paper No. 16592, Cambridge, MA, NBER Working Paper Series, National Bureau of Economic Research.

WHO. 1998. *Malnutrition and the Causes of Childhood Mortality*. Geneva: WHO.

WHO. 2006. *Responding to the Tsunami – The Tamil Nadu Experience*. Delhi: WHO Country Office, http://www.whoindia.org/EN/Section2/Section407.htm.

WHO. 2009. *Safer Pregnancy in Tamil Nadu. From Vision to Reality*, World Health Organization, Regional Office for South-East Asia.

Wilson, Rob A. and Geoff Briscoe. 2004. 'The Impact of Human Capital on Economic Growth: A Review', in P. Descy and M. Tessaring (eds), *Evaluation and Impact of Education and Training: The Value of Learning*, Third Report on Vocational Training Research in Europe. Synthesis Report. Luxembourg. Office for Official Publications of the European Communities Cedefop Reference Series.

World Bank. 1993. *World Development Report. Investing in Health*. Oxford University Press.

Younger, S. 2001. 'Cross-Country Determinants of Declines in Infant Mortality. A Growth Regression Approach', Cornell University Food and Nutrition Program Working Paper No. 130.

Zachariah, K. C., Irudaya Rajan S., P. S. Sarma, K. Navneethan, P. S. Gopinathan Nair and U. S. Mishra. 1994. *Demographic Transition in Kerala in the. 1980s*, Centre for Development Studies-Monograph Series. Trivandrum: Tilak Baker.

Zerinini-Brotel, J. 1998. 'The BJP in Uttar Pradesh: From Hindutva to Consensual Politics?', in C. Jaffrelot and T. B. Hansen (eds), *The BJP and the Compulsions of Politics in India*. Delhi: Oxford University Press, pp. 71–100.

Index

For Product Safety Concerns and Information please contact our EU
representative GPSR@taylorandfrancis.com
Taylor & Francis Verlag GmbH, Kaufingerstraße 24, 80331 München, Germany

www.ingramcontent.com/pod-product-compliance
Ingram Content Group UK Ltd.
Pitfield, Milton Keynes, MK11 3LW, UK
UKHW021633240425
457818UK00018BA/381